Yoga Therapy

Yoga Therapy: Theory and Practice is a vital guidebook for any clinician or scholar looking to integrate yoga into the medical and mental health fields. Chapters are written by expert yoga therapy practitioners and offer theoretical, historical, and practice-based instruction on cutting-edge topics such as the application of yoga therapy to anger management and the intersection of yoga therapy and epigenetics; many chapters also include Q&A "self-inquiries." Readers will find that *Yoga Therapy* is the perfect guide for practitioners looking for new techniques as well as those hoping to begin from scratch with yoga therapy.

Ellen G. Horovitz, PhD, is professor and director of the graduate art therapy program at Nazareth College in Rochester, New York. She is the author of seven books, served on the American Art Therapy Association's board of directors and as president-elect, and is past media editor of *Arts & Health: An International Journal of Research, Policy and Practice.*

Staffan Elgelid, PhD, is an associate professor of physical therapy at Nazareth College in Rochester, New York and has served on the board of the North America Feldenkrais Guild, the advisory board of the International Association of Yoga Therapists, and on the editorial board of several journals.

Yoga Therapy: Theory and Practice

Edited by Ellen G. Horovitz and Staffan Elgelid

Routledge
Taylor & Francis Group
NEW YORK AND LONDON

First published 2015
by Routledge
711 Third Avenue, New York, NY 10017

and by Routledge
27 Church Road, Hove, East Sussex BN3 2FA

Routledge is an imprint of the Taylor & Francis Group,
an informa business

All chapter introductory images except for that of Chapter 5 were produced by Paolo E. Marino

Library of Congress Cataloging-in-Publication Data
Yoga therapy : theory and practice / [edited] by Ellen G. Horovitz and Staffan Elgelid.
p. ; cm.
Includes bibliographical references and index.
I. Horovitz, Ellen G., editor. II. Elgelid, Staffan, editor.
[DNLM: 1. Yoga. QT 260.5.Y7]
RA781.7
613.7'046—dc23
2014040305

ISBN: 978-1-138-81615-2 (hbk)
ISBN: 978-1-138-81616-9 (pbk)
ISBN: 978-1-315-74629-6 (ebk)

Typeset in Baskerville
by Florence Production Ltd, Stoodleigh, Devon

For Karen Armstrong and Janet Rock: you contain me in spirit and word. Without you, this book would never have seen the light of day.

E.G.H.

To my friend Matt: My involvement in this book could not have happened without your guidance and support through the years. You let me find the right direction at SYTAR 2011 and life has not been the same since!

S.E.

Contents

Illustrations

Tables

Figures

Contributors

Frances Sommer Anderson, PhD is a psychoanalyst and licensed psychologist, and also holds a Practitioner Certificate (SEP) from the Somatic Experiencing Trauma Institute. The body—disabled, disfigured, and in pain—has been the focus of her clinical work, beginning with a clinical psychology internship in physical rehabilitation medicine at Rusk Institute–NYU Langone Medical Center in 1974. Specializing in treating pain and other mindbody disorders since 1979, she integrates relational psychoanalytic theory, research in the neuroscience of emotional and cognitive processing, and the neurobiology of attachment, trauma and pain. She has been recognized internationally for her experiential teaching style and for leading edge publications regarding the body in psychoanalytic theory and practice: *Relational Pespectives on the Body* and *Bodies in Treatment: The Unspoken Dimension*. Her new book, *Pathways to Pain Relief*, is co-authored with Eric Sherman, PsyD. She is a founding Member of the Board of Directors of a newly incorporated non-profit educational corporation, the Psychophysiologic Disorders Association (PPDA).

Scott Blossom, L.Ac., Dipl.Ac., Dipl.C.H. Dr. Blossom is a licensed practitioner of Traditional Chinese Medicine (TCM), an Ayurvedic consultant, and a Shadow Yoga teacher. He has been fortunate to have excellent teachers in the areas of TCM, Ayurveda, and yoga and weaves these modalities together in his clinical practice and yoga teaching. He is on the faculty of the Kripalu School of Ayurveda and regularly contributes to magazines and conferences on these subjects. Scott is particularly grateful to Zhander Remete, founder of Shadow Yoga, with whom he has studied for 14 years, and Dr. Robert Svoboda, renowned Ayurvedic doctor and scholar, with whom he has studied for 15 years. Scott graduated with a Master's degree in Traditional Chinese Medicine in 1997 from the Santa Barbara College of Oriental Medicine. During this time, he also completed a three-year extracurricular training in Chinese Herbology under Master herbalist Dr. Henry Han. Scott specializes in women's health specifically, as well as the musculoskeletal, immune, and digestive systems. His 14 years of clinical experience have laid a foundation for the therapies and practices that he shares on DoctorBlossom.com.

Richard P. Brown, MD. Dr. Brown is Associate Clinical Professor of Psychiatry at Columbia University. After receiving his MD in 1977 from Columbia University College of Physicians and Surgeons, Dr. Brown completed his Residency in Psychiatry and a Fellowship in Psychobiology and Psychopharmacology at New York Hospital. He is the recipient of numerous awards and has authored over 80 articles and book chapters on pharmacological treatments, clinical studies, and complementary approaches in psychiatry. In 1999, Dr. Brown introduced S-adenosyl-methionine (SAM-e) for treatment of depression at the New York Academy of Medicine. He coauthored, *Stop Depression Now*, presenting a holistic approach to depression. Dr. Brown's chapters include "Alternative Treatments in Brain Injury" in *Neuropsychiatry of Traumatic Brain Injury* (American Psychiatric Press 2004) and "Complementary and Alternative Treatments in Psychiatry," in *Psychiatry* Second and Third Editions (John Wiley & Sons 2003 and 2007). Books by Dr. Brown and his wife, Patricia Gerbarg, MD, are: *Non-Drug Treatments for ADHD, New Options for Kids, Adults, and Clinicians* (2012); *How to Use Herbs Nutrients, and Yoga in Mental Health Care* (2010) and *The Healing Power of the Breath* (Shambhala 2012).

Robert Butera, M.Div., PhD, Founder, YogaLife Institute and Co-Creator of Comprehensive Yoga Therapist Training. Dr. Robert ("Bob") Butera trains yoga students, yoga teachers, and yoga therapists in yoga and meditation, leads topic-based seminars, and organizes yoga retreats. Programs at YogaLife in Devon, Pennsylvania are based on the teachings published in Butera's previous books, *The Classical Yoga Study Guide (I, 2000)* and *The Pure Heart of Yoga: 10 Essential Steps for Personal Transformation* (Llewellyn, 2009) and *Meditation for Your Life: Creating a Plan that Suits Your Style* (Llewellyn, 2012).

Butera is also editor-in-chief and publisher of Philadelphia's popular 72-page holistic lifestyle magazine *Yoga Living*, currently celebrating its 14th year in publication. Butera was certified to teach yoga and meditation by the Yoga Institute of Mumbai in India, where he lived for six months in 1989. His doctorate work (1998) at the California Institute of Integral Studies focused on a yoga healing program for the immune system. Butera also holds a Masters of Divinity (1993) from The Earlham School of Religion and has studied Buddhist psychotherapy, meditation, and personal growth in Japan and Taiwan. Butera is also a member of the International Association of Yoga Therapists' Board of Directors. After studying and teaching yoga and meditation for more than twenty-five years, Butera approaches the subject with passion and an understanding that every client is unique. He teaches his clients how to understand their own needs and then, how to apply the appropriate practices based on those needs. It is a simple yet deep process, which over the years has helped many learn to live to their greater potential.

Erin Byron, MA is an insightful psychotherapist, theatrical public speaker, and the innovative Director of the first yoga center in Brantford, Ontario: Welkin YogaLife Institute and Co-Creator of Comprehensive Yoga Therapist Training Program. Erin adeptly guides the authentic yoga training programs at the Institute, certifying yoga teachers, meditation teachers, and professional comprehensive yoga therapists. Erin has over twenty years of experience counseling people with Post-Traumatic Stress and associated symptoms, where she gained esteem for her dynamic, creative approach to healing. Her magazine articles, online interviews, and engaging podcasts about mental health and yoga have inspired many in Self-Realization. Due to the popularity of her counseling practice, Erin became a sought-after, multi-modal public speaker helping companies reduce stress in their employees and motivating people to take control of their lives and create a quality existence through realized knowledge. Erin is enthusiastic about the changes she has seen in the lives of her clients and the companies she has assisted and is looking forward to publishing her first book on Karma Yoga.

Erin E. Casperson, BS is the Coordinator of the Kripalu School of Ayurveda. She is a Kripalu Certified Ayurvedic Health Counselor and 500-hr Kripalu Certified Yoga Teacher. After a major life transition, Erin was advised to go to yoga to learn to breathe. Her experience of the breath was transformational and lead her to complete a 200-hr yoga teacher training program. In this program, she was exposed to and fell in love with the traditional practices of Ayurveda. She has since dedicated her life to studying Ayurveda at the Kripalu Center for Yoga and Health and is a Kripalu Certified Lifestyle Consultant and Ayurvedic Yoga Specialist. She spent two years as a resident intern for the Kripalu School of Ayurveda where she completed her 500-hr Kripalu Yoga Teacher Training with a focus on Ayurveda. In her tenure as intern she maintained her intensive self study through the lens of yoga and Ayurveda and dived deeply into advanced training in clinical work, research, curriculum writing, and managing the Kripalu School of Ayurveda classroom. She is currently on the faculty for the Kripalu School of Ayurveda. She is available for workshops and private consultations.

Lisa Conboy, MA, MS, ScD is a Clinical Instructor at Beth Israel Deaconess Medical Center, Harvard Medical School and the Director of the Research Department and part-time faculty at The New England School of Acupunctures. She is a social epidemiologist and a sociologist with an interest in the associations between social factors and health. She is published in the areas of Women's Health, Mind–Body Medicine, and qualitative research methodology. Dr. Conboy is also a founding member of the Kripalu research collaborative which examines the mental, physical, and spiritual benefits of yoga, meditation, Ayurveda and other holistic and mind-body therapies.

Staffan Elgelid, PhD, PT, GCFP, RYT-500. Dr. Staffan Elgelid is an Associate Professor of Physical Therapy at Nazareth College. At Nazareth College, he teaches a wide variety of courses and is in charge of the Nazareth College Wellness initiative. Dr. Elgelid has been a physical therapist for 20+ years. A native of Sweden and graduate of the University of Central Arkansas, Dr. Elgelid has worked in a wide variety of settings, including owning his own clinics, and has presented at conferences on a wide variety of topics such as Complementary Approaches to Health, Guided Imagery, Healthy Aging, Mentoring, Awareness, Core Strengthening, and Feldenkrais, both in the US and in Europe. Dr. Elgelid has produced videos on different approaches to core strengthening. He has held several positions within the North America and International Feldenkrais Community. Currently, he is on the advisory board of the International Association of Yoga Therapists, and on the editorial board of several journals.

Hilary Garivaltis, BA founder and former Dean of the Kripalu School of Ayurveda, has more than 12 years of experience in teaching Ayurvedic daily living tools and Ayurvedic therapy techniques. She received her training at the New England Institute of Ayurvedic Medicine with advanced training in India from the Rishikesh College of Ayurveda and the Jiva Institute. She continues to train with the world's leading teachers in the United States and in India. www.hilarygarivaltis.com

Patricia L. Gerbarg, MD, Assistant Professor in Psychiatry NY Medical College, graduate Harvard Medical School and Boston Psychoanalytic Institute, integrates standard and complementary treatments for mental health. She serves on the APA task force on Complementary and Alternative Medicine and on the board of the American Botanical Council. Her research focuses on mind–body practices for stress, anxiety, depression, PTSD, military combat stress, and for survivors of mass disasters. Dr. Gerbarg and Dr. Richard P. Brown teach unique stress reduction and healing techniques in their Breath~Body~Mind workshops. With Dr. Brown she co-authored *How to Use Herbs, Nutrients, and Yoga in Mental Health Care* (National Best Book Awards 2009 First Place and International Book Awards 2010 First Place), *Non-Drug Treatments for ADHD* (Nautilus 2013 Gold Award), and *The Healing Power of the Breath* book and CD set (Nautilus 2013 Silver Award).

Ellen G. Horovitz, PhD, ATR-BC, LCAT, E-RYT, LFYP is Professor/ Director of Graduate Art Therapy at Nazareth College of Rochester. She has had over thirty-five years of experience with myriad patient populations and is a registered yoga teacher and yoga therapist. She is the author of numerous articles, book chapters and the following books: *Spiritual Art Therapy: An Alternate Path*; *A Leap of Faith: The Call to Art*; *Art Therapy As Witness: A Sacred Guide*; *Visually Speaking: Art Therapy and the Deaf*; *The Art Therapists' Primer: A Clinical Guide to Writing Assessments, Diagnosis and Treatment* (2nd edition) and *Digital Image Transfer: Creating Art with Your Photography*. She is past President Elect of the American Art Therapy Association (AATA) and past Media Editor for the Society for the Arts in Healthcare journal, *Arts and Health: Research, Policy and Practice.* Ellen offers workshops, lectures, and trainings in art therapy and yoga therapy. She also sees clients through the Creative Arts Therapy Department yoga/art therapy clinic at Nazareth College and is in private practice.

Sheri Kreher, LMSW, PRYT is a Certified Phoenix Rising Yoga Therapist and Group Facilitator, representing over 1500 hours of training. She has also mentored Phoenix Rising students-in-training. Sheri provides individual sessions, group classes, workshops, and retreats. She has over 15 years as a Licensed Master of Social Work, with experience with anger management, family interventions, eating disorders, and bereavement. Sheri is a Licensed Clinical Social Worker, specializing in stress management and anger management therapy. She has a private practice in Geneseo, NY and provides individual, couples and group psychotherapy, yoga therapy, workshops, and retreats. Sheri also works in a busy community mental health clinic, providing individual and group psychotherapy to seriously and chronically mentally ill patients. She facilitates the clinic's Anger Management Group, incorporating yoga therapy techniques into each session. *Meditations and Yoga for Anger Management* CDs available at: www.SheriKreher.com

Judith Hanson Lasater, PhD, PT, has taught yoga since 1971. She is a founder of the Iyengar Yoga Institute in San Francisco, CA, as well as the most-popular yoga magazine in the world, *Yoga Journal.* Ms. Lasater frequently trains teachers in virtually every state of the union, teaches internationally, and is often an invited guest speaker at yoga conventions. She is president of the California Yoga Teachers' Association as well as the author of numerous articles on yoga and health for nationally recognized magazines. She is the author of: *What We Say Matters: Practicing Nonviolent Communication* (with Ike Lasater) 2009; *Yogabody: Anatomy, Kinesiology, and Asana* (2009); *A Year of Living Your Yoga* (2006); *Yoga Abs* (2005), *Yoga for Pregnancy: What Every Mom-to-Be Needs to Know* (2004); *30 Essential Yoga Poses: for beginning students and their teachers* (2003); *Relax and Renew: restful yoga for stressful times*; and *Living Your Yoga: finding the spiritual in everyday life.*

Benjamin Lorr, MS grew up in Silver Spring, Maryland. He attended Columbia University, where he earned a BA in Biology and Creative Writing. After graduating, he spent six years as a high school science teacher in Bushwick, Brooklyn. His first book *Hell-Bent: Obsession, Pain, and the Search for Something Like Transcendence in Competitive Yoga* was called "witty and wise" by the New York Times Book Review and an "incredible," "hilarious" and "addictive read" by *USA Today*, *Men's Fitness*, and *People Magazine*, respectively. He is now at work on his second book, an exploration of the grocery industry.

François Raoult MA, RIYT is dedicated to teaching yoga with awareness, integrity, and compassion. He first felt the call to yoga at age 19, on a pilgrimage to the sacred sites of India. For a decade, he toured Europe with an avant garde puppet theater and composed music for the plays. The manipulation of string puppets led him to explore yoga and tai chi. A certified Iyengar teacher until 2010, François began teaching in 1975. A year later, he started extensive training with the great yogi Sri B.K.S. Iyengar. A graduate of the Ecole Nationale de Yoga in Paris and a Certified Iyengar Instructor, he has studied meditation with Zen Master Thich Nhat Hanh, Ayurveda with Dr. Robert Svoboda, and anatomy with Thomas Myers. After studying architecture and philosophy, trekking and recording sacred music in the Himalayas, he completed a Masters in ethnomusicology. In addition to directing the Open Sky Yoga Center and its creative Teacher Training program in Rochester, NY, he teaches yoga seminars worldwide. François is also certified in Gong Yoga and in "Laughing for no reason."

Richard Rosen began his practice of yoga in 1980, and is a graduate of the BKS Iyengar Yoga Institute in San Francisco, CA. In 1987, with his good friend Rodney Yee, he co-founded the Piedmont Yoga Studio in Oakland, CA (www.piedmontyoga.com/), where he still teaches today and serves as the school's director. He's a Contributing Editor at *Yoga Journal* magazine and the author of three books on yoga, including *The Yoga of Breath* (Shambhala, 2002) and *Pranayama: Beyond the Fundamentals* (Shambhala, 2006), as well as a set of seven instructional CDs for pranayama. His latest book, *Original Yoga: Rediscovering Traditional Practices of Hatha Yoga*, was published in May, 2012. Richard lives in Berkeley, CA.

Daniel D. Seitz, JD, EdD, has worked for over 25 years in the field of complementary and alternative medicine education, accreditation, and regulation. He currently serves as the executive director of the Council on Naturopathic Medical Education, consults with alternative medicine colleges and organizations on accreditation, strategic planning, marketing, administration, and other matters, and does professional facilitation. Dan previously served as the founding dean for the *School of Acupuncture and Oriental Medicine at New York Chiropractic College*, chair of the *Accreditation Commission for Acupuncture and Oriental Medicine*, president of *New England School of Acupuncture*, and chief of the Acupuncture Unit for the *Massachusetts Board of Medicine.*

Matthew J. Taylor PT, PhD, owner of Dynamic Systems Rehabilitation Clinic and creator of the DSR Method, has 29 years of sports medicine/orthopedic experience and a wellness/integrative medicine practice. As a leader in integrative rehabilitation, his practice has been featured in national publications for both patient care delivery and administrative design. His futuristic mind–body clinic is based on a fusion of orthopedic rehabilitation, classical yoga therapeutic principles and his doctoral work in modern transformation learning theory. He uses yoga as a practical, simple method of using new science discoveries to address pain and movement challenges for all types of conditions. Dr. Taylor led a 2-year research study at the Courage Center in Minnesota to measure change in organizational consciousness. He is also past president of the board of directors of the International Association of Yoga Therapists (IAYT.org) where during his board time the association created the Council of Schools to initiate the standards process, as well supporting funding for peer review journal status and the online digital resource library. As a programming committee member of the first three Symposiums on Yoga Therapy and Research, he chaired the first research committee that has since grown to become the Symposium of Yoga Research. Details on his yoga therapy background are available at www.drofyoga.com.

Amy Weintraub, MFA, E-RYT 500 is the founding director of the LifeForce Yoga Healing Institute and has been a pioneer in the field of yoga and mental health for over 20 years. She is the author of *Yoga for Depression* (Broadway Books) and *Yoga Skills for Therapists: Effective Practices for Mood Management* (W.W. Norton, 2012). She offers professional trainings and workshops for mental health and yoga professionals and speaks at medical and psychological conferences internationally. She is involved in on-going research on the effects of yoga on mood. Amy's evidence-based LifeForce Yoga protocol is in use in healthcare settings worldwide and is featured on the award-winning CD and the DVD series *LifeForce Yoga to Beat the Blues*. She edits a newsletter that includes current research, news and media reviews on yoga and mental health, archived on her website, yogafordepression.com.

Joanne Wu, MD, E-RYT, CHHC. Dr. Joanne Wu is a rehabilitation medicine physician, experienced registered yoga teacher (E-RYT), wellness consultant, and fitness expert who is passionate about exercise as prescription for healing. Her training includes holistic health coaching (CHHC) through Integrative Nutrition, Medical Acupuncture through Harvard University, and board certification in Integrative and Holistic Medicine. She has a foundation in Anusara Yoga, and continues to broaden her practice through Yoga for Seniors with Duke University, Iyengar Yoga for Scoliosis and Back Care, Baptiste Yoga for Athletes, Restorative Yoga Therapeutics and Thai Yoga Massage. Through these diverse pathways, she has established a vibrant and comprehensive approach to her yoga journey and teaching. Her philosophy of "movement for healthful living" is supported by her background in endurance sports, Spinning, Pilates, Barre, and Hoop. Through her roles as a Lululemon Athletica Ambassador and Acroyoga JAMbassador, Dr. Wu enjoys helping to build a community in which supported play, exploration, and inspiration can be achieved on and off the mat. She currently teaches a variety of fitness classes as well as private mind/body medicine clients, and leads workshops in Aerial Yoga, Partner Yoga and Acroyoga in upstate NY.

Acknowledgments

Books take time and constant seasoning until they are baked, just like a good meal. But this treatise has been a wholly different order since the concoction being stirred was not only my words and work but also that of my collective colleagues and contributors who contributed to the chapters herein. Numerous people encouraged this book, but Dr. Judith Hanson Lasater pushed me towards the finish line and connected me with the seminal authors, whose words grace these pages. And of course, I wish to thank my co-editor, Staffan Elgelid, for being with me every step of the way.

It goes without saying that I am extremely indebted to my agent, Michael Harriot. If it weren't for Michael, this book might still be lurking aimlessly on my hard drive. Thank you, Michael for believing in me and helping me share this work with others. I am especially thankful to Anna Moore, Senior Editor at Routledge, for believing in this book and assigning Elizabeth Graber to the manuscript. I am honored to be a part of this publishing house.

Yet, categorically, I need to thank some very important people who continue to sustain me and have been in my life for the long haul, my immediate family and friends: my husband, Eugene (Jay) V. Marino, Jr., my sister, Dr. Nancy Bachrach, my brother, Dr. Len Horovitz, my brother-in-law, Orin Wechsberg, my sister-in-law, Valerie Saalbach, my mother, Maida Horovitz, my children, Kaitlyn Leah Darby, Bryan James Darby, Nick Marino, and "*The* Paolo" Marino, my cheering squad and closest friends, Karen Armstrong, Janet Rock, and Dr. Jessie Drew-Cates. At work, I am held by numerous supports, specifically Lynn Boucher, Dr. Bryan Hunter, Dr. Shirley Szekeres, and Dr. Sara Varhus. And I thank Marget Braun for leading me to my teacher, Sri François Raoult, who encouraged me onto my path of yoga.

Finally, I wish to thank my clients, whose stories and hearts I have held and entwined with mine, as we worked towards a trajectory of wellness. Thank you for giving meaning to my life.

E.G.H.

Introduction

Ellen G. Horovitz

> There was only ever both, and that is the one. There is no existence and non existence—all knowing is dependent on not knowing—ignorance is the foundation of knowing.
>
> Vishali Varga—May 15, 2012 (personal communication)

Lately, the topic of ignorance is everywhere, but its welcome presence has finally surfaced in the world of Science. You see, for years, scientists have touted their assumptions, hypotheses, and theorems on what we think we know as hard science. But according to recent publications by Kahneman (2011) and Firestein (2012), decision-making (and especially scientific inquiry) is incredibly flawed.

It takes abundant humility to admit one's mistakes and fallibilities. But as we amass more knowledge, humanity's reception seems to be opening up to a deeper questioning of how we function. From the genetic predisposition that propels us unknowingly toward action and being in the world to the final recesses of understanding the brain, scientists are readily admitting that not only are the facts not in but also our investigation of such matters may indeed be flawed.

Frances Sommer Anderson (2008) talked about this in her opening introduction of *Bodies in Treatment*. As editor, she amassed a brilliant collection of writings on relational therapy and as far as I can see, advanced psychoanalysis into the 21st century. Her contributors were talking about the body, how it shaped the "analysand" (analytic patient), willy-nilly, whether invited or not. (Like it or not, the body and the mind are ever so uncomfortably entwined as one working (or non-working) entity.)

I was so struck by Anderson's book, that it initiated collegiality with Fran and germinated the beginnings of this book; indeed this led to inviting some of her influential authors to collaborate in this treatise. But my friendship with Judith Hanson Lasater opened the floodgates to this book's fruition. It was because of her encouragement and connections that several authors jumped into the fold. (It should be noted that there are numerous yoga therapy theorists and practitioners and this volume is not meant as an end point but a beginning conversation. Instead, this collection of expert voices bears witness to some of the science, theories, history, and practice of yoga therapy.) The book is divided into two sections. The first section covers the history and philosophy of yoga, as well as the definition and regulation of yoga therapy. The second section offers a wellspring of chapters on models of practice. Following each of the chapters in the second section, the reader is offered suggestions/questions for practice.

One of my teachers, Vishali Varga said above, "ignorance is the foundation of knowing." It freed me to admit that there is great power in ignorance. If you always do what you have done, the results will always be the same. But conducting yoga from the vantage point of the mind/body/spirit merge is about flexing the brain. To boot, operating from an interoceptive, proprioceptive, kinesthetic experience of being with another human being provides a secondary gain for the yoga therapist, and an unexpected surprise.

Change, not always a welcome harbinger to the homogenous folds of societal directionality, is generally fraught with uncertainty and doubt. But from such inquiry unfolds discovery, invention, and creativity. Such parameters are the breeding ground of health.

While Western treatment as usual (TAU) still appears to be medication coupled with psychotherapy, it is the imagery and creativity of both therapist and client to which one should attend. Functioning from this posture is the platform of yoga therapy. Regardless of whether or not our clients are being treated with pharmaceutical, psychotherapeutic, or alternative methodologies, it is important to operate from the plane of investigation of self, the self-that-is and the self that observes the self-that-is. Csikszentmihalyi (1993, p. 191) talked about this as the "flow experience":

> in the human mind, meeting difficult challenges became genetically linked with a form of pleasure. Just as we have learned to enjoy what is necessary to survive and preserve the species, like eating and sex, so we might have learned to enjoy the flow experience, which spurs us to master increasingly complex challenges. This *cor irrequietus,* this Faustian engine, could be the source of what we count as human progress.

Without this inquiry, there will be stagnation, no growth, and just an addition to the tide of ineffective, deleterious treatment.

Levinthal (1988, p.191) further clarified that through "effective surprise" there is:

> a new placement, perhaps merely a rearrangement, that yields in the end a new perspective, so that we can be transported beyond the everyday ways of experiencing the world. As a result, the world is changed, never to be quite the same again.

It has also been suggested that during this *ah-ha* state there is a temporary loss of ego: often we ignore the cries of our body for sleep, food, drink, and even rest. Instead, we can get caught up in the more celebratory aspects of the work itself. (Of course this state of euphoria can have a flip side to it: depression. Take Alexander the Great who wept at the end of his conquests because he felt there were no more worlds to conquer.)

Oftentimes, when immersed in a yogic or artistic state, time elasticizes. This state is no different than the pleasure derived from food, sex, or any of the other bodily needs as stated above. Perhaps that is why the yogic state is so highly addictive. As Levinthal (1988, pp. 194–195) suggests:

> The similarities to drug addiction may be only suggestive and the evidence circumstantial, but nevertheless, it is plausible that we are dealing with the functioning of brain endorphins . . . the endorphins system in the brain have succeeded in allowing the emergence of a peculiarly human attribute: the pleasure of creating . . .

Levinthal (1988) went so far as suggesting that as a species we are in fact ill named. He gingerly suggested replacing the term *Homo sapiens* (which translates into Latin as "the wise one") with the more accurate *Homo ludens* (which means "the one who plays"). Hammer (1990) would most likely agree wholeheartedly to this idea of *Homo ludens* since he is a major proponent of incorporating laughter and humor into the therapeutic arena. (And as we know, now one can even be certified in Gong Yoga (laughing for no reason.)) The science of laughter in curing dis-ease has been touted for years (Caruth, 1995; Leiber, 1986). In 1999, I discussed the concept of embracing *elemental play* as therapy (Horovitz, 1999).

Sweet (1990, p. 21) writes determinedly about embracing this state in such a forthright manner that donning sunglasses is practically prerequisite. He advises:

> make a list of cultural taboos, find one that personally makes you sweat the most – ones that you've repeatedly dreamed about night and day – and then assume yourself sufficiently energized to explore that tension. After all, . . . (it) . . . is a form of ripping, exposing, revealing, of exorcising what one's particular society and what one's particular self has trouble forbidding. . . creativity.

But in order to enfold elemental play, one must be yoga: otherwise the message is recursive and ill received. So the concept behind elemental play (and being yoga) is that of circularity—completing the loop within the self, indeed a perfect example of yoking, or the yogic state. This concept simply begs that one's inner "yoke" be the healing agent. It is a powerful and medicinal agent. And in the case of inculcating the yogic state with one's clients, one is merely the message-orator: nothing more, nothing less. It is this temporary loss of ego that unfurls the artful bodily/mind state that churns the catalyst toward healing. This is yoga.

In talking about *letting go*, yogi Marc Holzman (2013) stated, "The ultimate definition of yoga is a reunion where we are longing for consciousness. We are longing to feel that connection."

In the US alone, most of the healthcare dollar is spent on lifestyle disease. Modern medicine has not managed stress-related lifestyle. Heart disease, depression, and stroke are slated to be amongst the leading causes of death by 2020 (Hoyert & Xu, 2011; Murray & Lopez, 1997). Since yoga therapy positively elevates hormones that counteract these diseases, prescribing this cost-effect medicinal uptake offers economic, physical, and spiritual recovery for our overwhelmingly complex world. This book sets the present table of yoga therapy, what the field has to offer, where it is heading, and offers expert commentary, analysis, and case studies from the foremost practitioners in the field. May this book open the dialogue and propel a spirited conversation of health and wellbeing.

References

Caruth, C. (1995). *Trauma: Explorations in memory*. Baltimore, MD: Johns Hopkins University Press.

Firestein, S. (2013). *Ignorance: How it drives science*. New York: Oxford University Press.

Hammer, E. (1990). *Reaching the affect/style in psychodynamic therapies*. New York: Aronson Inc.

Holzman, M. (2013). *Precision, gentleness and the ability to let go*. Retrieved October 18, 2014 from www.yogaglo.com/online-class-3202-Precision-Gentleness—The-Ability-to-Let-Go.html

Horovitz, E.G. (1999). *A leap of faith: The call to art*. Springfield, IL: Charles C Thomas.

Hoyert, D.L., and Xu, J. (2011). Deaths: Preliminary data for 2011. *National Vital Statistics Report*, 61(6), 1–6.

Kahneman, D. (2011). *Thinking, fast and slow*. New York: Farrar, Straus and Giroux.

Leiber, D. B. (1986). Laughter and humor in critical care. *Dimensions of Critical Care Nursing*, 5(3), 132–191.

Levinthal, C. (1988). *Messengers of paradise: Opiates and the brain: The struggle over opium, rage, uncertainty and addiction*. New York: Anchor Books.

Murray, C. J., & Lopez, A. D. (1997). Alternative projections of mortality and disability by cause 1990–2020. *Lancet*, 349(9064), 1498–1504.

Sommer Anderson, F. (Ed.) (2008). *Bodies in treatment: The unspoken dimension*. New York: Routledge Press.

Sweet, R.B. (1990). *Writing towards wisdom. The writer as Shaman*. Carmichael, Ca.: Helios House.

Varga, V. (2012). Personal communication.

Section I

History, Philosophy, and Regulation of Yoga Therapy

1 Yoga

History and Philosophy in the West

Richard Rosen

History will be kind to me, for I intend to write it.

Winston Churchill

Figure 1.1

Back in the spring of 1990, the popular magazine *Yoga Journal* triumphantly announced a significant milestone in the history of yoga. "YOGA IN AMERICA," its cover trumpeted in big bold capital letters, with the subtitle, "The First 100 Years" (Dass, 1990). A centennial like this was certainly one to be proud of, more than deserving of the issue's expansive two-part, 18-page report chronicling our yoga beginnings in "How the Swamis Came to the States" and the "spirit" of the contemporary American yoga scene in "From Sea to Shining Sea." There was only one small problem with all this excitement. It's generally agreed that "yoga" first landed on these shores, in the person of one Swami Vivekananda (1863–1902) in 1893, not 1890 (Feuerstein, 2001). To be fair, the magazine acknowledged it was caught up in a "burst of . . . enthusiasm" over its own fifteenth anniversary (founded in 1975 by one of the other contributors to this volume, Judith Hanson Lasater). No doubt the editorial staff decided a look back at, well, almost a century of American yoga would be an appropriate way to put an exclamation point on their own special occasion. And three years later in 1993, Leviton acknowledged the actual anniversary with another, albeit shorter piece in YJ (*Yoga Journal*) "Celebrating 100 Years of Yoga in America."

I imagine most non-yoga people, and maybe a fair number of casual students, would be surprised to learn that yoga has been with us, in one form or another, for 120 years (as I write this in 2015). I say "in one form or another" here because there have actually been two quite different models of yoga introduced to us from India. The first, the one that occasioned *Yoga Journal*'s premature jubilation, came to town with the then 30-year-old Vivekananda (Bharathi, 1998). The story of his epic journey to the US and its aftermath is rich in both inspiration and humor (Urban, 2003).

He was born Narendranath Datta to an upper-class family in Calcutta in 1863. As was typical for young Indian men of his station in those days, he attended British-run schools; consequently his education was thoroughly Western. Apparently he was both highly intelligent and artistically talented, and seemed destined for a successful career whether in the colonial government or the private sector. But in 1881, at the age of 18, he had what proved to be a life-changing run-in with an extremely odd duck by the name of Ramakrishna. Twenty-seven years his senior, Ramakrishna was . . . well, it's hard to pin down just exactly what he was; in fact for a time, because of his unpredictable behavior brought on by fits of ecstatic devotion, he was suspected of being insane. Investigators were dispatched to check him out and decide whether or not to have him institutionalized. Fortunately in the end he was judged to be an enlightened soul and appointed caretaker of a local Hindu temple, a position he held to the end of his life.

Details of the relationship between Naren and Ramakrishna are beyond the scope of this chapter (Isherwood, 1965). Let's just say that at the outset, the big-city, Western-educated teenager was freaked out by the illiterate eccentric from the backcountry, but eventually Ramakrishna's unstinting affection wore down Naren's resistance and he was slowly and inexorably drawn to join the guru's inner circle. When Ramakrishna died in 1886, leaving behind a ragtag community of young disciples, Naren stepped into the void and assumed the leadership role. He designated himself a swami and took the name by which all India still remembers and reveres him, Swami Vivekananda, the "Bliss of Discrimination."

After Ramakrishna's death, Vivekananda followed a monkish custom and set out on a five-year walkabout through all of India, where he was deeply moved by the trials and tribulations of the population. He decided to dedicate himself to alleviating the suffering he saw, and solicited funds from the people of means he met to finance his projects, but received little support. One of his disciples urged him to go to the US, where he might attract the interest of wealthy Americans. It was decided he would attend and speak at the momentous gathering of 1893, the World Parliament of Religion (WPR), an auxiliary event of the Chicago World's Fair, organized to commemorate the 400th anniversary of Columbus's "discovery" of the New World (while *Yoga Journal* jumped the gun by three years on Vivekananda's anniversary, the Fair was a year late because of construction delays). The WPR was the first of its kind in history, a convocation of representatives of ten of the world's major religions, invited to come together in the spirit of cooperation and exchange ideas and perhaps find some common footing. (The footing though turned out to be mostly in each other's backsides, as the dominant Christian delegation didn't take kindly to the deservedly harsh criticism of their missionary efforts from representatives of Western colonized countries, including India).

What Vivekananda didn't know, because he never bothered to find out, was that speaking at the WPR was by invitation only, and not only was he not invited, the program line-up had already been set for several weeks by the time he reached Chicago in the summer of 1893. The story of how this penniless, self-appointed swami, barely out of his twenties and the spiritual offspring of, by Western standards, a mad man, managed to get himself installed on the speakers' platform for one of the most prestigious religious events of the nineteenth century should by now have been made into a Hollywood movie; sadly, we don't have world enough or time to go into it, except to say that he was either blessed with astonishingly good karma, or he was the luckiest guy alive. But what he lacked in foresight and planning he more than made up for with charisma. His talks at the Parliament brought down the house and made him an instant celebrity. He did what celebrities nowadays do to maximize their exposure, he hired an agent and spent the next couple of years in on the road, mostly along the East Coast but also venturing into the Midwestern hinterlands to places like Detroit and Des Moines.

His teaching was loosely based on Classical Yoga, so called because it's counted as one of the six traditional orthodox "viewpoints" (*darshana*) or philosophical systems of India. Had this been the only yoga model to reach our shores, it's quite unlikely it would have made much of a splash in our mainstream culture. With its unbending, puritanical moral code and demanding regimen of sitting meditation, it's best suited to those with a self-denying, ascetic bent, which certainly disqualifies the vast majority of Americans. Indeed, Vivekananda's second foray to the US a few years later was much less successful. He'd had, as we say, his 15 minutes of fame, and though the centers he established here, headed by monks of his order, are still active today, his brand of yoga has taken a back seat to the second model, which for simplicity sake, we can say arrived here in the late 1940s.

This is, of course, what we somewhat inaccurately call Hatha Yoga. To be painstakingly precise, it's better thought of as a modern offshoot we'll call Neo-Hatha Yoga. Oh, you thought everyone was doing the real thing, and now here's someone claiming it's an "offshoot"? I hate to be the bringer of bad news, but what's being passed off in this country as "Hatha Yoga" bears as much resemblance to the traditional practice as an orange does to an apple. Yes, there are some superficial similarities, they're both round for example, and both are fruits, but there are a whole lot of essential differences as well. Let me explain.

Traditional Hatha Yoga emerged in India round about 1000 CE, give or take, as is usual with these old Indian dates, a century on either side (de Michels,

2005). Now we have to be careful when we talk about "Hatha Yoga," because over its thousand-year run it assumed a host of variegated forms and guises. It's best to think of it as an umbrella term rather than as a monolithic praxis, covering an ever evolving cast of typically outrageous methods and characters. Now for a number of reasons way beyond the scope of this chapter, by the end of the nineteenth century in India, traditional Hatha had fallen on hard times and was on its last, wobbly leg, persecuted by the country's British rulers and scorned by respectable citizens, including, ironically enough considering its current popularity, our friend Vivekananda. In an attempt to preserve and propagate some semblance of the ancient discipline, a handful of Indian teachers set out to revive and then popularize the downtrodden, bed-ridden patient, among them the so-called "father of modern yoga," the imposing scholar-yogi Tirumalai Krishnamacharya (1888–1989) (Mohan & Mohan; 2010). But to do that the teachers faced a conundrum. In general, like its Classical cousin, traditional Hatha was intended for a select group of renunciate males who were strictly supervised by self-realized gurus (although it appears that as time went on, householders and women were admitted to the fold). Several of its key individual practices were either too complicated or too dangerous for an unsupervised mass audience. In the name of safety, these then had to be deleted from the practice repertoire. They were replaced by a trainload of exercises co-opted from areas like Indian wrestling and European gymnastics, which were christened with Sanskrit names to "yoga them up" and magically transformed into "postures" (*asana*). The result is that unlike traditional Hatha, which relied on only a relative handful of postures as preparations for the real focus of the practice, controlled breathing (*pranayama*) and sitting meditation, our most popular schools of Neo-Hatha lean heavily on the asanas, so that most "yoga" classes in this country are in fact more accurately described as "asana" classes (for a fascinating account of the development of modern yoga, see Singleton, 2010).

American teachers are often bitterly accused by traditionalists of "distorting" the purity of yoga, turning it into nothing more than gymnastics, but it was the Indian Neo-Hatha innovators who started the ball rolling in the 1930s. Representatives of the new order began showing up here en masse after 1965, the year Congress passed an Immigration Act abolishing quotas for immigrants based on national origin, which had been in effect for the previous 40 years. Like its traditional predecessor, Neo-Hatha covers a bewildering variety of styles. A quick check of the *Yoga Journal* website (yogajournal.com) provides us with a potpourri of current schools. Some take the name of their leading light, and so we have Bikram Yoga, named after its fiery and controversial inventor, Bikram Choudhury, or Iyengar Yoga, named after perhaps the most influential teacher of the twentieth century, B.K.S. Iyengar, selected in 2004 by *Time Magazine* as one of the top 100 people in its heroes and icons category (Stengel, 2004). Other American-born schools assume Sanskrit names, like Purna Yoga or Anusara Yoga, to lend themselves an aura of tradition and authenticity, or names that presumably appeal to Americans' love of sweaty and/or high-tech workouts, like Hot Yoga (a spin-off of Bikram) or Synergy Yoga.

So while we can technically claim for our own satisfaction, as well as for marketing purposes on special occasions, that we're two decades into our second yoga century, we have to add that it's only been over the last 50 years or so that yoga has been embraced by and made its mark on our mainstream culture. Compared to our ancient Indian predecessors, we're no more than yoga babies, figuratively lying in our cribs wiggling our fingers and toes. But we're growing up fast. Across the country, in large cities and small towns alike, yoga schools are becoming as ubiquitous as gas stations and fast food chains. Moreover, these schools aren't the only venues offering classes, and hale and hearty 25-year-olds who can touch their toes without bending their knees aren't the only ones taking classes. Just about any empty room with bare floor space can accommodate a yoga class, and just about any person, whatever his or her age or physical condition, is a candidate for participation. Accordingly, we find classes hosted in health clubs, college gymnasiums, senior citizen, veteran, and pre-school day care centers, corporate meeting rooms, homeless shelters, hospitals, churches and synagogues, even jails and prisons.

This raises two questions for non-yogis: what exactly is "yoga," and how many of us actually "practice" it? If we ask any moderately experienced student to define the Sanskrit word "yoga," we'll inevitably get an answers like "yoking" (yoga is cognate with this word) or "union" (but not with this one). The implication is that the culmination of a successful yoga practice, at least as it's framed by the long tradition, results in the "union" of two totally immaterial entities. One is typically described as the "embodied self," the animating soul or spirit of the individual person, and the other the "great" or "cosmic Self," which is treated as the corresponding pervasive soul or spirit of the universe.

But there's a usually unrecognized shortcoming with the yoga-as-union definition. A quick check of "yoga" in the Sanskrit–English dictionary shows it's packed with multiple meanings, a common feature of many words in the yoga lexicon (Monier-Williams, 1976). In addition to the "act of yoking, joining, attaching, harnessing," we also find a string of definitions along the line of "means, expedient, device, way, manner, method," that are almost always overlooked. This tells us that yoga-as-union is only half the story. While "union" signifies the *goal* of the practice, the Indian yogis insist there must also always be a *practical method* to reach that goal. The two go together like a horse and carriage. We can't reach the goal without a marked path to follow, and without an intended goal the path will just be a long and winding road with no destination. So to be more precise, yoga should ideally be rendered as "union-method."

Of course, the traditional spiritual goal of "yoga-as-union" has little or nothing to do with why most Americans practice yoga. We have in general far more mundane reasons, such as improving physical strength and flexibility, for temporary relief of job-related stress, or increasingly as a modality in some kind of therapeutic program. We even now have a class of teachers known as "yoga therapists" trained in the use of individual techniques like posture, conscious breathing, and meditation, to help heal the body–mind. I hasten to add that there's absolutely nothing wrong with these applications. While some conservative elements of the yoga community criticize our yoga motives as a distortion of the original intent, in fact the old yoga books have plenty of references to the health benefits, both physical and emotional, of yoga.

If you're not a student yourself, there's a good chance you have a friend or colleague or relative that is. A recent survey (posted online at www.statisticbrain.com/yoga-statistics/) projected the number of American yogis at 15 million, just under 5% of our population, though I've seen estimates go as high as 20 million. Unfortunately the survey doesn't specify what it means by "practice." Is it a bare minimum, like once-a-week attendance (except when the relatives are in town or the family dog is ill) at a 90-minute public class? Or something more substantial, like a dedicated, once-a-day, hour-long, at-home session (even if Fido has the sniffles)? It's impossible to say for sure, but having taught now for more than 26 years, I'd guess the definition of "practice" is closer to the former than the latter. Even so, no matter what the practice entails, 15 million is an eye-catching number, especially when we consider the relatively short time yoga's been accepted in this country by John and Jane Q. Public. But what makes the number even more astonishing is the survey's finding that nearly three-quarters of our yogis are college graduates, and just about the same percentage earn upwards of $75,000 yearly.

If it were possible to conduct this same survey among the Indian yogis of, say, 1500 CE, we would come out with much different results. As I mentioned earlier, the traditional yogi was typically a male who had permanently renounced family, friends, and material possessions, except for a ragged loin cloth to wrap his privates (though some went about naked, wearing nothing but a coat of ashes), a staff, and the top of a human skull used as a begging bowl (it's a long story), and wandered homeless through the cities and countryside living hand-to-mouth. Today in the US, with the possible exception of a few throwbacks lurking around the fringes of "straight" society, the once severe and uncompromising yogic life is a thing of the distant past. Our modern survey estimates that the annual hand-to-cash-register expenditure on yoga and yoga "products" is $27 billion, the same as earnings accumulated in recent years by Apple and Exxon, an average expense of $1800 for each and every yogin and yogini.

You might first think that the word "billion" in the previous sentence is a misprint, which it's not. So the next the question arises, how is it possible to spend that much money on yoga classes? It would be a stretch, so to speak, if all the money did go just to classes, but once the American entrepreneurial spirit got wind of that alluring amount of disposable income, it wasn't long before the yoga "industry" was open for business. What did good old Yankee ingenuity come up with? For starters, just like computer nerds, real estate agents, and Star Trek enthusiasts, yogis can attend big-city or resort-hosted "conventions." There they gather by the hundreds to see and be seen, cramming into cavernous hotel ballrooms for the chance to "study" with superstar instructors. There are also the many yoga "retreats," or more accurately vacations, which may be drive-to local affairs in woodsy settings organized by popular local area favorites, or fly-to jaunts with those same convention superstars to exotic locales in Hawaii, Mexico, Greece, and the motherland of yoga itself, India. Next, we can't overlook all the accouterments of modern yoga practice, starting with the mat. The evolution of the yoga mat over the last 30 years would be a spellbinding tale. In 1987, when I opened up my yoga school in Oakland, California, a large roll of sticky mat material could be had for around $100, a princely sum back then, especially on a yoga teacher's earnings. Shortening the standard five-foot-long mat by a few inches, strictly for ecological purposes, we could cut 8 to 10 mats from the roll, costing us about $10 per mat. Depending on the frequency and intensity of their usage in our classes, one of these mats would last for a few months before it started shredding and shedding little green "snowflakes" all over the classroom floor. Nowadays some single mats are priced at $100, but they are made out of some indestructible rubbery material that will likely outlast you and can be handed down to kids and grand kids as a family heirloom.

But mats are just the tip of the yoga props iceberg. Props are nothing new, yogis have been using them for hundreds of years. When sitting cross-leg for long bouts of meditation, for example, the old yogis might have wrapped a cloth band around their lower back and knees to ease their stay in the posture. Others might have used a short crutch-like tool on which to rest their chin while sitting in meditation, so those who slipped off to sleep during the practice wouldn't nosedive down to earth. Now there are two general schools of thought about props in the modern yoga community. One insists that props of whatever kind are "crutches" that, if used long and often enough, encourage dependence and ultimately inhibit "progress," however that's defined. The other school believes just the opposite. Props, comes their retort, help students, particularly beginners or disabled people hold onto or balance in postures more safely and for a longer time, which speeds "progress." Who's right? I tend to throw in with the latter position, but I can understand the rationale behind the former, and don't dismiss it totally. In any case, some schools use few or no props, while others (like the Iyengar school) use them in profusion. It's not uncommon that the practice space at the end of an Iyengar class looks like a kindergarten room after an unsupervised play period: metal folding chairs, foam blocks and wedges, blankets and round bolsters, cotton straps, and 10-pound sand bags are scattered helter-skelter about the floor. Props like these, along with specialty items like pelvic slings, head standers, back benders, and "trestles" or "horses"—to the uninitiated this must sound like some exquisite form of yogic torture—can run to thousands of dollars for the well-stocked yoga school, hundreds for the individual practitioner.

Wait, there's more. Yogis have produced instructional manuals for hundreds of years, though customarily they were few and far between, and never intended for mass consumption, only for a relative handful of cognoscenti. But when yoga became a mass movement in the mid-twentieth century, the instructional manual underwent a radical change. Now if you search for "yoga" in Amazon's book section you'll get over 25,000 results (including somewhere in there the four books I've written). Along with books we can buy magazines, like *Yoga Journal*, and instructional CDs and DVDs. The latter might feature one of our superstars in a high-end production on a beach in Hawaii with sweeping panoramas of the Pacific, or an up-and-coming but relative unknown teacher with high hopes and a shoestring budget. These vids, as I call them, have multiplied like Tribbles over the past 20 years, which is how long I've been reviewing them for *Yoga Journal*. My total passed 300 a few years back, and I've looked at but not reviewed at least half again as many. Finally, last but by no means least—in fact, I strongly suspect this is where the lion's share of the money is going—are the yoga "fashions," the colorful $80 tights, the $60 tops and $50 tanks, even a $40 towel, aimed for the most part at, guess who?

Who indeed. Because of women's low-class status in pre-twentieth-century India, female yogis were scarce. Nowadays however in this country, male dominance has been flipped upside down, as if doing a headstand. Anyone who regularly attends a yoga class can verify what our survey found: that a substantial majority of our 15 million practitioners, somewhere in the neighborhood of 75% or between 10 and 11 million, are female. This is amazing, especially because relative to traditional Hatha Yoga's approximately thousand year run, it happened in a handful of decades, an historical wink of the eye. Consider that as late as the 1930s, modern yoga dad Krishnamacharya refused to accept women as his students, and only reluctantly accepted his first after being pressured by his patron to take her on (Mohan & Mohan, 2010).

We might pause briefly at this point to wonder who this wonder woman was, someone who should well serve as inspiration to all female practitioners (and open-minded male students as well). Her given name was Eugenie Peterson. Born in Russia (though by today's geography, it would be Latvia) in 1899, she was better known to the world as Indra Devi (this might be taken as a "spiritual name," but in fact it was an assumed stage name for her acting roles in several Indian movies). Devi was sort of the Lewis and Clark of female yoga, an intrepid adventurer who ventured into what was for her gender uncharted territory, which had been dominated for a millennium by male misogynists; moreover she took as her guide a man who was by all accounts the sternest of taskmasters. In the end, through her dedication and perseverance, she won him over completely. In 1948, she made her way to the US and opened one of our first public yoga schools in—where better?— Hollywood, and eventually became the first "yoga teacher to the stars," attracting such motion picture luminaries as Gloria Swanson and Marilyn Monroe. Surely as a tribute to her yoga practice and clean-living lifestyle, she lived for over 100 years, passing on in 2002 (Aboy, 2002).

Explanations for this great disparity in yoga attendance between the sexes are legion. We get different responses depending on who we're asking, and since there are no surveys on this question (that I'm aware of) to confirm or disprove the theories, every one of them should be taken but with a grain of salt. One popular position—popular, that is, with women—is that yoga demands a high degree of flexibility, and since women are generally more flexible than men (both physically and psychologically, some will argue), they're more naturally drawn to the practice. The reverse side of this coin is that men, who are presumed to be innately competitive by nature, are turned off by yoga because, as the stiffer gender, they unconsciously believe they're "losing" the one-sided "battle" for class superiority to women (and here I offer my apologies to all the male readers, we don't for a minute believe any of this is true).

Whatever the reasons for the preponderance of women in modern yoga, we can surely expect that the feminine element will have a sizable influence on the development of yoga in this country and in the West in the coming decades. We already see one result in the work of Angela Farmer who, along with husband Victor van Kooten, form one of yoga's most dynamic teaching duos. Early in her career Farmer was a dyed-in-the-wool Iyengar-ite, trained by the Boss himself in that rigorous method with its emphasis on physical alignment and stability. But over time, though she was one of the world's foremost practitioners of Iyengar Yoga, she became more and more dissatisfied with what she considered its relatively rigid "masculine" influence. Then one day, as she relates the story, she had an epiphany while visiting a Hindu temple decorated with zaftig, sensual female carvings. The experience re-inspired and transformed her teaching and practice, and physically controlled postures gave way to free-flowing, serpentine-like, "feminine" performances (the word posture just doesn't seem to suit what she does) that has had a significant impact on the way both genders approach the practice.

As I see it, and remember I have no crystal ball that confirms these predictions, there are two "streams" of practice in American yoga that will take us into the future. On the one hand we have what we can call "exercise yoga," which is now extremely popular with the younger generation, and some older folks too, who might not yet be experiencing the ravages of time and tide. This yoga is, as the name suggests, practice for no other purpose than physical development, such as strength, flexibility, endurance, and the like. While many in the yoga community decry this approach, there's actually plenty of precedent for it in the Hatha tradition. One practice manual, for example, dating from the mid-fifteenth century, promises that a simple sitting forward bend will "flatten" your belly and "bring good health" (Hatha Yoga Pradipika (HYP) 1.29; Svatmarama, 2000), or that a particular breathing exercise will turn you into Kama, the Hindu god of love (you might want to check this out at HYP 2.54). Another later text assures us that by regular practice of a certain exercise, we can eradicate old-age wrinkles and remain eternally youthful (Gheranda Samhita 3.52; Anonymous, 2004). Neo-Hatha, with its many challenging postures, which can be linked together in "flowing" sequences as a strenuous asana "workout," is actually ideally suited to this kind of activity. No doubt this style of yoga will continue to appeal to the majority of American students for a long time to come. The real objection to exercise yoga is, other than from the sticklers who hold that since it's not ultimately "spiritually inclined," then technically it's not truly yoga as tradition defines it, that there are occasions, in certain schools with certain overly enthusiastic teachers, that students are encouraged to push well beyond their reasonable physical limits, and the result not infrequently is, predictably, minor to more or less serious injuries. However, to be fair, exercise yoga when instructed intelligently and performed consciously is an excellent way to stay in tip-top physical condition.

The other "stream" we can call, for lack of a better term, "neo-traditional yoga," yoga that seeks to re-establish the original intent of the discipline, self-transformation or self-realization, but in ways suited to the exigencies of the modern West. No doubt there are some modern schools whose leaders will adamantly insist that their raison d'être has been "spiritual" from the very get-go. Be that as it may, neo-traditional yoga seems to me, over the past few years, to be picking up a chugging head of steam, as more and more students become interested in the "deeper dimension" of yoga, to borrow a phrase from the title of a book by the late Georg Feuerstein (1947–2012), who during his life was one of our leading advocates for a return to yoga's spiritual roots (Feuerstein, 2003). Many of these students started their practice swimming in the exercise stream, but have now dipped a toe or even dived head first into the neo-traditional, and I fully expect many more will follow. But I want to be sure, in closing, to make it clear that neither of these streams is "better" or "more yogic" than the other. Neo-Hatha Yoga is proving to be a near infinitely adaptable and flexible discipline, which can accommodate pretty much the entire spectrum of the American public, whatever are their yoga needs or desires. In my experience over the last 30+ years of practice, I haven't run across anyone who, by age or physical condition, couldn't in some way engage in a yoga practice that would positively affect his or her life on some level, whether physical or spiritual or both. What will neo-traditional yoga look like? Let's agree to return in 200 years and find out.

References

Aboy, A. (2002). Indra Devi's legacy. *Hinduism Today*. Retrieved September 1, 2014: www.hinduismtoday.com/modules/smartsection/item.php?itemid=3846.

Anonymous (2004). Gheranda Samhita. In S. Ghosh (Ed.) *The original yoga* (pp. 103–165). New Delhi: Munshiram Manoharlal.

Bharathi, K. S. (1998). *Encyclopaedia of eminent thinkers: The political thought of Vivekananda*. New Delhi, India: Concept Publishers.

Dass, B. H. (1990). Yoga in America: The first 100 years. *Yoga Journal*, March/April, 42.

de Michelis, E. (2005). *A history of modern yoga*. New York: Continuum.

Feuerstein, G. (2001). *The yoga tradition: Its history, literature, philosophy, and practice*. Prescott: AZ: Hohm Press.

Feuerstein, G. (2003). *The deeper dimension of yoga: Theory and practice*. Boston, MA: Shambhala Publications.

Isherwood, C. (1965). *Ramakrishna and his disciples*. Hollywood, CA: Vedanta Press.

Leviton, R. (1993). Celebrating 100 years of yoga in America. *Yoga Journal*, May/June, 67–71.

Mohan, A. G., & Mohan, G. (2010). *Krishnamacharya: His life and teachings.* Boston, MA: Shambhala Publications.

Monier-Williams, M. (1976). *Sanskrit–English dictionary* (p. 856). New Delhi: Munshiram Manoharlal Publishers.

Singleton, M. (2010). *Yoga body: The origins of modern posture practice.* New York, NY: Oxford University Press.

Stengel, R. (2004). The 2004 Time 100: Heroes & icons. *Time.* April, 61.

Svatmarama, Y. (2000). *The Hatha Yoga pradipika.* Chennai, India: The Adyar Library and Research Centre.

Urban, H. (2003). Deodorized tantra: Sex, scandal, secrecy, and censorship. In J. Woodroffe (Ed.), & Swami Vivekananda, *Tantra: Sex, secrecy, politics, and power in the study of tantra* (pp. 134–164). Berkeley: University of California Press.

2 Yoga Therapy, Defined

Staffan Elgelid and Erin Byron

Our scientific age demands that we provide definitions, measurements, and statistics in order to be taken seriously. Yet most of the important things in life cannot be precisely defined or measured. Can we define or measure love, beauty, friendship, or decency, for example?

Dennis Prager

Figure 2.1

Definitions

Yoga is growing rapidly in the Western world. Mostly it is yoga in the form of asana, pranayama, and some meditation. Also growing, albeit not as fast as yoga, is the field of yoga therapy. As more and more people are being exposed to the field of yoga therapy the question becomes what is yoga therapy, how is it different from regular yoga and how does it fit into today's society and Western medicine? Just as with any other definitions, people and organizations will have different ways to define the same thing. This is especially true for a newer profession such as yoga therapy.

In the United States the International Association of Yoga Therapists (IAYT) have defined (the educational standards) of yoga therapy as follows (IAYT, 2012):

> Yoga therapy is the process of empowering individuals to progress toward improved health and wellbeing through the application of the teachings and practices of Yoga.

In addition, in the educational standards the IAYT (IAYT, 2010) states that:

> Yoga therapy is the appropriate application of these teachings and practices in a therapeutic context in order to support a consistent yoga practice that will increase self-awareness and engage the client/student's energy in the direction of desired goals. The goals of yoga therapy include eliminating, reducing, or managing symptoms that cause suffering; improving function; helping to prevent the occurrence or re-occurrence of underlying causes of illness; and moving toward improved health and wellbeing. Yoga therapy also helps clients/students change their relationship to and identification with their condition.

On the IAYT website (IAYT, 2010), other selected definitions of contemporary yoga therapy are also found:

> Yoga therapy is a self-empowering process, where the care-seeker, with the help of the Yoga therapist, implements a personalized and evolving Yoga practice, that not only addresses the illness in a multi-dimensional manner, but also aims to alleviate his/her suffering in a progressive, non-invasive and complementary manner. Depending upon the nature of the illness, Yoga therapy can not only be preventative or curative, but also serve as a means to manage the illness, or facilitate healing in the person at all levels.
>
> TKV Desikachar & Kausthub Desikachar

> Yoga therapy, derived from the Yoga tradition of Patanjali and the Ayurvedic system of health care, refers to the adaptation and application of Yoga techniques and practices to help individuals facing health challenges at any level manage their condition, reduce symptoms, restore balance, increase vitality, and improve attitude.
>
> Gray Kraftsow, American Viniyoga Institute (USA)

> Yoga therapy is that facet of the ancient science of Yoga that focuses on health and wellness at all levels of the person: physical, psychological, and spiritual. Yoga therapy focuses on the path of Yoga as a healing journey that brings balance to the body and mind through an experiential understanding of the primary intention of Yoga: awakening of Spirit, our essential nature.
>
> Joseph LePage, Integrative Yoga Therapy (USA)

> Yoga therapy adapts the practice of Yoga to the needs of people with specific or persistent health problems not usually addressed in a group class.
>
> Larry Payne, Samata Yoga Center (USA)

Yoga therapy is the adaptation of yoga practices for people with health challenges. Yoga therapists prescribe specific regimens of postures, breathing exercises, and relaxation techniques to suit individual needs. Medical research shows that Yoga therapy is among the most effective complementary therapies for several common aliments. The challenges may be an illness, a temporary condition like pregnancy or childbirth, or a chronic condition associated with old age or infirmity.

Robin Monro, PhD, Yoga Biomedical Trust (England)

Yoga comprises a wide range of mind/body practices, from postural and breathing exercises to deep relaxation and meditation. Yoga therapy tailors these to the health needs of the individual. It helps to promote all-round positive health, as well as assisting particular medical conditions. The therapy is particularly appropriate for many chronic conditions that persist despite conventional medical treatment.

Marie Quail, Yoga Therapy and Training Center (Ireland)

The use of the techniques of Yoga to create, stimulate, and maintain an optimum state of physical, emotional, mental, and spiritual health.

Judith Hanson Lasater, PhD

Yoga therapy consists of the application of yogic principles, methods, and techniques to specific human ailments. In its ideal application, Yoga therapy is preventive in nature, as is Yoga itself, but it is also restorative in many instances, palliative in others, and curative in many others.

Art Brownstein, MD

Yoga therapy may be defined as the application of yogic principles to a particular person with the objective of achieving a particular spiritual, psychological, or physiological goal. The means employed are comprised of intelligently conceived steps that include but are not limited to the components of Ashtanga Yoga, which includes the educational teachings of *yama*, *niyama*, *asana*, *pranayama*, *pratyahara*, *dharana*, *dhyana*, and *samadhi*. Also included are the application of meditation, textual study, spiritual or psychological counseling, chanting, imagery, prayer, and ritual to meet the needs of the individual. Yoga therapy respects individual differences in age, culture, religion, philosophy, occupation, and mental and physical health. The knowledgeable and competent yogin or yogini applies Yoga Therapy according to the period, the place, and the practitioner's age, strength, and activities.

Richard Miller, PhD

Yoga therapy is of modern coinage and represents a first effort to integrate traditional yogic concepts and techniques with Western medical and psychological knowledge. Whereas traditional Yoga is primarily concerned with personal transcendence on the part of a "normal" or healthy

> individual, Yoga therapy aims at the holistic treatment of various kinds of psychological or somatic dysfunctions ranging from back problems to emotional distress. Both approaches, however, share an understanding of the human being as an integrated body–mind system, which can function optimally only when there is a state of dynamic balance.
>
> Georg Feurstein, PhD

> Yoga therapy is a holistic healing art. Rather than prescribe treatments, it invites presence and awareness. Using age-old yogic approaches to deeper presence and awareness, we are able to know ourselves more fully. Out of that knowing, we are more easily moved to embrace the opportunity for change, growth, and enhanced wellbeing in body, feelings, thought, and spirit.
>
> Michael Lee, Phoenix Rising Yoga Therapy

> Yoga therapy is the application of Yoga to individuals to empower them to progress toward greater health and freedom from disease.
>
> Ganesh Mohan, Svastha Yoga and Ayurveda

In addition, Butera (2012) of YogaLife has defined yoga therapy as follows:

> Comprehensive Yoga Therapy applies to self-realization from classical Yoga traditions to alleviate suffering through harmonization of body, energy, mind and intellect.

While other schools and individuals may have different definitions of what yoga therapy is, most of the above definitions include terms such as empowering, holistic, all level healing (physical, psychological, emotional, and spiritual), alleviate suffering, and applying the principles of Yoga. Yoga therapy is grounded in classical, philosophical texts such as the Vedas, *Yoga Sutras of Patanajli*, and *Bhagavad Gita*. While not specifically defining yoga therapy, the *Yoga Sutras* (chapter 1 verse 2) define yoga as "the suppression of the modifications of the mind" (Mukeri, 1983), or the stilling of the waves of the mind (Butera, 2012). Butera (2012) goes on to state that for yoga therapy to "still the waves of the mind: the practices chosen should yield an internal steadiness and lead the practitioner to transcend the suffering of the body and unite with pure consciousness" (p. 1). To accomplish this stilling of the waves of the mind, the yoga therapist will apply the "teachings and practices of yoga" according to the teachings of Patanjali.

What Are Considered the Teachings and Practices of Yoga?

The teachings and practices of yoga are much more than asana, pranayama, and meditation. While asanas, pranayama, and meditation techniques are a part of yoga therapy, yoga therapy encompasses all eight limbs of yoga to improve the client's awareness of how lifestyle choices affect all aspects of life, and ultimately leads to suffering. The eight limbs of yoga are yamas (restraints), niyamas (observances), asana (mind–body postures), pranayama (breath control), pratayahara (sensory withdrawal), dharana (concentration), dhyana (meditation), and samadhi (pure awareness) (Butera, 2010). The yoga therapist will utilize all the eight limbs of yoga to increase the person's awareness of his/her own unique needs and how lifestyle choices can impact health, harmony, and consciousness in all aspects of life. While all eight limbs are important tools for the yoga therapist, the first two limbs, yamas and niyamas, might be the most important, and often overlooked, branches of yoga for successful lifestyle changes. As one moves through the limbs the practices become more personally driven, while the yamas and niyamas are more specific and universal. A person who follows the yamas and niyamas will live a lifestyle that is conducive to comprehensive health and wellbeing.

The yamas (restraints) are ahimsa (non-violence), satya (truthfulness), asteya (non-stealing), bramacharya (moderation), and aparigraha (non-attachment) (Butera, 2010).

Non-violence (ahimsa) is commonly thought of as violence towards others, but also included in the yoga concept of non-violence is refraining from violence towards ourselves. Many people practice non-violence towards others, but are blind towards the violence they do to themselves. The violence towards self can take the form of pushing too hard at work, sports, or asanas. Non-violence can also take the form of the person being overly self-critical, comparing themselves to others at all times, or creating an internal climate of negativity.

Truthfulness (satya) is more than speaking the truth. Truthfulness also includes honoring the truth towards ourselves. That includes breaking habits and patterns that are not fostering health and wellbeing, and looking out for the wellbeing of everyone including ourselves.

Non-stealing (asteya) is another restraint that seems obvious, but included in non-stealing is not desiring what others have. Most people don't steal, but we desire what we don't have, or what someone else has and that mental form of stealing robs our own contentment.

Moderation and non-attachment (bramacharya) can be realized when we don't desire what we don't have. Once we have silenced our desires (non-stealing) we can live a life of moderation and non-attachment, directing our energies towards self-realization rather than squandering it on frivolities. All the yamas are interdependent, in that living the concept of one tends to lead to improvements in the other yamas too. The same is also true of the niyamas.

The niyamas (observances) are saucha (purity), santosha (contentment), tapas (discipline), svadhyaya (introspection), and ishvara pranidhana (surrender to an infinite reality) (Butera, 2010).

Purity (saucha) includes many of our daily actions such as the food we eat, the activities we perform, and physical hygiene; but purity also includes *mental hygiene*. Consider what we absorb mentally on a daily basis: movies we watch, news reports we hear, music we listen to, even the people we spend time with (voluntarily or otherwise) have a direct impact on our state of mind and general attitude. Asana practice contributes to purity by improving the blood flow of the body and increasing the elimination of physical toxins through deep breathing and movement. Yoga therapy helps us consider how to purify the mental toxins that accumulate on a daily basis.

Contentment (santosha) offers an abiding sense of wellbeing. It is closely connected to not desiring what we don't have. A great deal of effort goes into chasing the things that we do not have but are sure will bring us happiness; but unlike contentment, this kind of happiness is fleeting. Through the restraints and observances, yoga poses and breathing, and uplifted state of mind we can be happy with who we are and what we have.

Discipline (tapas) is needed to be able to still the waves of the mind, and maintain physical and mental purity. The idea of this discipline is that it sparks the fire of enthusiasm within us, so that we enjoy our healthy routines and what they do for us. Sometimes we resist yoga practice and other beneficial lifestyle choices; this is the burn of that purifying fire of discipline. That little sting reminds us that this personal purpose is worth the effort. Clients of yoga therapy evaluate their own priorities and situations to make healthy routines a part of everyday life.

Introspection (svadhyaya) gives us a chance to observe ourselves as we are without making judgments. We observe the choices that we make, and can from that determine if we are true to ourselves, the yamas and niyamas, and if we are on the path to a lifestyle that leads to wellness and harmony in all aspects of our lives. Introspection will also allow us to observe how our responses to external events (stress) influence us. The last niyama, *surrender* (ishvara pranidhana) is a way for us to let go of all the burdens that affect us. It is the realization that we cannot control everything and that there is a point where we just have to let go and have faith that God, the Universe, or whatever larger than ourselves deity/principle we believe in will take care of all beings.

Many yoga therapists will evaluate the person's yamas and niyamas as part of the initial visit, since they form the foundation of yoga therapy. The assessment of the yamas and niyamas can guide the yoga therapist towards what lifestyle changes are needed for a life where the client can transform stress, form healthy relationships, deal with setbacks, and eventually reach the stillness of mind that leads to decreased suffering, and self-realization/enlightenment.

Why Do We Need Lifestyle Changes?

The needs for lifestyle changes become more and more important in today's society, and guiding our clients towards lifestyle changes may be where yoga therapy can make the biggest impact today and in the future. The yoga therapist will guide the client towards an individualized comprehensive life style approach that will help the client reach his/her personal goals. Similar outcomes can arise from varying yoga lifestyle interventions, as each client follows his or her own strengths, aptitudes, and interests. Through the support of a yoga therapist and self-reliant action, the client becomes an active student of her/his own beneficial routines.

Yoga therapy does not treat disease as an acute illness, that is the role of the medical profession, or in the case of psychological dysfunction the role of psychologists and psychiatrists. The yoga therapist is aware that the yoga therapist's job is not to diagnose and "fix" what is "wrong" with the client, or to just treat the client's symptoms. Instead the yoga therapist looks at, evaluates, and guides the client towards physical, psychological, mental, and spiritual wellness. The yoga therapist offers education and practices to restore harmony and consciousness to all those facets of the client's life, and looks at what is "right" with the client. This does not mean that yoga therapy will not have an impact on diseases, acute illnesses, and psychological conditions, but it does so through lifestyle changes, increased awareness, and uncovering of ineffective, habitual behaviors and thought patterns. The yoga therapist is more interested in the distinct intention of the client and the resources available to the client and how they can be utilized to improve the person's health, and less interested in the disease process. To be able to guide the client towards this improved level of health the yoga therapist must have an understanding of the client's physical, mental, and emotional status, the client's goals and intention, and then guide the client towards finding the path of yoga that is right for him/her. This guidance is informed by assessments based on yogic and Ayurvedic concepts such as the five paths of yoga, the gunas, chakras, kosha, and the kleshas.[1]

What Type of Assessments Does the Yoga Therapist Use?

When a client goes to see a yoga therapist, the therapist might have the client complete several assessment forms that will guide the therapist in the work with the client. The forms will give the therapist an idea of where the client is right now, as well as which of the paths of yoga the client might be most receptive to. Yoga can be said to have five major paths: Jnana Yoga (the path of yoga and intellect), Bhakti Yoga (the path of love and devotion), Karma Yoga (the path of action and selfless service), Raja Yoga (the path of discipline and meditation), and Tantra Yoga (the path of health and wellbeing) (Swami Rama, 1982; Butera 2012). Each individual has a path/practice that he/she is more inclined to follow at each phase of life. Based on the client's answer to the questions in regards to the five paths of yoga, the therapist can then suggest activities for the client that is in line with the client's preferred path of yoga. The assessment and awareness of the five paths of yoga is something that sets yoga therapy apart from "regular" yoga. Complete yoga should ideally use all eight limbs of yoga, but only a yoga therapist tends to evaluate and take into consideration the five paths of yoga. While evaluation of the different paths will guide the therapist as to what kind of general overall approach might be the most appropriate for the client's temperament and needs, assessment of gunas (quality of existence), chakras (balance between energy centers), koshas (concerns within each of the five sheaths that constitutes the client), and kleshas (what psychological blocks are present?) will direct the yoga therapist towards the client's strengths and weaknesses and give more detailed information about what might be blocking the progress of the client and what specific activities might be the most appropriate for the client (Butera, 2010, 2012).

Not all yoga therapists will utilize all of the different assessment methods. Some yoga therapists might not use any written assessment forms, while others might use different assessment forms depending on the needs of the clients. However, a thorough assessment can give the therapist insights into how the client functions from a yogic perspective and how the client functions at so many different levels. Until the yoga therapist understands the client at a deep level it is difficult to work out an effective yoga therapy course of action. Not to be forgotten is that the yoga therapist could also, and probably should, use modern assessments tools too. The yoga therapist should know basic medical information such as past medical history, medications (including supplements) that the client takes, activity levels, and treatments that the client is undergoing or has undergone prior to the visit to the yoga therapist. Once the yoga therapist has an understanding of the client from a yogic and medical perspective the yoga therapist can create a unique, individualized plan for the client.

How is Yoga Therapy Different from Western/ Allopathic Medicine?

Yoga therapy is different from allopathic medicine, but they need to work hand in hand for the maximum benefit of the client. According to Webster's Dictionary, allopathic is defined as: a system of medicine that aims to combat disease by using remedies (as drugs or surgery) which produce effects that are different from or incompatible with those of the disease being treated (Merriam-Webster, 2014). In the above definition there is no mention of the basic element included in the definition of yoga therapy such as empowering individuals, having the patient progress towards health and wellbeing, healing at different levels, or of applying a philosophy and practice (IAYT, 2010). Allopathic medicine tends to be more about combating the acute phase of the disease or reducing the intensity of its symptoms, while yoga therapy is more about empowering the individual, healing at multiple levels, etc. Let's make it clear that allopathic medicine does a wonderful job combating a large variety of diseases and conditions. For a fractured bone we want to see the orthopedic surgeon if surgery is needed. Antibiotics (although over-prescribed at the present time) are helping millions of people combat acute disease processes and infections. Other pharmaceutical and medical procedures perform miracles against a whole host of diseases and conditions. From the above it should be clear that the treatment of acute conditions and symptoms is the responsibility of medical professionals and *not* the yoga therapist, although yoga therapy can help in the acute phase of a disease too, by working on stilling the waves of the mind. This inner peace gives the illness context and helps these clients live worthy lives alongside it. The yoga therapist's job is not to fix the client's disease, and yoga therapy cannot cure all that makes our clients suffer. The yoga therapist must be clear about what he/she can and cannot help with and refer out to more appropriate practitioners as needed.

Where yoga therapy can really be beneficial is in the chronic phase of a disease and in "lifestyle" disease. Many patients continue their medication for the rest of their lives after going through an acute episode of an illness. Examples of where this might happen is people with breathing conditions such as asthma, COPD, etc., high blood pressure and other cardiovascular diseases, and non-insulin dependent diabetes. This dependency on medication comes at a high cost to society and the individual in the form of suffering, increased cost of medications, medical insurance, and lost productivity. In addition many of the medications create side effects that have to be treated with other medications, leading to other side effects. The answer to many of these chronic disease conditions is lifestyle changes, and that is where yoga therapy can really make a big difference in today's society and healthcare system. Of course the biggest difference would happen if the lifestyle changes occurred *before* the person's system is affected from the chosen lifestyle, but even *after* the disease has occurred yoga therapy *can* help. A client undergoing yoga therapy might not necessarily get off medications, or go back to his/her normal functioning, but there is a good chance that if the yoga therapist works closely with a physician or other medical practitioners that the amount of medication that the person needs can be decreased. As mentioned before yoga therapy is emphasizing what is right with the person and what resources the person has, so a person seeking yoga therapy is more an active student of health than a passive patient of disease.

In summary, yoga therapy can be defined as "the process of empowering individuals to progress toward improved health and wellbeing through the application of the teachings and practices of Yoga" (IAYT, 2012). The aim of yoga therapy is a lifestyle approach that guides the client through increased self-awareness towards overall health and wellbeing and ultimately towards self-realization.

Editors' Note

1 While the Yoga Alliance requires schools to mention these ideas, a student coming out of a 200-hour training may learn these models but does not necessarily know how to assess these ideas in his/ her client. While the student *might* be able to apply the concepts to him or herself, he/she may not understand how to assess these constructs in a client.

References

Butera, R. (2010). *The pure heart of yoga. Ten essential steps for personal transformation.* Woodbury, MN: Llewellyn Publications.

Butera, R. (2012). *Comprehensive yoga therapy manual.* Devon, PA: YogaLife.

International Association of Yoga Therapists (IAYT) (2010) *Contemporary definitions of yoga therapy.* Retrieved April 10, 2014 from www.iayt.org/?page=ContemporaryDefiniti.

International Association of Yoga Therapists (IAYT) (2012) *Educational standards for the training of yoga therapists.* Retrieved April 19, 2014 from www.iayt.org/resource/resmgr/accreditationmaterials/iayt_educational_standards_7.pdf.

Merriam-Webster (2014). Definition of allopathic. Retrieved April 19, 2014 from www.merriam-webster.com/dictionary/allopathic.

Mukeri, P. N. (1983). *Yoga philosophy of Patanjali.* Albany, NY: State University of New York Press.

Swami Rama (1982). *Choosing a path.* Honesdale, PA: Himalayan Institute Press.

3 Regulating Yoga Therapy

Acceptance in the West

Daniel D. Seitz

> What matters is this: Being fearless of failure arms you to break the rules. In doing so, you may change the culture and just possibly, for a moment, change life itself.
>
> Malcolm Mclaren

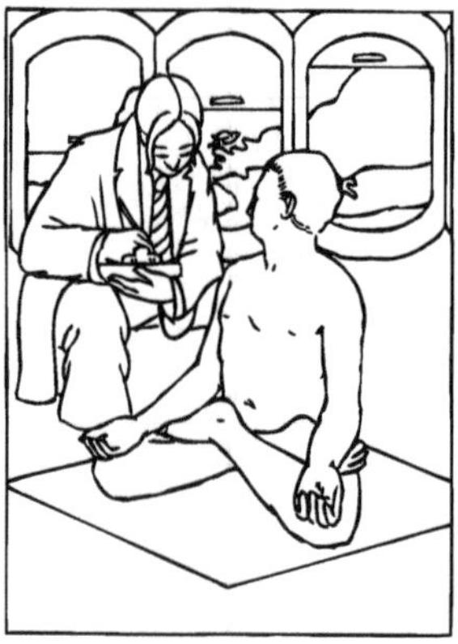

Figure 3.1

Introduction

In order to gain greater credibility, emerging healthcare and health-related fields usually establish a variety of self-regulatory structures and organizations. These structures serve to promote safe and effective practice, strengthen the field's legal status, expand professional opportunities, increase the profession's political influence, and legitimize a field in the eyes of potential patients, potential students, governmental entities, and the healthcare industry. Self-regulatory structures can also set the groundwork for professional licensure and other types of external recognition. Developing self-regulatory structures, however, can pose significant challenges and invariably involve trade-offs. Therefore, practitioners and educators within emerging fields should engage in inclusive, representational, and transparent decision-making processes to build support for any self-regulatory measures being considered.

The purpose of this chapter is twofold: (1) to explore several of the key professional/regulatory issues associated with the acceptance and recognition of yoga, yoga therapy, and Ayurveda in the United States, and (2) to outline and analyze the options available to these professions to engage in a process of self-regulation.

In the United States, emerging medical fields and fields that are healthcare-related or health enhancing—such as traditional Chinese medicine, naturopathic medicine, Ayurveda, yoga, and yoga therapy—often follow a similar trajectory in their development as a formal profession. This developmental process helps move the field from the fringes of society to a place of greater visibility, credibility, and impact. Over time, movement along this trajectory typically involves creating a variety of professional organizations and regulatory structures to better define the range of practices associated with a field. By doing so, a professional organization:

- promotes safe and effective practice;
- legitimizes a field in the eyes of potential patients, the general public, governmental entities, and the healthcare industry;
- legally safeguards the right to practice;
- increases the political influence of the practitioner community; and
- expands the range and attractiveness of professional opportunities for practitioners.

Once in place, these organizations and regulatory structures serve a key function: they provide a starting place or basis for the ongoing development of the field through upgrading educational standards and related requirements for practice. In turn, this leads to enhanced knowledge and skills on the part of practitioners.

The formal development of a profession is usually accompanied by strong reactions from practitioners within the emerging field who may disagree on the fundamental goals to pursue or the pragmatic directions to take. There may also be strong reactions from conventional physicians and others who may perceive their professional interests as being threatened or who are opposed to the paradigm represented by the emerging field. There are often rhetorical battles as an emerging field grows in prominence. Proponents characterize their practices in neutral or positive terms such as "complementary and alternative medicine" (CAM), "integrative," "health and wellness," "natural," "holistic," "traditional," or "mind–body–spirit," while opponents—in an attempt to discredit the field—may use terms like "unconventional," "non-evidence-based," "unscientific," or, at an extreme, "quackery."

Political and legal battles also routinely occur as practitioners of CAM and health-related and health-enhancing fields seek greater legal recognition and expanded professional opportunities. Conventional practitioners may seek to co-opt, limit, or outlaw the practice of certain therapies and even to legally own the use of certain words like "physician" and "diagnose." At an extreme, a state board of medicine may seek the prosecution of unregulated practitioners for practicing medicine without a license. Conversely, conventional physicians who integrate alternative therapies may be targeted by their licensing board for practicing outside of their scope of practice.

In addition to conflicts with conventional healthcare professions, there are often rivalries among emerging professions due to overlapping practices. Sometimes, newer professions are forced by more established professions to impose limitations on what they consider their rightful scope of practice. For example, naturopathic doctors study acupuncture, but may not utilize this modality in states where acupuncture is a licensed profession without having a separate acupuncture license. The examples above demonstrate that there is an unavoidable messiness associated with professional recognition and regulation due to the many competing interests and stakeholders. Nonetheless, a variety of pragmatic options and strategies are open to practitioners, educators, and professional organizations within an emerging field to develop a stronger, more coherent professional identity. Gaining greater public recognition and credibility, improving the overall quality of practice, opening up new professional opportunities, and strengthening the legal status of a field are, for most practitioners and educators, compelling motives to create some sort of regulatory structure, whether or not the structure is used at a later time as a basis for seeking a state-sanctioned or mandated role in the healthcare system.

Despite the challenges in gaining respect and recognition, leaders within an emerging field should take heart in the well-known quote of Mahatma Gandhi: "First they ignore you, then they ridicule you, then they fight you, then you win" (Ogubemi, & Lee, 2011, p. 359).

Internal Versus External Regulation

To better understand the options for professional and regulatory structures, it's useful to distinguish between *internal* (or self-regulatory) and *external* structures. These can be defined as follows.

Internal structures are developed by a profession on its own without involvement of governmental entities or organizations unrelated to the profession; examples of this are an accrediting agency for schools and a professional association's registry of practitioners.

External structures are developed through political action and negotiation with outside entities; an example of this is state licensure of a healthcare field.

Of course, virtually no organization is totally free of the need to interact with external entities. For example, state boards or departments of education have regulatory requirements and processes that would likely apply to formal training programs in an emerging field; establishing a nonprofit organization requires state incorporation; and gaining tax-exempt status or some other special classification requires IRS approval. Also, as a field develops, the distinction between internal and external regulation may shift in regard to an organization. For example, a private, nonprofit accrediting agency might, after having been in existence for a number of years, seek recognition by the U.S. Department of Education (DOE) in order to gain greater credibility in the eyes of regulators and/or provide students with access to federal loans.

Whatever organizational structures an emerging profession may choose to establish, it's safe to say that the profession will initially need to focus its efforts more inwardly to develop educational and practice standards and to define its identity. External recognition is impractical—if not impossible—to achieve until reasonably solid structures are in place.

Even before a profession can develop internal and external regulatory structures, it must first develop organizations that can provide a vehicle for pursuing collective goals and interests. Two of the most basic types of organizations are practitioner associations and school associations. Such organizations provide a forum for the open discussion and the foundational visioning that eventually leads to the creation of a more formal regulatory process. It is beyond the scope of this chapter to analyze in depth how emerging professions coalesce into formal organizations and how these organizations, in turn, embark on the task of creating internal regulatory structures and processes. However, it should be noted that, as touched upon earlier, efforts toward formalizing a profession are likely to cause apprehension and even conflict within practitioner and school communities. Thus, as regulatory structures are being developed, it is important to design reasonably inclusive, representational, and transparent decision-making processes that allow ample opportunity for comment on any proposed standards or requirements.

With the distinction between internal and external regulation in mind, we can now turn to the main subject: (1) a review of the primary options for internal/self-regulation of an emerging medical or health-related profession, and (2) a discussion of the benefits and challenges associated with these options. Internal efforts at self-regulation, if carefully carried out, can lay the necessary groundwork for future efforts to establish external regulatory structures that enhance the recognition and legal status of a field, should the profession choose to pursue these goals.

Primary Types of Internal Regulatory Structures

Registration of Practitioners and Schools

Perhaps the most basic approach to self-regulation within a profession is for a professional membership organization to establish a registry of practitioners. Eligibility for registration may initially be as simple as being a dues-paying member of the organization, or may involve demonstrating completion of certain educational requirements. Usually registration is based on the submission of required documentation that is reviewed for compliance with requirements, accuracy, and authenticity. There are, of course, limitations inherent in any regulatory process based solely on a paper review, since there may be no independent way of verifying the applicant's education.

Because educational approaches in emerging fields often vary widely in terms of content, duration, philosophy, and delivery, the type of education that qualifies a practitioner for registration is often defined broadly and inclusively at the outset. This is generally a good thing. The pioneers of a field in the US are often engaged in a grand experiment of transplanting traditional arts to a new cultural and legal environment, and diversity allows for creative space to find what works effectively. There are many crosscurrents inherent in this initial experimental phase: traditionalists may question the adaptations that educators make to run programs in the US (e.g., offering shorter programs than exist in the country of origin, eliminating certain practices that may raise issues in a Western culture); the creation of diploma mills and abbreviated training programs (often widespread in the early years of an emerging profession) may compromise the field's reputation by producing substandard practitioners; new theories and techniques may be developed under the rubric of traditional practices; and a welter of professional titles may dilute the professional identity of a field, causing confusion to the consumer.

These sorts of issues point to the ultimate tension in professional regulation: the need to seek a balance between the freedom for individuals to innovate, teach, and practice as they wish, and the collective desire among educators and practitioners to create a reasonably unified set of professional standards that support safe and effective practice and that promote public awareness and confidence.

Registration of schools often develops hand-in-hand with registration of practitioners. Graduates of registered schools are eligible to be registered practitioners, and registered practitioners are seen as qualified to teach at registered schools. While the main goal for registering practitioners is to provide the public with contact information on practitioners, the main goal of school registration is to provide potential students information on training opportunities for the profession.

Once an emerging field starts to attain some measure of stature and public attention, it is natural for the field to reexamine the basic regulatory structures that characterized the initial phase of development. There are typically a number of individuals involved with the field who are knowledgeable about professional education and regulation in the US, and some or many members of the practitioner community have aspirations for further growth and recognition of the field. Also, some organizations will start to develop discretionary financial resources beyond what is needed simply to survive and can invest them in building the profession.

Almost inevitably, during this evolutionary stage, a group of people within the profession starts questioning the adequacy of the initial registration requirements: paradoxically, the very breadth and inclusivity that helped get the field off the ground are now seen as a *limiting factor* to its success. This, in turn, often leads to a push to upgrade the registration requirements and/or to develop other approaches to self-regulation. The push to upgrade educational and practice requirements can cause considerable conflict within a profession unless there is extensive open discussion and careful consideration of how to equitably include practitioners trained under the old requirements who are interested in being recognized at a higher level. Even when decisions are arrived at through a genuinely inclusive process, a field may still experience a difficult and perhaps divisive transition to increased standards.

Certification of Practitioners

Certification is a process, often voluntary, by which individuals who have demonstrated the level of knowledge and skill required in a given profession, occupation, role, or skill are identified to the public and other stakeholders. Typically, a single private entity grants recognition—a certificate—to an individual who has met a set of qualifications established by that agency. These qualifications often consist of meeting certain educational standards and passing an examination. The examination may be entirely written or may have both written and practical components.

It should be noted that the word "certification," as it relates to professional education and practice, causes confusion. In an emerging profession, before schools gain authorization to grant degrees, they generally issue a certificate or diploma signifying completion of the training. This may lead schools to state that they are certifying practitioners. However, certification within a profession is meant to be a uniform, objective credential, not one that varies from training program to training program. In fact, until an agreed upon certification process is established, the "certification" of practitioners by individual schools and other organizations can, paradoxically, create a "race to the bottom," as it is likely that some schools will issue a certificate for completion of relatively cursory training programs. The very creation of a certification examination has a *de facto* defining and constraining effect on the educational programs in the field and on the profession's scope of practice. This is because the certification agency *must* articulate with reasonable specificity the subject matter that the exam will cover. While individual programs may continue to teach a wide variety of approaches and philosophies, their need to equip students with the knowledge and skills to pass the exam will naturally lead to a greater conformity among programs over time.

Moreover, the outliers (those programs whose philosophies and practices are furthest from the mainstream) will face the challenge of ensuring that students gain sufficient knowledge of the material that will be tested in the exam, while staying true to their vision. Any emerging profession developing a certification exam will have to work painstakingly and inclusively to ensure buy-in among a critical mass of stakeholders. The process will benefit from seeking an acceptable balance between being prescriptive in terms of subject matter and providing latitude for some non-mainstream approaches in the field.

Creating a reliable certification exam is no small task, and at the outset, the legitimacy of any certification process can be contested, both as to the level or type of education that qualifies someone for certification and the soundness of the exam itself. The challenges of creating a satisfactory certification process include defining the content of the exam, developing a pool of carefully formulated questions, establishing exam policies and secure testing sites and procedures, developing statistically reliable and defensible means to set passing scores, and ensuring sufficient funding to cover start-up expenses and ongoing operations. For a profession that wishes to establish a certification agency and exam, there is a substantial body of technical knowledge available as well as experts in the area of professional testing who can provide advice. However, accessing such resources can be expensive.

Given the complexity of developing a reliable certification process, the credibility of the process can always be questioned. One way that an agency may seek to gain greater credibility is through external "accreditation" of the certification process. Such an accreditation service is offered by the National Commission for Certifying Agencies (NCCA), which is the accrediting division of the Institute for Credentialing Excellence (Institute for Credentialing Excellence, 2005). This agency sets quality standards and accredits certification programs covering hundreds of professions and occupations. In seeking external recognition such as NCCA accreditation, there is a natural trade-off for an agency. The costs and time involved, not insubstantial, must be weighed against the perceived need to demonstrate the credibility of the certification process to important stakeholders.

There is also an international standard, ISO/IEC 17024 (ISO is the International Organization for Standardization), that sets forth criteria for certification agencies that offer "certification of persons" (International Organization for Standardization, 2014). The purpose of such a standard is to foster worldwide consistency in how certification agencies conduct their work. Such a standard may pave the way for recognition of professional training across national boundaries—a goal that some governmental entities and other organizations are actively promoting.

Within a medical or healthcare-related field there is sometimes pressure to develop a practical exam component in addition to the written component. This is especially true if minimally trained individuals (or individuals whose training is not easily verified) may be allowed to take the exam. Since a written exam only tests theoretical knowledge at one point in time, there is always a concern that a person could pass the exam regardless of his or her practical skills and abilities; such skills and abilities are, of course, at the heart of being a competent practitioner in any health- care-related field. Developing a reliable practical exam is, however, even more challenging than developing a reliable written exam, and administering such an exam is costly for applicants. Such exams are also more likely to be challenged by examinees on the basis of inconsistency or bias. For these reasons, some certification agencies choose to use a written format exclusively.

Regardless of whether an agency uses a written exam format or a combination of written and practical components, the agency must address the issue of what educational credentials will qualify someone to sit for the exam.

In more well-established fields in the US, such as naturopathic medicine and acupuncture, graduation from, or current attendance in, an accredited U.S. program is the primary qualification. The stronger the educational requirements for taking a certification exam, the less pressure there is to ensure that a certification test covers the full range of theoretical knowledge and practical skills, since there is an assumption that the examinees' formal education ensures basic competence in a wide range of areas. In an emerging field, educational requirements for taking a certification exam tend to be looser, especially if accreditation or some other more rigorous school approval process does not yet exist.

As with a registration process, there is typically some sort of "grandfathering" (also referred to as "grandparenting") provision at the time when a certification process is implemented that applies to more senior practitioners trained at an earlier time when educational levels and programs were different. The grandfathering process can be applied in two ways: (1) a person who is grandfathered is deemed qualified to take the exam based on educational requirements and/or professional experience that is appropriate to the era in which he or she was trained, or (2) a person who is grandfathered is not required to take the exam at all based on satisfying era-appropriate educational requirements and/or professional experience. Generally speaking, designing a grandfathering process to be reasonably inclusive will help promote buy-in by a larger proportion of the profession. However, there is almost inevitably a trade-off, since some grandfathered practitioners may be deficient in the knowledge and skills considered necessary for safe and effective practice.

Accreditation of Educational Programs and Institutions

The primary purpose of registration and certification is to identify and qualify individual practitioners of a profession. As noted above, schools, training programs, and instructors can be registered as well. If this process involves making a determination that the school or program is legitimate and offers an acceptable level of training, then school registration is also a de facto approval process aimed at ensuring the quality and rigor of the education.

Accreditation is a widely used approval process for higher education in the US. Accreditation can be defined as the granting of national public recognition to an institution or program of study that meets or exceeds an established set of standards. (Note that "accreditation" in this context is different from the accreditation of certification agencies discussed in the previous section, and use of the same word in a different but related context often causes confusion in the regulatory arena.) The determination of whether the institution or program meets or exceeds the accreditation standards is based on a review of detailed reports and documentation submitted by the institution and a subsequent on-site evaluation conducted by a team of qualified experts, which includes educators and practitioners. Accreditation is primarily a quality control mechanism: a credible, objective third party gives its public stamp of approval to an educational program and/or institution. Additionally, accreditation is a peer-review process that supports the ongoing improvement of institutions and programs.

Accreditation for a healthcare or health-related field in the US is generally carried out by a nongovernmental agency that is initially established by a professional association or a group of schools. The agency's board of directors is responsible for developing a set of standards that include educational requirements specifying the necessary baseline or entry level knowledge and skills for the field. To ensure their acceptance, accreditation standards are generally developed through an open process involving representatives of the key stakeholders in the field, including educators and practitioners. An opportunity to comment is given to those not engaged directly in the standards development process.

Accreditors are often divided into two categories: *institutional* and *programmatic*. Institutional accreditors grant accreditation to an entire institution, such as the University of Massachusetts, while programmatic accreditors deal with specific academic programs, such as a medical or chiropractic degree. In some cases, an accrediting agency will combine these functions when dealing with what are called "single purpose institutions": schools that offer programs in only one field of study. In this case, the accrediting agency grants both an umbrella accreditation for the entire institution and also accredits one or more specific programs.

Programmatic accrediting agencies that focus on a specific profession are also often referred to as "specialized" or "professional" accreditors. The primary focus of the accreditation standards of such agencies is on the content of educational and training programs. However, the accreditation standards of these agencies typically cover a wide range of other areas, including faculty, administrative and governance structures, finances, facilities, and other facets of educational institutions. For example, in the area of faculty, an accreditation agency might have requirements pertaining to educational degrees/credentials of the faculty, the proportion of full-time/core faculty hired by an institution, and the involvement of faculty in academic matters.

It is important to note that in recent years, accreditors have shifted the emphasis from simply listing the required subject areas and hours of study for programs to identifying the range of competencies that students must attain during the course of study in order to be adequately or comprehensively trained. The main idea behind a competencies-oriented approach is that, at the end of the day, the graduate of a training program should be able to demonstrate that he or she has actually learned the knowledge base and skills associated with the field and has not merely spent a prescribed number of hours in a classroom or a clinical setting.

Despite the greater emphasis on competencies, accreditors still normally specify certain broad requirements in terms of classroom hours and/or credits (for example: the total minimum length of the program and the time that must be devoted to clinical instruction and internship). This is to guard against a program's claim that its students are able to master a complex set of competencies within what experts in the field would consider an unreasonably short period of time.

State higher education departments have the responsibility for authorizing schools to grant academic degrees (e.g., bachelor's, master's, and doctoral degrees). However, programmatic accreditors specify the degree level of the programs they accredit. Therefore, one of the key questions that the educational and practitioner communities within a field must address is *what degree level* is an appropriate starting point for the field. For example, the accrediting agency for acupuncture and Oriental medicine started out by developing educational standards for a single type of program: a master's degree-level training in acupuncture. The same agency subsequently developed educational standards for a master's degree-level program in Oriental medicine and, more recently, for a doctoral degree program. The accrediting agency for naturopathic medicine, by contrast, started out accrediting programs at the doctoral degree level and has not markedly changed or extended this mission in three decades—though it has periodically revised its educational requirements.

An agency has the option to create one or more sets of educational standards for a given field that correspond to different scopes of practice, different sets of competencies, and different degree levels. An *emerging field* (e.g., yoga, yoga therapy, and Ayurveda) needs to consider very strategically what educational program requirements and degree levels are realistically achievable for a critical mass of the programs that it hopes to attract into the accreditation process.

Accreditation is considered a voluntary process. However, once the accreditation process within a field is widely accepted by consumers and practitioners in the field (as well as by practitioners in other healthcare-related fields), schools that forgo accreditation will lose their competitive edge. If a field becomes *licensed,* gaining accreditation is even more important to a school's competitiveness, as graduation from an accredited program is typically a requirement for licensure within most jurisdictions.

Many accrediting agencies, though not all, choose to seek recognition from the U.S. Department of Education (DOE) once they are solidly up and running. DOE recognition of an institution's accrediting body is the basis upon which an institution may be authorized to provide federal financial aid to students. Since federal financial aid greatly increases the marketability of educational programs, many fields are committed to seeking DOE recognition for their accrediting body.

DOE recognition also greatly enhances the credibility and legitimacy of an accrediting agency in the eyes of potential students, external regulators, and the general public. This is because DOE recognition is a demanding regulatory process that requires accreditors to demonstrate conformance to a stringent set of criteria as well as a high degree of professionalism. Generally, if a profession is seeking state licensure, establishing a DOE-recognized accrediting agency is almost a mandatory prerequisite. Otherwise, a state legislature or administrative agency has no independent way of determining whether the accrediting process is legitimate and effective. In fields where there are numerous diploma-mill operations, the owners of these operations often establish sham accrediting bodies (referred to as "accreditation mills") that endorse their programs. The existence of multiple accrediting bodies within a field can cause confusion to state officials.

Establishing an accreditation agency (like establishing a certification agency) requires solid financial resources as well as sufficient expertise regarding higher education practices. Typically, an accreditation agency has a board of directors consisting of representatives of schools, practitioners, and members of the public who are responsible for developing educational standards and agency policies and for making accreditation decisions. Additionally, an agency needs to assemble and train a pool of individuals who will have the knowledge and skills needed to assess the quality of programs during an onsite visit. Finally, an agency needs administrative staff, which at the outset, often consists of a single part-time employee. The costs of running an agency are typically borne by the accredited schools through annual fees. In some cases, professional associations and individuals may also provide financial support, and supporting organizations may also allocate some staffing, space, and other resources.

Unlike registration and certification of practitioners, accreditors do *not* grandfather schools/programs. This is partly because accreditation is an ongoing process that includes periodic reevaluation and re-accreditation of schools, and partly because the DOE requires recognized accrediting agencies to enforce their standards with equal consistency. However, the initial accreditation standards may be set at a level that is within reach of most of the institutions in existence at the time. Setting the standards at a realistically achievable level encourages buy-in to the process.

Conclusion

The fact that the emerging professions of yoga, yoga therapy, and Ayurveda have established (or are in the process of establishing) their own registration, credentialing, and/or school-approval processes is an implicit acknowledgment that the forward movement of a profession, at least in the US, requires creating a professional regulatory structure and identity. Typically, taking these steps will synergistically raise the quality of practice, increase public awareness and trust of these fields, extend the political influence of the practitioner community, and expand professional opportunities.

For these emerging professions, there is no right answer regarding whether and how to self-regulate or, for that matter, whether it might be advantageous to seek external recognition via professional licensure at some point in the future. Any self-regulatory structure involves a variety of trade-offs and financial costs that can be substantial. Additionally, establishing a self-regulatory structure demands extensive internal discussion: discussion that is open, respectful, and inclusive in order to ensure a reasonable degree of acceptance by practitioners and educators and to minimize the risk of creating schisms within the field.

While there are tried-and-true approaches to self-regulation that emerging professions can use as models, no emerging profession should be a slave to convention. New paradigms of health and wellness may well require the creation of new regulatory paradigms. At a minimum, efforts to create a conventional self-regulatory structure may benefit from a healthy degree of skepticism and experimentation so that the soul of the field is honored and nurtured as the profession becomes increasingly established and recognized.

The work of self-regulation is never complete. As soon as an emerging profession creates any regulatory structure, the weaknesses and omissions of the structure will start to become apparent. Also, the growing experience and expertise of practitioners and educators will bring about new aspirations for the development of the field. The sheer growth and success of a profession will, over time, necessitate the reformulation of structures and standards. This ongoing work, painstaking as it usually is, should be welcomed, as it often results in continued improvement in education and in quality of services offered by practitioners.

References

Institute for Accrediting Excellence (2005). Retrieved September 4, 2014 from www.credentialingexcellence.org.

International Organization for Standardization (2014). Retrieved September 4, 2014 from www.iso.org/iso/home.html.

Ogubemi, S., & Lee, T. (2011). *Accountability through public opinion: Inertia to public action.* Washington, DC: The World Bank.

4 Organizational Yoga Therapy

The Unfoldment of Institutional YogaMind in the World

Matthew J. Taylor

The blind spot in the twentieth-century toolkit of economics and management can be summarized in a single word: consciousness.

Otto Scharmer

Figure 4.1

Introduction

The current efforts to bring yoga into institutions are important, but fall well short of what is possible. One significant reason for this shortcoming is a form of asmita (mistaking the self for the Self, or small mind for the big mind) that is prevalent both in our Western culture and the yoga community embedded within that same culture. This chapter is intended to inspire, provoke and challenge the reader's understanding of "what could be" in what might be described as "organizational yoga therapy" in contrast to yoga asana classes at institutions. Beginning with a brief summary of current context of the situation today followed by present day discoveries, this chapter will then offer resources and suggestions for the future unfoldment of consciousness through human institutions.

Where Are We Now?

For all of the talk about unity and being one, it is fascinating to observe how almost all yoga is then practiced and delivered from the perspective of the rugged individual and focused on the suffering of that individual. There are literally books written on why this is the focus, which include *Yoga in the modern world* (Singleton & Byrne, 2009), *Yoga body* (Singleton, 2010), and *Yoga PhD* (Horton, 2013) as what I consider three of the best. The best phrase for capturing why this is comes from a study I read in my doctoral studies where the authors used the term "velvet paradigmatic rut" or in yoga, "samskara." These ruts of the small mind (self) keep us from remembering the yogamind of unity (Self). Our minds, lined with velvet, result in our silently and softly falling into the pattern of the asmita (Sanskrit for ego) of the individual, like silverware into slots in a fine velvet silver chest. We don't hear it, we don't realize it, but sure enough, without awareness we are prescribing yoga for a backache to move a score on the individual's comfort and function scale. Who addresses all of the other relationships/yokings that are now known to contribute to back pain in the individual and society at large?

The Western models of health and wellness, to include much of what is sold as "integrative," are in fact mired in these same ruts. These ruts keep us focused on the parts, be they the individual system of the person practicing yoga or a class sharing a common diagnosis or ailment. This focus *on the parts* prevents yoga teachers from seeing the paradigmatically invisible unity of relationships that weaves the cloth of the whole of yogamind. Such misdirection in the *rut* prevents participants from themselves discovering and then addressing those relationships that could begin to unsnarl them from the yoking/network linkage that generates the suffering at work and home.

For instance, trying to keep one's hypertension under control at a work-based yoga class will have the individual trying to stretch tight muscles, breathe properly, and even sit more at ease. But who addresses the corporate culture (mind) of 24/7 vigilance for email/pages to address business issues while juggling meaningless reports no one reads and annual reviews that demean the loyalty and dedication of not using any sick leave and staying over/working weekends throughout the year? Is there a voice for the collective institutional culture to correct these wellness issues or is it even safe from a job security perspective for the individual to point to these threads that generate the stress and pressure that push the blood pressure higher despite a few good OMs (aums)?

In a parts-centric/mechanistic culture, yoga has the potential in institutions to become yet another band-aid to unstable corporate yogamind rather than the transformational fire it could become if presented differently. Reducing health costs or increasing productivity via a regular yoga practice without mechanisms for altering institutional culture/mind would merely perpetuate the unintended, but silent violence of present day institutions. The following section offers insights into new discoveries that should challenge each of us individually and the larger yoga community in general to acclimatize the present day strategies to reach the full potential of the practice.

Current Discoveries Fostering New Possibilities

This chapter shares the highlights of these discoveries and will hopefully lead the reader to explore the topics as part of their Jnana (Sanskrit for path of knowledge) Yoga. When glimpsed through a yoga-lens of possibilities, such discoveries are remarkable, but to date have largely remained silent with the exception to *parts application*. Here are the highlights.

Mind Is Not Limited to the Individual Human

In 2007, Daniel Siegel, MD and co-director of the UCLA Mindful Awareness Research Center, defined mind as, "a process that regulates the flow of energy and information" and that has, "both intrapersonal quality (i.e., the process within an individual human) and interpersonal (the same process between humans)." This very functional definition shatters the atomistic description of mind beyond the individual. The school and the research that supports this definition are of high quality. And largely no one has noticed. This definition reflects the yogic definitions of mind as being beyond the mere individual and points toward Aurobindo's 20th century description of super-mind (yogamind?). If mind exists between humans, what are the yogic technologies to promote stability of such a mind?

Three years earlier, Senge, Scharmer, Jaworksi, and Flowers (2004) published *Presence: human purpose and the field of the future* and described multinational corporations as potentially the highest level of evolutionary development displacing the individual human. At the time, Senge et al. (along with MIT's Sloan School of Management) were inviting inquiry into how to best change the consciousness of these institutions as their present day level of mind was wreaking environmental, economic, social, and political havoc around the globe. Each of the authors has gone on to produce additional works with tools that are now being used with Fortune 50 companies. In Scharmer's (2009) *Theory U*, he proposes allowing best future ideas and processes to come forward for executives and management teams; in this reading, the yoga teacher will recognize the embodied process that includes somatic awareness, witnessing processes of the mano and vijna koshas (sheaths of the mind and wisdom), and surrender to Silence as being very nidra-like (guided) in practice. These experiences are then shared and modified to lead to actions of change, powered by processes of building corporate narrative à la Senge et al. These actions of prototyping are scrutinized just as individual asana allows for feedback loops of enhancement and further discovery, ultimately leading to transformed individuals and institutions. How and why this might work can be connected to what Siegel describes as interpersonal neurobiology.

Mind Does Not Equal Brain, But Brain Points to Aspects of Mind

A word of caution regarding the following information: so easily we can slip back into our rut of asmita when presented with the emerging neuroscience typically based on imaging and recording brain activity. Terms like neuroplasticity, mirror neurons, compassion studies, and lizard brain lure us into wanting to understand in order to be able to fix. Rather than study to fix (and granted there's value in that too), go beyond the fluff of the headline and ask deeper, more yoga oriented questions. Are there classical writings that pointed to this? If this is true, then how might it change my practice or teaching? What don't we understand about this? As a species and even broader life evolutionary process, how did/does this benefit life and what might advance the development in the future for both individuals and institutions? With those types of questions in mind, consider the following snippets:

Neuroplasticity: Brain imaging studies are the hot ticket to getting what little funding there is available at this time. Too often these get misinterpreted as the mind is in the brain, brain creates the mind, etc. Beware such simplicity. Brain anatomy, relationships, the physical body, the environment, nutrition, and so much more appear to be woven into this fabric of mind. So with that said, it is amazing that there are great studies demonstrating the practice of attention changing neural structures (neuro-plastics) and how movement habits can alter neural connections leading to enhanced movement strategies with measureable outcomes of function. The novelty and diversity of movement strategies from just a postural asana class utilizes these capacities, let alone the additional breadth of stimuli from a full-spectrum yoga therapeutic process including the many other yoga technologies. The chronic pain literature is a wellspring of yogic inquiry as conventional rehabilitation literally rediscovers the influences of the koshas (sheaths) by other names (i.e., biopsychosocial relationships) (Flynn & Olson, 2009). Neil Pearson and Marlysa Sullivan are two yoga-based physical therapists who have written widely on these principles (see, for example, Pearson, 2012; Sullivan, 2012). The take away from the neuroplasticity discoveries is that we continue to discover that the previously held rigidity around identifying and fixing just the broken parts continues to shift with the impermanence of structure as well!

Mirror neurons: While hyped as pointing toward group mind or societal yogamind, very little research has been done with humans. The primate studies are fascinating and they suggest potential implications and evolutionary efficiencies for humans, but we really don't know much yet. If we do have neurons that mirror goal-directed behaviors of others, what are the implications (and responsibilities) that these suggest for the many layers of individuals that make up organizations from frontline delivery staff to CEOs? What behaviors do we emulate as teachers or therapists and how do they influence our students or the members of the institutions we are serving? If teachers, healthcare providers, politicians, celebrities, and business leaders are harried, distracted, and reactive, how does that behavior get mirrored in society? If the research does demonstrate this invisible web of yogamind connectedness, how do we best harness its power for good and ahimsa (Sanskrit for to do no harm)?

Compassion studies: There is very promising research coming forward demonstrating the ability to teach compassion and empathy to individuals from as young as four years old. Also demonstrated are the health benefits to the person practicing compassion, positive brain state changes, and anatomical remodeling. Good additional study resources are Stanford's Center for Compassion and Altruism Research and Education (2014); the work of Kristin Neff, PhD (2011); and the University of Wisconsin's Center for Studying Healthy Minds (2013) led by Richard Davidson, PhD. Literally building a fabric of compassion and empathy in not just behavior, but anatomy too, ought to be the work of institutional yoga in the future it would seem.

Mind Outcomes for Institutional Needs

Our culture is results and/or outcomes oriented. "If I do X, what do I get?" is the question anyone approaching an institution must be ready to answer. In addition to all of the above, there are additional outcomes to "sell" the decision makers. Critical in today's rapidly changing environments are the buzzwords of resilience, social creativity, transformational learning, and sustainability. Every institution is under pressure to adapt and re-create itself as markets, funding, and political climates shift. If yoga teachers added to their list of benefits the five traits of creative individuals by Frank Barron (1968, 1995) that are enhanced or generated by a yoga practice beyond just "stress management," getting in the door would be that much easier. The traits are:

- independence of judgment;
- tolerance for ambiguity;
- from polarizations and oppositions thinking to complex thinking;
- androgyny (clarity on gender attributes and roles);
- complexity of outlook, symmetry/asymmetry.

Wonderful archived resources are available for free at the Wisdom 2.0 websites where you can watch leaders from every field discuss and explore how their institutions are already trying to adopt and utilize yoga-like practices at every level. As you will read below, while these traits might initially seem attractive for bottom line results, they also are the sparks of change of consciousness for both the individuals and the corporate mind itself and can bring unexpected transformations in behavior.

How Might the Future of Organizational Yoga Therapy Look?

In 2008, this author and Matthew Sanford led a two-year study at the Courage Center Rehabilitation facility in Golden Valley, MN. Rather than just teach caregivers yoga, I suggested we try some of the above principles to see if we might affect the consciousness of the organization (Taylor, 2014). Utilizing a collaborative inquiry methodology we worked with all levels of the organization inviting them to a daily practice of simple awareness combining mindfulness, restorative yoga postures, *Theory U* concepts, and corporate narrative work. The results were encouraging and presented at a national rehabilitation conference in 2010. Unfortunately the 2008 economic downturn exhausted funding and the research had to be terminated. In addition to the many positive benefits for the staff and the transference of behavior to patients, we also discovered that when the yogamind is stabilized in an organization, there must be adaptations by the institution. When the individual members began to sense across their entire being, it also gives them voice for change. This results in participants speaking up for what isn't healthy and demanding change from their discoveries within the practice. While the changes were accepted at some levels, other times members discovered their need to change employment and, in one instance, career. Leaders need to be cautioned that organizational yoga is not just keeping the troops calm, but a powerful igniter of change that often includes Shiva-like (fire-like) destruction as part of the growth.

Conclusion

Consciousness is said to be our next frontier. As yoga teachers we can be well positioned to lead such an exploration not just within the individual, but the yogamind of human institutions. It is incumbent for us as the vanguard of bringing organizational yoga therapy to institutions that we quicken the pace of our own evolution, broadening our context to match our culture and our skills to include those touched on above. The benefits for the individual, institution, and greater community are all in great need right now. The same fervor that fueled our early asana and classical study now needs to spread into becoming culturally competent to discover and deliver practices that incorporate the best of the above practices and also create innovative systems of delivery not even imagined today. How do we do this? Within the complexity of our circumstance lies the simplicity of the sutras and modern day organizational change: we practice daily. Peter Senge wrote in response to the question of how do we change organizational consciousness, "What is most systemic is most local . . . that's why personal cultivation [practice] is so important" (Senge et al., 2004). It is that simple. This isn't some New Age thinking or Eastern koan, just our charge to step and foster the next unfoldment of this art and science we have dedicated our lives to sharing. We stand on the shoulders of the great teachers, only to become the shoulders for the next generations to climb.

References

Aurobindo, S. (1990). *Synthesis of yoga*. Twin Lakes, WI: Lotus Light Publications.
Barron, F. (1968). *Creativity and personal freedom* (Insight series on Psychology). New York, NY: Van Nostrand Reinhold, Inc.

Barron, F. (1995). *No rootless flower: An ecology of creativity* (Perspectives on creativity research). Creskill, NJ: Hampton Press.

Flynn, N., & Olson, N. (2009). *Courage Center Study: "New age" solutions to age old problems in rehabilitation: staff retention and stress reduction.* Notes from presentation, AMRPA, San Antonio, TX: October.

Horton, C. (2013). *Yoga PhD: Integrating the life of the mind and the wisdom of the body.* Amazon Digital Service, Inc.: Kleio Books.

Neff, K. (2011). *Self-compassion: The proven power of being kind to yourself.* New York: Harper Collins.

Pearson, N. (2012). Know pain? A brief guide to understanding pain for yoga therapists. *Yoga Therapy Today*, 8(2), 14–16.

Scharmer, O. C. (2009). *Theory U: Learning from the future as it emerges* (Bk Business). Amazon Digital Services: Berrete-Koehler Publisher,

Senge, P.M., Scharmer, C. O., Jaworksi, J., & Flowers, B. S. (2004). *Presence: Human purpose and the field of the future.* New York, NY: Doubleday Books.

Siegel, D. (2007). Personal communication.

Singleton, M. (2010). *Yoga body: The origins of modern posture practice.* New York, NY: Oxford University Press.

Singleton, M., & Byrne, J. (Eds.) (2009). *Yoga in the modern world: Contemporary perspectives* (Routledge Hundu Studies Series). New York, NY: Routledge.

Stanford Center for Compassion and Altruism Research and Education. Retrieved September 2, 2014 from http://ccare.stanford.edu/.

Sullivan, M. (2012). The significance of studying anatomy for yoga therapists: A doorway into self-inquiry and transformation. *Yoga Therapy Today*, 8(2), 17–18.

Taylor, M. (2014). *Re-membering our back pain: A collaborative inquiry back school for individuals with chronic back pain.* Retrieved September 2, 2014 from http://matthewjtaylor institute.com/researchprojects.php#courage.

University of Wisconsin's Center for Studying Healthy Minds (2013). Retrieved September 2, 2014 from www.investigatinghealthyminds.org/.

Section II

Models of Practice

5 Yoga and Neuronal Pathways to Enhance Stress Response, Emotion Regulation, Bonding, and Spirituality

Patricia L. Gerbarg and Richard P. Brown

> Practicing is not only playing your instrument, either by yourself or rehearsing with others – it also includes imagining yourself practicing. Your brain forms the same neural connections and muscle memory whether you are imagining the task or actually doing it.
>
> Yo-Yo Ma

Figure 5.1

Introduction

Although the methods, concepts, and terminology used in psychotherapy, yoga, and neuroscience differ, each discipline sheds light on aspects of the mind, body, and spirit. Studying their points of convergence enriches our understanding and generates fresh approaches to maintaining and restoring physical, psychological, emotional, and spiritual wellness.

Traditional psychotherapies consider the bodily presence of both the patient and the therapist, but have relied predominantly on verbal communication between the mind of the therapist and the mind of the patient. Body-centered treatments such as Emotional Freedom Techniques (EFT), Eye Movement Desensitization and Reprocessing (EMDR) (Shapiro, 2001), Somatic

Experiencing (Levine, 2005), and "energy work" are being used more in Western health practices, although their roots are in Eastern traditions. In contrast, the eight limbs of yoga engage and seek to unite the mind, body, and spirit. Based on the assumption that the mind is an expression of brain function, neuroscience probes the activity of anatomic structures, neural pathways, neurohormones, and brain chemistry.

As with all human knowledge, the science of the mind begins with observing inexplicable events that compel us to find explanations. Here we will examine what neuroscience has to say about the effects of mind–body practices on wellness and how to incorporate specific practices into psychotherapy. The main focus will be on breathing practices because they are essential in yoga, Qigong, meditation, Judaism, Christianity, Islam, and tribal religious practices worldwide (Brown & Gerbarg, 2009, 2012). Our interest in how specific breath practices help restore physical, emotional, and spiritual health grew out of listening to people describe transformative experiences during and after yoga breathing workshops and from working with survivors of mass disasters such as the September 11, 2001 terrorist attacks on the World Trade Center. In addition, teaching selected breath practices to patients in treatment for anxiety, depression, or PTSD appeared to enhance their capacity to tolerate and benefit from treatment. Initial responses included reduced anxiety and worry, as well as improved sleep, mood, concentration, and wellbeing. Over time, the daily use of breath practices enabled patients to experience more positive emotions such as love and compassion. Some became more aware of other people's feelings, more insightful about their own emotions, and better partners in close relationships. This discussion will include our clinical observations, the results of research studies, and our evolving hypotheses about how breath practices affect stress response and emotion regulatory systems. The central theme will be bonding, a human capacity that is essential for physical, emotional, psychological, cognitive, and spiritual wellbeing.

Human Bonding and Love

Human bonding usually refers to the process of developing a close, interpersonal relationship or attachment, most commonly between family members, partners or friends, but it also exists among groups such as military units, first responders, sports teams, co-workers, theater ensembles, community volunteers, and others engaged in intense collaborative efforts. Bonding usually involves trust, loyalty, commitment, love, empathy, and caretaking (Bowlby, 1969). People can also bond with animals, sometimes more deeply than with humans.

Plato proposed that love directs the bonds of human society. In The Symposium (c. 385–380 BC), he said that the highest form of love "is directed, in temperance and justice, towards the good, whether in heaven or on earth: happiness and good fortune, the bonds of human society, concord with the gods above." Socrates asserted that the highest purpose of love is to become a philosopher or, a lover of wisdom. In other words, to Socrates, there is no higher bond than the bond of love between a philosopher and wisdom.

We suggest that the neural substrates for human interpersonal bonding may also support other kinds of deeply meaningful attachments, for example, to a cherished belief, an idea, a deity, a higher power, a community, a nation, all of humanity, or the universe. Consider how many people have been willing to die in defense of an idea that they love more than life itself. In this sense, meaningful bonding is essential for human love relationships with others, self-love, and spiritual love, all of which can be impaired by stress, trauma, neglect, or betrayal. Such adverse experiences are known to cause temporary and long-term dysfunctions in stress responses, emotion regulatory systems, and the capacity for healthy relationships. The authors propose that interventions that enhance or correct the functioning of these impaired systems should be therapeutic or restorative in any or all domains of bonding.

Stress Responses and Homeostasis

Stress and trauma challenge the capacity of regulatory systems to maintain homeostasis and optimal levels of functioning. Wellbeing can be viewed as a healthy, predominantly positive subjective sense of one's physical, psychological, and relational state that depends upon the ability to effectively respond to stress or perceived danger, endure the burden of allostasis/adaptation to stress, and return to a normal homeostatic condition upon resolution of the stress or threat. Acute or cumulative stressors may overwhelm the capacity to restore homeostasis, resulting in dysfunction in autonomic and neuroendocrine systems (McEwen, 2007). When this occurs, the systems become less efficient and less flexible, burn more energy, generate more free radicals, and lead to damage to the organism. Acute over activity of the sympathetic nervous system (SNS) may be necessary to survive immediate danger through fight-or-flight responses. However, chronic over activity of the SNS and hypothalamic-pituitary-adrenal (HPA) axis can result in illnesses such as cardiovascular or gastrointestinal disease, inflammation, and neuronal damage due to excess levels of excitatory neurotransmitters, free radicals, and cortisol (Streeter, Gerbarg, Saper, Ciraulo, & Brown, 2012).

The Autonomic Nervous System

The autonomic nervous system is well known for maintaining automatic functions including respiratory, cardiovascular, digestive, and glandular. More recent research on evolution and neurobiology is revealing that it also plays a major role in positive social behaviors such as bonding, care-giving, social communication, and emotional expression (Carter, 1998; Porges, 2009). The autonomic system has two main branches, the sympathetic nervous system (SNS) and the parasympathetic nervous system (PNS). The SNS contains both a behavioral activation system (BAS) that motivates us to seek rewards and a behavioral inhibition system (BIS) that protects us from acting too impulsively and helps us to avoid harm (Beauchaine, 2001). Activation of the SNS leads to increases in adrenaline and glucocorticoids in preparation for fighting or fleeing. Once the threat has passed, the SNS should quiet down and its counterpart, the PNS, should become active to slow the respirations and heart rate, restore resting patterns of blood flow, rebuild energy reserves, and reduce inflammation.

The main pathway of the PNS is through the two vagal nerves (10th cranial nerves), which innervate all the internal organs and other internal tissues. Each vagal nerve contains multiple pathways. About 30% of vagal fibers (efferents) carry messages descending from the brain to the body. These messages regulate the autonomic functions such as heart rate, respiratory rate, vasodilation, vasoconstriction, digestion, inflammation, and energy utilization. Approximately 70% of vagal fibers (afferents) carry sensory information from inside the body (*interoception*) up to the brain. These ascending messages strongly influence stress response, emotion, and neurohormonal regulatory networks that include the thalamus, limbic system, hypothalamus, prefrontal cortex, and other critical regions of the cerebral cortex (including the prefrontal cortex). The PNS affects facial expression, communication, emotional expression, and love (Berntson, Sarter, & Cacioppo, 2003; Carter, 1998; Porges, 2009).

Interoception is the perception of sensations from inside the body such as air hunger, visceral pain, cramps, heat, cold, vibration, intense sensual touch, food hunger, nausea, satiety, and others. Based on neuroanatomic mapping, Craig postulates that the Sylvian fissure inside the insular cortex, which he calls the *interoceptive cortex*, receives the information about the internal state of the body and forms a kind of interoceptive map or homunculus. Perception of this information becomes the basis for the subjective experience of the body (Craig, 2003; Critchley, 2005).

The Respiratory System

The respiratory system is rich in sensory receptors, which send millisecond-to-millisecond information through interoceptive pathways where they affect the centers of autonomic, and emotion regulation (Brown & Gerbarg 2005b; Yu, 2005). Neural pathways between the brain and the respiratory apparatus are phylogenetically old, rapid, and strong. The authors hypothesize that changes in respiratory patterns may induce powerful, rapid changes in mood and cognition because signals about breathing receive top priority. Breathing is vital to survival. If anything goes wrong with respiration, the brain must immediately focus all of its attention and resources on resolving the problem or the organism will be dead within minutes. Among the millions of signals processed in the brain, respiratory messages must gain immediate attention and cause widespread effects in order to coordinate survival behaviors.

Most anxiolytic (anti-anxiety), anti-depressant, and anti-psychotic medications reduce the activity of the SNS. To date, there are no psychotropic medications that have been shown to elevate the activity of the PNS. However, certain mind–body practices, positive emotional experiences, and supportive social activities have been shown to activate the PNS.

Heart rate variability (HRV) is the rate at which the heart rate changes. Normally, the heart rate increases during inspiration and decreases during expiration. Higher HRV correlates with health and wellbeing, but it diminishes with age, illness, stress, and lack of exercise. Respiratory sinus arrhythmia (RSA) has been used to estimate SNS and PNS activity, but currently researchers mainly use HRV. PNS activity, as measured by HRV, tends to be low in anxiety disorders, panic disorder, depression, and stress-related medical conditions such as irritable bowel syndrome, cardiovascular disease, and obesity (Friedman & Thayer, 1998; Thayer & Brosschot, 2005). Studies showing that mind–body practices can reduce SNS and increase PNS activity, as indicated by increases in high frequency HRV have been reviewed elsewhere (Brown & Gerbarg, 2009; Brown, Gerbarg, & Muskin, 2009; Streeter et al., 2012).

Certain mind–body practices have been shown to reduce SNS and increase PNS activity, thereby increasing HRV (Satyanarayana, Rajeswari, Rani, Krishna, & Rao, 1992; Telles & Desiraju, 1992). This action is thought to be a significant mechanism by which these practices may improve emotional regulation and alleviate stress, anxiety, and depression. Furthermore, emerging evidence suggests that improving the balance between the SNS and PNS may strengthen the capacities for bonding, love, compassion, and empathy.

Polyvagal Theory, Stress, and Paced Breathing

In humans, there are three phylogenetic vagal systems. The newest and highest level evolved with the neocortex and the myelinated vagal pathways within the PNS. These pathways regulate facial expression, head movements, vocalization (verbal communication), and oxygenation of cortical areas involved in communication, empathy, and caregiving. Under conditions of threat, this high level stress response system keeps the mind and body calm while attempting to deal with the situation by evaluating the perceived threat, *mentalization* (see below), and using verbal communication to resolve conflict. However, if the stress is too intense or prolonged, the PNS component may become less active such that the system reverts to the phylogenetically older SNS response. This state, called *parasympathetic withdrawal*, leaves the SNS unopposed as it tries to counteract the perceived threat by activating arousal networks in the mind, speeding up the heart and respirations, and generating angry fight or fearful flight reactions. In situations where there is no possibility of fighting or running away, the SNS may default to the lowest level of defense, the *vagal brake*, expressed as freezing, becoming paralyzed, playing dead, fainting, or passive behavior. The following study is consistent with the authors' proposals that slow paced breathing could help maintain sympatho-vagal balance and prevent anxiety, emotional and cognitive regression, and other stress-related symptoms.

A randomized study of 30 healthy college students exposed to a threat of electric shock showed that paced breathing at 8 bpm increased cardiac parasympathetic tone as indicated by increasing HRV significantly more than nonpaced spontaneous breathing or breathing paced at 15 bpm (Sakakibara & Hayano, 1996). The authors suggest that by stimulating the PNS activity, the slower breathing prevented parasympathetic withdrawal. This helps explain how certain yoga practices could ameliorate anxiety states and enable people to feel calmer and more clear-headed during periods of stress or threat (Clark & Hirschman, 1990).

Steve Porges hypothesizes that physiological states, characterized by increased vagal influence on HRV, support social engagement and bonding. Stimuli that increase feelings of safety can recruit neural circuits that support social engagement and inhibit defensive limbic activity (Porges, 2009). Evidence indicates that mind–body practices, especially slow (3 to 6 bpm) breathing techniques, can activate PNS pathways that induce feelings of safety and bonding while reducing defensive (angry and fearful) emotions and behaviors (Brown & Gerbarg, 2012). Furthermore, resistance breathing could enhance these calming vagal effects and further improve heart rate variability (HRV). For example, slow chanting of "OM" induces internal vibrations, which stimulate the vagal nerves. In an fMRI study, chanting "OM" was associated with significant deactivation in the amygdala, anterior cingulate, parahippocampal gyrus, thalamus, and hippocampus (Kalyani et al., 2011).

Emotion Regulation

Western research confirms teachings of the Indo-Tibetan and Traditional Chinese Medicine that breathing and emotion have a reciprocal relationship (Brown & Gerbarg, 2009; Shih, 1994). Emotional states affect respiratory patterns. Conversely, changes in the breathing pattern can affect emotional states (Philippot, Chapelle, & Blairy, 2002).

Most mind–body programs include breathing, movement, and meditation, making it difficult to determine which specific components have the greatest effect on sympatho-vagal balance. Breathing, the only autonomic function easily controlled through voluntary effort, can be used as a portal through which imbalances in the stress-response system are corrected. By changing the pattern of the breath, the body changes the messages being sent to the brain. For example, slowing respiration down to 5 to 8 bpm increases PNS activity, decreases SNS activity, and tells the brain that conditions are safe (Lehrer, Sasaki, & Saito, 1999; Sakakibara & Hayano, 1996). Calming, soothing messages of safety dissolve anxiety and worry, reduce defensive behaviors, and enable more loving, affiliative emotions to influence behavior (Brown & Gerbarg 2005a, 2005b, 2012; Streeter et al. 2012).

Drs. Brown and Gerbarg combined three breath techniques into one to maximize HRV, autonomic balance, emotion regulation, and bonding: coherent breathing, resistance breathing and breath moving (Brown & Gerbarg 2012; Calabrese, Perrault, Dinh, Eberhard, & Benchetrit, 2000). Coherent breathing is a gentle abdominal breathing with eyes closed. Each breath consists of 6 seconds inspiration and 6 seconds expiration at a rate of about 5 bpm. As the person continues coherent breathing, resistance is employed with a slight contraction of the laryngeal muscles and partial closure of the glottis. Resistance breathing creates a sound like the ocean and is called ocean breath, victory breath, or Ujjayi in Sanskrit. As the coherent with resistance breathing continues, the imagination is engaged to move the breath in circuits through different parts of the body. During Breath~Body~Mind workshops, participants are guided through repeated rounds of simple Qigong movements, periods of coherent plus resistance plus breath moving, and a body scan or open focus meditation (Fehmi, 2008). These practices have been shown to rapidly reduce scores on standardized tests of anxiety, depression, and PTSD in studies of patients with severe Generalized Anxiety Disorder (Katzman et al., 2012a, 2012b), First Responders and others affected by the 2001 World Trade Center attacks, survivors of war and slavery in South Sudan, and Mississippi caregivers under stress following the Horizon Gulf Oil Spill (Gerbarg, Streeter, Whitfield, & Brown, 2012; Gerbarg, Wallace, & Brown, 2011).

Neurohormones Oxytocin and Arginine Vasopressin

Pro-social neurohormones affect the HPA axis and the autonomic nervous system. Oxytocin, the "cuddle hormone," promotes bonding. It is released when infants breastfeed and strengthens the maternal-infant bond (Depue & Morrone-Strupinsky, 2005; Nelson & Panksepp, 1998). Oxytocin (OT) is also released during childbirth and orgasm. Positive interpersonal experiences such as hugging, stroking, or sharing a meal with friends can increase oxytocin levels. Oxytocin receptors are widespread throughout the central nervous system including in the central extended nucleus of the amygdala where they participate in the processing and integration of cognitive and emotional responses. Arginine vasopressin (AVP) regulates water, glucose, and salt concentration in the blood. There is evidence that it is also involved in male-to male aggression, and in protective, guarding, and pair-bonding behavior. In monogamous animal studies, vasopressin receptors in the reward circuit pathway are activated when AVP is released during social interactions such as mating, reinforcing partner preference and formation of a pair bond.

Evidence suggests that OT and AVP are found in the source nuclei of the myelinated vagus. These hormones affect the vagal/PNS activities, RSA and HRV (Norman et al., 2011). Under conditions of emotion dysregulation, OT and AVP down-regulate the amygdala. Porges and Carter present evidence to support their hypotheses that oxytocin counteracts defensive behaviors

Table 5.1 Correlates of Stress and Counteracting Stress with Regulatory Systems

Stress, Threat, Danger		*Slow Breathing, Caretaking, Supportive Social Interactions*	
Regulatory Systems	*Correlates of Stress*	*Regulatory Systems*	*Counter-stress Correlates*
ANS imbalance ≠ SNS ↓ PNS ↓ HRV	Defensive, Unsafe Fight or Flight ↓ mentalization	ANS Balance ≠ PNS (SNS ≠ HRV	Affiliative, Safe ≠ Bonding ≠ verbal communication ≠ mentalization
≠ HPA ≠ adrenaline ≠ cortisol	≠ HR, BP	↓ HPA ↓ adrenaline ↓ cortisol ≠ oxytocin, ≠ vasopressin	↓ HR, ↓ BP ≠ Bonding ≠ Caretaking
↓ inhibitory control of amygdala by PFC, insular cortex, and OT	↓ emotion regulation ≠ over reactivity ≠ fear, anger	≠ inhibitory control of amygdala by PFC, insular cortex, and OT	≠ emotion regulation ↓ over reactivity ≠ calmness, love, empathy, compassion

Key for Table 5.1: ANS = autonomic nervous system; SNS = sympathetic nervous system; PNS = parasympathetic nervous system; HPA= hypothalamic-pituitary-adrenal; HRV = heart rate variability; PFC = prefrontal cortex; OT = oxytocin; HR = heart rate; BP = blood pressure; ↓ = decreases; ≠ = increases.

associated with stress and plays a critical role in stress management and in facilitation of social behaviors (Porges, 2009; Porges & Carter, 2011). They propose that an *integrated social engagement system* coordinates the body's regulatory systems with neural structures and networks involved in social and emotional behaviors (Porges, 2009; Porges & Carter, 2011). Table 5.1 shows the physiological and behavioral effects of stress, threat, or danger compared with the effects of activities, such as coherent breathing, caretaking, and supportive social interactions.

Incorporating Mind–Body Practices into Psychotherapies

Mind–body practices augment psychotherapy in several important ways. Common obstacles to therapeutic progress are mistrust, difficulty bonding, fear of self-exposure, fear of painful memories, inability to regulate or control emotions, shame, self-blame, self-punishment, inability to experience feelings for the self or for others, fear of overreactions during or after sessions, and intolerance of intense anxiety, anger, or sadness. Issues within the therapist that may contribute to therapeutic impasses include therapist stress, professional burn-out, fatigue, secondary or caregiver trauma, loss of empathy, inattention, impatience, irritability, or unrecognized counter-transference.

Based upon studies noted above, mind–body practices can reduce many of the obstacles to treatment by reducing the levels of fear, anxiety, and anger as well as by improving emotion regulation and control. Moreover, the increase in parasympathetic activity and release of pro-social neurohormones, such as oxytocin and vasopressin, facilitates the development of trust, the patient-therapist bond, connectedness to the self and to others, and the ability to experience and tolerate positive emotions, including love, empathy, and compassion (Gerbarg, 2008). The capacity to have compassion for oneself is key for overcoming self-hatred, self-blame, self-criticism, shame, self-punishment, and self-destructive behaviors. In addition to using breathing and movement in regular daily practice, patients can also learn to pace their breath to dissolve acute anxiety and strengthen mastery of their emotions.

The Threat of Compassion

Paul Gilbert and colleagues recognized that self-criticism can obstruct progress in psychotherapy and that some individuals are afraid and intolerant of compassion, particularly if they have been highly self-critical or experienced abuse (Gilbert, McEwan, Matos, & Rivis, 2011). They discovered that Compassion Focused Imagery (CFI) could stimulate the soothing PNS and reduce HPA axis activity in some patients, but not in those who were more self-critical and who had insecure attachment issues. In the latter group, compassion was experienced as a threat and was associated with a decrease in HRV (Rockliff et al., 2011).

Compassion may be experienced as dangerous for many reasons. Firstly, compassion opens the door for feeling vulnerable and for being hurt, particularly by unpredictable, abusive parents or partners. Secondly, compassion involves feeling pain for the suffering of oneself or others and that pain may be unbearable. Thirdly, compassion can trigger intolerable memories or flashbacks of disappointment, abuse, or betrayal of trust. Fourthly, compassion involves closeness, which may trigger anxiety, panic, rage, or loss of control.

Developing compassion for oneself is an important step in working though guilt, self-blame, and self-defeating behaviors. However, in abuse survivors, talking about compassion can serve as a trigger setting off disturbing memories, and physiological reactions. In such cases, it is necessary to first reduce the SNS over reactivity and stimulate the PNS to enhance feelings of safety. This can be done by teaching the patient coherent breathing at 5 to 6 bpm. The patient is instructed to practice by pacing his or her breathing with a CD, iPhone, or Android application, or other device for 20 minutes once or twice daily. In addition, during therapy sessions, the patient uses coherent breathing if over reactivity or re-experiencing occur. This calms the emotions and restores the sense of safety and self-control. Over time, the patient becomes more able to discuss and experience feelings of compassion with a concomitant lessening of guilt, shame, and self-blame.

An fMRI study in which individuals were instructed to imagine being self-critical or self-reassuring found an association between self-criticism and increased activity in the dorsolateral prefrontal cortex (PFC) and the dorsal anterior cingulate, areas involved in error processing and behavioral inhibition. Imagining self-reassurance was associated with activation of the left temporal lobe and insula, areas involved in expressing compassion and empathy. Self-reassurance was positively correlated with increased ventrolateral PFC activity (Longe et al., 2010).

Mentalization, Affiliative System, Bonding

Mentalization refers to the ability to understand the mental state of oneself and others and to use mental representations of our own and other people's emotional states. As a kind of imaginative mental activity, mentalization enables us to perceive and interpret human behavior as an expression of intentional mental states (e.g. needs, desires, feelings, beliefs, goals, and reasons).

According to Peter Fonagy and colleagues, individuals with certain attachment styles (e.g. due to physical, psychological, or sexual abuse) can have greater difficulties in the development of mentalization-abilities (Fonagy, Gergely, Jurist, & Target, 2002). Attachment history partially determines the strength of mentalizing capacity. Securely attached individuals tend to have had a mentalizing primary caregiver, and consequently have more robust capacities to represent the states of their own and other people's minds. Bad and insufficient parenting, leading to insecure attachment styles, can result in children being unable to modulate and interpret their own feelings, as well as the feelings of others. These inabilities to mentalize and regulate affect have implications for problems of self-confidence, and sense of self (Fonagy et al., 2002).

Stimuli that activate the PNS, increase feelings of safety, and improve emotion regulation may enhance mentalizing, a capacity that is essential for self-observation, controlling impulsive overreactions, reassessment of threats, and generating appropriate behaviors. When emotional regression occurs, cognitive functions, such as mentalization, are compromised. The level of mentalization that predominates depends upon the subjective experience and meaning of the social relationship. The following example shows how shifts from the patient's usual high level of mentalization and function to more childlike levels of mentalization were triggered by interactions, which she subjectively and unconsciously experienced as "the same" as childhood experiences with her emotionally abusive parents.

Case #1

Allyson, a successful lawyer, was well liked and respected by co-workers for her ability to remain calm and clear-minded during conflicts not only between clients, but also between members of the large legal firm where she had worked for over 25 years. Alyson never lost her composure, was able to see both sides of an issue, and deftly found her way through mine fields of anger that clients and colleagues brought to the table. Over time, even bullies and narcissists worked with her productively. No one knew that she had been in psychotherapy all of her adult life for PTSD due to emotional and physical abuse by her parents.

Allyson was extremely self-critical and afraid of displeasing others such that she began and ended every conversation with a string of apologies. Her intellectual abilities and insights were excellent. Nevertheless, in the presence of a demanding or critical supervisor, she rapidly regressed to feeling like an inadequate child hopelessly trying to please a disapproving parent. Her cognitive functions also regressed, as evidenced by all-or-nothing thinking, magical thinking, blaming herself for things that could not possibly be her fault. Once caught in a regression, she could not find a way out until the next therapy session. In the safe, reassuring presence of her therapist, Allyson would come out of the regression with restoration of her higher mentalizating capacities.

In therapy, Allyson learned to identify situations that were likely to trigger regression and to better maintain her adult awareness. Once she learned how to use coherent breathing to reduce her anxiety, she was better able to prevent the anxiety from tipping her into a regression.

Mentalization is strongly affected by the experience of threat or safety in social relationships (Liotti & Gilbert, 2011). Impairments in mentalization make it difficult to solve problems and to navigate the adult world. Such deficits can also impede progress in psychotherapy. Creating an atmosphere of trust is critical to successful treatment. Feelings of safety help sustain higher levels of mentalization and the self-observation needed for a patient to tolerate negative emotions that emerge in treatment rather than acting out or breaking the therapeutic bond.

Stimuli that support feelings of emotional and physical safety promote higher levels of mentalization and may counteract or prevent emotional/cognitive regression. In this sense, mind–body treatments that stimulate the PNS and neuroendocrine systems involved in soothing, reassurance, bonding, and safety can contribute to progress and recovery.

Compassion Fatigue

Work burnout and compassion fatigue are hazards of the helping professions. Therapists and teachers need to counteract the daily wear and tear of exposure to the emotional struggles of their patients. Many find that even a short daily practice of 30 minutes of movement and breathing practices can improve stress resiliency, energy, mental alertness, and emotional attunement. In a study of 84 healthcare providers in Mississippi working with people experiencing emotional distress related to the 2011 Horizon Gulf oil Spill, a three-day training, the Breath~Body~Mind workshop, significantly improved mean scores on the Perceived Stress Scale (PSS) and the Exercise Induced Feeling Inventory (EIFI). Initial PSS scores were well above norms. After the training workshop, mean scores were below comparative norms. On the EIFI significant increases ($p < .001$) occurred in scores for positive engagement, revitalization, and tranquility, while physical exhaustion decreased significantly (Gerbarg et al., 2012). In the program evaluation by the Mississippi State Department of Mental Health, participants indicated that they would use what they had learned in their clinical practice.

Potential Complications and Adverse Reactions

Slow, gentle breathing practices are safe for most people. However, those with acute asthma, obstructive lung disease, and other respiratory problems may need special adaptations to avoid exacerbating their conditions. Rapid and forceful breathing that expels too much carbon dioxide can cause tingling, cramping, anxiety, panic, or flashbacks. Physically healthy individuals, without serious psychiatric problems, best use such techniques. Slow paced breathing is emphasized here because it is effective and generally safe even for people with serious medical or psychiatric illnesses.

Therapists and yoga teachers who obtain competence in teaching simple movement and breathing practices to their clients can minimize adverse reactions. First, care providers should learn and practice the techniques to become proficient and to ameliorate their own stress. Second, they should obtain training in how to teach the techniques and how to guide patients through any problems they may have in performing the exercises. Attending a live training is preferable. However, it is possible to get started with an instructional book and CD set (Brown & Gerbarg, 2012). Patients can also obtain a CD or download a soundtrack to guide their at-home practice (Respire-1 CD at www.coherence.com). Numerous devices and iPhone and Android applications are available to facilitate paced breathing using auditory or visual cues. Initially patients with anxiety, depression, or PTSD may need to practice 20 minutes twice daily for one to three months and then taper down to once daily when they feel better. In addition to the focused 20-minute practice with eyes closed, after one to six months, they can also do the breathing practices with eyes open as they go about their day at home, while commuting, at work, or at school. This can be done inconspicuously such that no one else is aware that the person is using the breath practices to remain calm, prevent stress, stop worrying, reduce performance anxiety, focus their mind, or increase work productivity.

Summary

Christian monks, Jewish mystics, Buddhists, yogis, and other religious devotees have used paced breathing as a prelude to prayer, to deepen meditative states, and to enhance spiritual experiences for thousands of years. Scientists now have the means to study ancient practices and to help develop therapeutic adaptations of them for modern life.

Neuroscientific exploration expands our understanding of neural pathways involved in stress response, emotion regulation, and symptoms associated with anxiety, depression, PTSD, and stress-related medical conditions. The scientific is moving toward a convergence with ancient and modern mind–body practices, which provide non-invasive techniques for studying autonomic, neuroendocrine, and emotion regulatory systems. The more we understand the modes of action that underlie the observable effects of specific mind–body techniques, the better we will be able to adapt such practices for prevention and treatment of a vast array of mental and somatic conditions.

Breath techniques can be seamlessly integrated with other mind–body practices such as yoga, Qigong, meditation, mindful walking, dancing, stretching, and joint mobility exercises, to increase the benefits of these activities. Training in the correct methods and the use of technologies for pacing assures efficacy while mitigating negative effects. The evolution of safe, effective, inexpensive mind–body programs holds promise for individual and global health.

Suggestions for the Reader from the Editors

Day 1: Start by practicing coherent breath for 6 minutes. (It may help to keep your eyes closed so you can withdraw into your internal senses.) After completing the 5-minute round, notice the effects in your body and mind. If you wish, journal about this.

Day 2: Increase your coherent breath to 12 minutes per day. Again, with eyes closed, notice the effects in your mind and body. If you wish, you can journal or draw your response to this exercise.

Day 3: Increase your coherent breath to 18 minutes per day. Again, with eyes closed, notice the effects in your mind and body. If you wish, you can journal or draw your response to this exercise.

Day 4: Increase your coherent breath to 20 minutes per day. Again, with eyes closed, notice the effects in your mind and body. Today, imagine what it would be like to lead a class or client(s) in coherent breath. Again, if you wish to journal about this do so.

Day 5: Conduct coherent breath during a class. If necessary, begin this concept as slowly as you did while training yourself. Dialogue with clients regarding the salutary effects in their bodies.

References

Beauchaine, T. (2001). Vagal tone, development, and Gray's motivational theory: Toward an integrated model of autonomic nervous system functioning in psychopathology [Research Support, U.S. Gov't, P.H.S.Review]. *Development and Psychopathology*, 13(2), 183–214.

Berntson, G. G., Sarter, M., & Cacioppo, J. T. (2003). Ascending visceral regulation of cortical affective information processing [Research Support, U.S. Gov't, P.H.S. Review]. *European Journal of Neuroscience*, 18(8), 2103–2109.

Bowlby, J. (1969). *Attachment: Attachment and loss* (vol. 1). London: Hogarth Press.

Brown, R. P., & Gerbarg, P. L. (2005a). Sudarshan Kriya Yogic breathing in the treatment of stress, anxiety, and depression. Part II—clinical applications and guidelines [Review]. *Journal of Alternative and Complementary Medicine*, 11(4), 711–717. doi: 10.1089/acm.2005.11.711.

Brown, R. P., & Gerbarg, P. L. (2005b). Sudarshan Kriya yogic breathing in the treatment of stress, anxiety, and depression. Part I—neurophysiologic model [Review]. *Journal of Alternative and Complementary Medicine, 11*(1), 189–201. doi: 10.1089/acm.2005.11.189.

Brown, R. P., & Gerbarg, P. L. (2009). Yoga breathing, meditation, and longevity [Review]. *Annals of the New York Academy of Sciences*, 1172, 54–62. doi: 10.1111/j.1749-6632.2009.04394.x.

Brown, R. P., & Gerbarg, P. L. (2012). *The healing power of the breath. Simple techniques to reduce stress and anxiety, enhance concentration, and balance your emotions.* Boston: Shambhala Publications, Inc.

Brown, R. P., Gerbarg, P. L., & Muskin, P. R. (2009). *How to use herbs, nutrients, and yoga in mental health care.* New York: W. W. Norton & Company.

Calabrese, P., Perrault, H., Dinh, T. P., Eberhard, A., & Benchetrit, G. (2000). Cardiorespiratory interactions during resistive load breathing. *American Journal of Physiology – Regulatory, Integrative and Comparative Physiology*, 279(6), R2208–2213.

Carter, C. S. (1998). Neuroendocrine perspectives on social attachment and love [Research Support, U.S. Gov't, Non-P.H.S. Review]. *Psychoneuroendocrinology*, 23(8), 779–818.

Clark, M. E., & Hirschman, R. (1990). Effects of paced respiration on anxiety reduction in a clinical population [Research Support, U.S. Gov't, Non-P.H.S.]. *Biofeedback and Self-Regulation*, 15(3), 273–284.

Craig, A. D. (2003). Interoception: The sense of the physiological condition of the body [Research Support, Non-U.S. Gov't Research Support, U.S. Gov't, P.H.S.Review]. *Current Opinion in Neurobiology*, 13(4), 500–505.

Critchley, H. D. (2005). Neural mechanisms of autonomic, affective, and cognitive integration [Research Support, Non-U.S. Gov't Review]. *Journal of Comparative Neurology*, 493(1), 154–166. doi: 10.1002/cne.20749.

Depue, R. A., & Morrone-Strupinsky, J. V. (2005). A neurobehavioral model of affiliative bonding: implications for conceptualizing a human trait of affiliation [Research Support, N.I.H., Extramural Research Support, U.S. Gov't, P.H.S.Review]. *Behavioral and Brain Science*, 28(3), 313–350; discussion 350–395. doi: 10.1017/S0140525X 05000063.

Fehmi, L. R. J. (2008). *The open focus brain. Harnessing the power of attention to heal mind and body.* Westminster, MD: Random House, Inc.

Fonagy, P., Gergely, G., Jurist, E. L., & Target, M. (2002). *Affect regulation, mentalization and the development of the self.* New York: Other Press.

Friedman, B. H., & Thayer, J. F. (1998). Autonomic balance revisited: Panic anxiety and heart rate variability [Research Support, Non-U.S. Gov't Review]. *Journal of Psychosomatic Research*, 44(1), 133–151.

Gerbarg, P. L. (2008). Yoga and neuro-psychoanalysis. In F. S. Anderson (Ed.), *Bodies in treatment: The unspoken dimension* (pp. 127–150). Hillsdale, NJ: The Analytic Press, Inc.

Gerbarg, P. L., Streeter, C. C., Whitfield, T., & Brown, R. P. (2012). *Breath-Body-Mind (B-B-M) Training for Healthcare Providers Post 2010 Gulf Oil Spill.* Paper presented at the 165th Annual Meeting American Psychiatric Association, Philadelphia, PA.

Gerbarg, P. L., Wallace, G., & Brown, R. P. (2011). Mass disasters and mind-body solutions: Evidence and field insights [Review]. *International Journal of Yoga Therapy*, 21, 97–107.

Gilbert, P., McEwan, K., Matos, M., & Rivis, A. (2011). Fears of compassion: Development of three self-report measures. *Psychology and Psychotherapy*, 84(3), 239–255. doi: 10.1348/147608310X526511.

Kalyani, B. G., Venkatasubramanian, G., Arasappa, R., Rao, N. P., Kalmady, S. V., Behere, R. V., . . . Gangadhar, B. N. (2011). Neurohemodynamic correlates of "OM" chanting: A pilot functional magnetic resonance imaging study. *International Journal of Yoga*, 4(1), 3-6. doi: 10.4103/0973-6131.78171.

Katzman, M. A., Vermani, M., Gerbarg, P. L., Brown, R. P., Iorio, C., Davis, M., Cameron, C., Pawluk, E. Tsirgielis, D. (2012a). A multicomponent yoga-based, breath intervention program as adjunctive treatment in patiens suffering from geberalized Anxiety Disorder (GAD) with or without comorbidities. *International Journal of Yoga*, *5*(1), 57–65.

Katzman, M. A., Vermani, M., Gerbarg, P. L., Brown, R. P., Tsirgielis, D., & D'Ambrosio, C. (2012b). *Breath-Body-Mind Workshop as adjunctive treatment in patients suffering from Generalized Anxiety Disorder (GAD) with or without comorbidities.* Paper presented at the 165th Annual Meeting American Psychiatric Association, Philadelphia, PA.

Lehrer, P., Sasaki, Y., & Saito, Y. (1999). Zazen and cardiac variability [Comparative study]. *Psychosomatic Medicine*, 61(6), 812–821.

Levine, P. A. (2005). *Healing trauma. A pioneering program for restoring the wisdom of your body.* Boulder, CO: Sounds True, Inc.

Liotti, G., & Gilbert, P. (2011). Mentalizing, motivation, and social mentalities: Theoretical considerations and implications for psychotherapy. *Psychology and Psychotherapy*, 84(1), 9–25. doi: 10.1348/147608310X520094.

Longe, O., Maratos, F. A., Gilbert, P., Evans, G., Volker, F., Rockliff, H., & Rippon, G. (2010). Having a word with yourself: Neural correlates of self-criticism and self-reassurance [Research Support, Non-U.S. Gov't]. *NeuroImage*, 49(2), 1849–1856. doi: 10.1016/j.neuroimage.2009.09.019.

McEwen, B. S. (2007). Physiology and neurobiology of stress and adaptation: Central role of the brain [Review]. *Physiological Review*, 87(3), 873–904. doi: 10.1152/physrev.00041.2006.

Nelson, E. E., & Panksepp, J. (1998). Brain substrates of infant-mother attachment: Contributions of opioids, oxytocin, and norepinephrine. *Neuroscience and Biobehavioral Reviews*, 22(3), 437-452.

Norman, G. J., Cacioppo, J. T., Morris, J. S., Malarkey, W. B., Berntson, G. G., & Devries, A. C. (2011). Oxytocin increases autonomic cardiac control: Moderation by loneliness [Research Support, N.I.H., Extramural Research Support, Non-U.S. Gov't]. *Biological Psychology*, 86(3), 174–180. doi: 10.1016/j.biopsycho.2010.11.006.

Philippot, P., Chapelle, C., & Blairy, S. (2002). Respiratory feedback in the generation of emotion. *Cognition & Emotion*, 16, 605–627.

Porges, S. W. (2009). The polyvagal theory: New insights into adaptive reactions of the autonomic nervous system [Research Support, N.I.H., Extramural Review]. *Cleveland Clinic Journal of Medicine*, 76 Suppl 2, S86–90. doi: 10.3949/ccjm.76.s2.17.

Porges, S. W., & Carter, C. S. . (2011). Neurobiology of evolution: Mechanisms, mediators, and adaptrive consequences of caregiving. In S. L. Brown, Brown, R. M. , Perner, L. A. (Ed.), *Self Interest and Beyond: Toward a New Understanding of Human Caregiving* (pp. 53–71). New York: Oxford University Press.

Rockliff, H., Karl, A., McEwan, K., Gilbert, J., Matos, M., & Gilbert, P. (2011). Effects of intranasal oxytocin on "compassion focused imagery" [Randomized Controlled Trial Research Support, Non-U.S. Gov't]. *Emotion*, 11(6), 1388–1396. doi: 10.1037/a0023861.

Sakakibara, M., & Hayano, J. (1996). Effect of slowed respiration on cardiac parasympathetic response to threat [Clinical Trial Randomized Controlled Trial Research Support, Non-U.S. Gov't]. *Psychosomatic Medicine*, 58(1), 32–37.

Satyanarayana, M., Rajeswari, K. R., Rani, N. J., Krishna, C. S., & Rao, P. V. (1992). Effect of Santhi Kriya on certain psychophysiological parameters: a preliminary study. *Indian Journal of Physiology and Pharmacology*, 36(2), 88–92.

Shapiro, S. (2001). Enhancing self-belief with EMDR: Developing a sense of mastery in the early phase of treatment. *American Journal of Psychotherapy*, 55(4), 531–542.

Shih, T. K. (1994). *The Chinese art of healing with energy Qi Gong therapy*. Barrytown, NY: Station Hill Press.

Streeter, C. C., Gerbarg, P. L., Saper, R. B., Ciraulo, D. A., & Brown, R. P. (2012). Effects of yoga on the autonomic nervous system, gamma-aminobutyric-acid, and allostasis in epilepsy, depression, and post-traumatic stress disorder [Research Support, N.I.H., Extramural Research Support, Non-U.S. Gov't]. *Medical Hypotheses*, 78(5), 571–579. doi: 10.1016/j.mehy.2012.01.021.

Telles, S., & Desiraju, T. (1992). Heart rate alterations in different types of pranayamas [Comparative study letter]. *Indian Journal of Physiology and Pharmacology*, 36(4), 287–288.

Thayer, J. F., & Brosschot, J. F. (2005). Psychosomatics and psychopathology: Looking up and down from the brain [Review]. *Psychoneuroendocrinology*, 30(10), 1050–1058. doi: 10.1016/j.psyneuen.2005.04.014.

Yu, J. (2005). Airway mechanosensors [Research Support, N.I.H., Extramural Research Support, Non-U.S. Gov't Research Support, U.S. Gov't, P.H.S. Review]. *Respiratory Physiology and Neurobiology*, 148(3), 217–243. doi: 10.1016/j.resp.2004.12.007.

6 Emotional Detox and Hot Yoga

Benjamin Lorr

The best way to detoxify is to stop putting toxic things into the body and depend upon its own mechanisms.

Andrew Weil

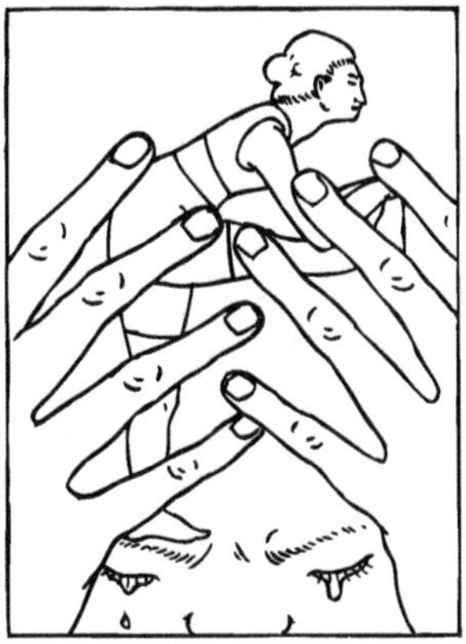

Figure 6.1

Background

Tracey Crosier is crumpled over sobbing her middle-aged brains out all over her middle-aged palms.[1] She is not a cry-y person, she would tell you if she wasn't crying. But today, most of her yoga class has co-existed with these tears: Tracey not so much maintaining composure, as letting her eyes "do their thing," continuing her practice while observing the unrelenting outflow down her cheeks. Now however, with the class concluding, she is just letting go and wailing.

This is the typical scene, as bizarre and bewildering as anything in the Bikram Yoga universe: a giant class steamed with sweat, jammed with bodies, and scattered with practitioners bawling their eyes out. They are so definitional, these sobbing yogis, as to be ignored, skin pouring sweat as their face pours out tears, all while the instructor plows forward without paying them even a moment of regard. And while this type of emotional release is found across all yoga styles, what might be a sporadic oddity in some studios—a sign of either a bad day or a "breakthrough"—is absolutely endemic in the hot room, routine as a SmartWater bottle or a muscle cramp. To practice Hot Yoga for any length of time is to find yourself next to one of these practitioners, or to unexpectedly bend into a posture and become one yourself.

But where do these emotional outbursts fit within the practice? What role do they serve? And what if anything mediates their release?

Tracey did not come to class with a sad thought in her mind. It was as normal a day as any. She arrived early, unfurled her mat, unfurled her towel, and lay on her back in savasana waiting for class to begin. Bikram Yoga involves performing a static series—the same 26 postures practiced each class to the same instructions. Even the atmosphere is controlled (if uncomfortably so) with high heat (100–105 degrees) and miserable humidity defining the experience. A veteran practitioner, Tracey knew exactly what was coming and what to expect.

The third posture in the series, awkward (or chair) posture, was never one Tracey attempted to its deepest expression. She had come to yoga with "crunchy" knees, and awkward with its deep flexion "killed from the beginning," she told me. Like an "ice pick through the knee cap." And so each class as it came up, even attempting this awkward posture represented a frustrating moment in the already hot, uncomfortable class. When instructors urged her to move deeper into the posture, Tracey often argued back mentally with them, priding herself on being stubborn, on "knowing her body" and therefore not pushing it too deeply. And this particular class, when awkward came, was no different: Tracey just slightly bending her knee, typically frustrated, typically anxious, definitely not in the full expression, when "blam!" something new happened, "a flash of violence hit my eyelids." Tears came. She wanted to flee the room. Then:

A memory awoke in her with the clarity of the present. Tracey was on her stomach, face-to-face with ankles and beer cans and peanut shells. She was 18 years old. Several of her ribs were broken, one kneecap cracked, the other displaced. Above her was a room packed with strangers; from the yoga room as she cried, she could hear them chattering, she could feel the strangers ignoring her. The memory was of a brutal hazing. Twenty-three years ago Tracey had joined her college marching band, and the initiation pledge had gone wrong. A group of senior boys were lifting her limp body up like a rag doll and throwing it on top of beer cans, pretending the full cans were grenades. As the scene enveloped her, she was able to shift perspective and "tour the memory from above," experiencing the emotional immediacy of the events as if it were happening all over again. Or as she said, "It was like I had never cried over this night before."

Which, point of fact, was not the case. The hazing incident was not some repressed demon; it was a known, if awful experience, from her past. A memory "handled" in therapy. She had cried over it many times during college, but she had also moved on, coming to terms with the experience, understanding it as the work of "a few evil, drunk cretins." At this point, Tracey could talk about it clearly, even joke if the right conversational moment came up. She did not blame herself for what happened, did not feel haunted. And yet now, twenty-three years later, she found herself sobbing about it on the yoga room floor: a memory back unbidden, with no warning, and almost supernatural clarity.

Trauma and the Fallout

Tracey was in the midst of what researchers call an "involuntary flashback," a type of memory characterized by hyper-vivid, highly personal recollection (Holland & Kensinger, 2010; Kent & Lamberts, 2008). Depending on your age, think about the moment you first heard about the Kennedy assassination, the Challenger explosion, or the 9/11 terrorism attacks. That immediate ability to place yourself at a scene, to remember contextual details—emotions both before and after the event—might provide a small reference point for the bright illumination characteristic of an involuntary flashback.

Perhaps the most famous representation of an involuntary flashback—literary or scientific—is Marcel Proust's madeleine. In the first chapter of *In Search of Lost Time*, Proust's narrator dips a particular seashell-shaped cookie (the madeleine) into his tea and takes a nibble. The unique crumbling taste sparks a flashback of such epic vividness that it leads directly into his narrator relating the entire rest of his 7 volume, 4,211 page masterpiece.

The madeleine—and the epic retrieval of those 4,211 pages—has come to stand for the powerful connection that taste and smell can have with vivid memory. It is an association we can all attest—swooning at the echoes of lovers' perfumes in crowded elevators, or lapsing into rapture when momma's lasagna comes out of the oven during a college furlough—even if it would seem to have little more than a cursory connection to the sobbing memories retrieved in Hot Yoga studios (ignoring, of course, the possibilities of mass tragedy in or around dirty laundry hampers).

Except that rather than being specific cases—smell, taste—Proust's literary observations foreshadowed much larger lessons about how we remember, store, and recall vivid emotional memories. It turns out that across the proverbial board, memories are more easily retrieved in situations similar to when they were formed (Laird, Wagener, Halal, & Szegda, 1982) as "perceptual information is stored in the sensory-motor neural units that were responsible for encoding the information."

Moreover, memories aroused through "sensory cues tend to elicit more emotional memories and stronger feelings of being 'brought back' than other cue types" (Herz, 2004).

This phenomenon is variously called "state dependent memory retrieval" and/or "mood congruent memory" and, in many circumstances, it is intuitive and obvious. If an experience happens when we are walking merrily under a bridge, it is more likely to come back to us when we are walking merrily under a different bridge. It extends across situations, from the external (like places with bridges), to the emotional (like merry walking), to all the associated sensory perceptions in-between (like the tastes, smells, and sounds associated with various situations). In particular, it has been experimentally validated with regards to body posture (Dijkstra, Kaschak, & Zwaan, 2007), physical motion (Riskind, 1983), and internal physiological states (like pulse rate when stimulated by a drug) (Southwick et al., 1993).

And what could be more relevant to Hot Yoga than those last three? Especially when coupled with the experimental observation that involuntary flashback memories are more likely to occur during periods of emotional arousal (Buchanan, 2007).

Hot Yoga is almost by definition uncomfortable: in the contortions of the particular postures, in the oppressive baking heat, in the vulnerability practitioners experience while they practice. The postures involve stretching, opening, and exposing intimate areas of the body. Tight revealing clothing is often worn on bodies neither tight nor used to being revealed. Even seemingly simple sounding postures can be maddeningly difficult to achieve. There is scrutiny, both of the self and by others. An instructor stands—often on pedestal—overseeing the entire class, and so even if there is an explicit understanding that judgment is not being applied, it is easy to understand how anxiety and frustration manifest.

Finally, due to the unique cardiac effects of heat, you have racing heart rates, sweat, and fatigue in otherwise static postures. You have struggling to maintain composure, acute pain, and muscle failure. Nausea, dizziness, and disorientation are common. Practitioners are repeatedly brought to liminal states and pushed beyond their comfort zone. Abstracted from the safe, incense-infused quarters of a 21st century yoga studio, these physiological states—innate to a Hot Yoga practice—bear a tremendous overlap with the physiological states associated with trauma.

Traumatic Memory

Even the earliest clinical descriptions of traumatic memory focused on an almost physical fragmentation of the self. Writing in 1912, Sigmund Freud noted that "Memory of the trauma . . . acts like a foreign body which long after its entry must be regarded as an agent that is still at work" (Freud, 1912, quoted in van der Kolk, 2000). In the face of such traumatic emotions—those forged in the face of uncontrollable, overwhelming events—individuals become unable to integrate the memories into their day-to-day consciousness, instead disassociating and storing fragments of these emotions in physical sensations, hallucinations, and generalized anxiety. Writing almost a century later, Bessel van der Kolk, MD, a Harvard trauma researcher, echoed the physicality of Freud's description saying, "What most people do not realize is that trauma is not the story of something awful that happened in the past, but the residue of imprints left behind in people's sensory and hormonal systems" (van der Kolk, 2009).

This imprinting can have profound effects. Those at the darkest end of the spectrum watch as their sense of self shatters and their emotions numb. Internal descriptions—"I do not know myself anymore; I feel like an object, not like a person" (Foa, Ehlers, Clark, Tolin, & Orsillo, 1999)—are mirrored by external observers, often describing loved ones as "deadened" or "robots." There is a literal abstracting of the human experience, where individuals so exhausted by overwhelming memories have difficulty labeling or participating in everyday emotional experiences. Simultaneously, residual, seemingly irrational emotional triggers can spur flashes of guilt, anger, or shame, leaving individuals frightened by their own bodies, dissociated from their own sensations.

It is as if a haunting occurs: an experience from the past remains physically imprinted on the present.

Processing these type of memories—even in *forme frustes* far below the clinical symptoms described above—might therefore require less of an abstract "breakthrough" of understanding, and more of a visceral "re-printing" or "reliving of the memory." If this sounds too new age, consider the scientific literature on emotional memories. "Retrieval" is a misnomer here. Emotional memories are not dug up and fetched like boxes from a neural attic, rather they are re-constructed and re-experienced at the point of recall: a similar neural storm and hormonal cocktail surging through the brain all over again (Holland & Kensinger, 2010; Kent & Lamberts, 2008). When left to unfold without support, such repeated reoccurrences of the trauma can sink individuals into a "black hole" re-enforcing the fragmentation and worsening their condition (van der Kolk, 1994). At the same time, within a more nurturing context, reconstruction can give a practitioner the opportunity to fully process the range of emotions raised during their traumatic event, many of which might have had to be repressed during the actual incident to increase survival or minimize the threat of the trauma.

Combine these observations with the vast scientific literature on neural plasticity and a picture begins to emerge of how what first appears as reckless sobbing in a Hot Yoga class might in fact be a calculated approach to therapeutic release—if not by removing Bessel van der Kolk's "residue" of trauma, then by replacing that residue with a newly created imprint, formed in a safe space which explicitly emphasizes integration and union.

Bikram Yoga and Detoxification

Beyond leveraging the heat to elicit these memories, and then offering a favorable space to re-experience their emotional weight, there are several distinct aspects of the Bikram Yoga practice, which I believe help students process emotional memories. I offer them here not to preach the benefits of Bikram Yoga (especially as several of these aspects come complete with corresponding negative attributes, while others are found across yoga styles and hardly unique to Bikram), but to better deconstruct the experience, and try to glean insight into the functional mechanisms behind a positive "emotional detox."

Mindfulness. All yoga shares an emphasis on generating mindfulness. Like many traditions, instructors in the Bikram Yoga tradition refer to their series as a "moving meditation," and explicitly instruct practitioners to observe both internal and external states from a non-judgmental, neutral perspective as they move through the series. To facilitate this approach, classes are held without music, without demonstrations by the teacher, and with repeated emphasis on the importance of quiet self-study.

Correlations in brain imaging point to the strong possibility that engaging in exactly this type of "mindful observing" can stimulate areas of the brain typically dulled by trauma (Frewen, Dozois, & Neufield, 2010). For instance, as discussed previously, traumatic memories are strongly associated with emotional numbing (a blankness known as alexithymia where people can no longer accurately name their emotional state). Brain imaging in patients with histories of traumatic memory strongly associates a specific area of the brain—the dorosmedial prefrontal cortex—with this dulling, showing severely decreased activity in sufferers of alexithymia (Lanius, Bluhm, & Frewen, 2010). Engaging in mindful observing, on the other hand, has been demonstrated to activate exactly the same areas of the brain (Frewen et al., 2010). While the exact mechanism is unknown, the obvious therapeutic implication is that mindfully thinking might be able to "reawaken" those areas of the brain typically inactive after trauma.

Similarly, the fragmentation inherent in traumatic memories can cause distortion in how everyday events are perceived. Moments of minor discomfort become paralyzing, evoking the emotional intensity of extreme trauma even if that is completely disproportionate to the actual real-world stimulus. A coherent sense of time and cause and effect can be lost.

Traditional descriptions of Hatha Yoga practice emphasize the importance of finding stillness—a transcendent peace—within the tension and discomfort of a posture (Mircea, 1970). Unlike the image of discomfort held in a mind warped by traumatic memory however, the discomfort of asana is always transitory: held momentarily, then released. Mindfulness in such a series teaches that the sensations in our bodies are transitory, that we can cope with them even if we might initially find them overwhelming, that a more helpful response to discomfort is to observe.

The mirror. Bikramites practice staring at a floor-to-ceiling mirror. While primarily serving as a guide for practitioners by providing feedback on their physical form, the mirror also has a significant cognitive function: it exists as an impassive reflection of reality, providing a constant visual connection to the self. It reflects without judgment, clearly delineating perceived flaws alongside narcissistic fixes and allows practitioners to observe the body moving calmly, even gracefully, while internally confronting panic and frustration.

This self-observation during posture can lead to more positive body image for practitioners. This is not a trivial factor for those suffering from traumatic memories. While anxieties around body image probably exist within any media saturated culture, negative self-image is often magnified to a pathological level by exposure to trauma. Women suffering from Post-Traumatic Stress Disorder report a disproportionate level of negative thoughts and associations when looking at themselves in the mirror (Frewen, Dozois, Neufield, & Densmore, 2011). Similarly when viewing their own face alongside either a positive or negative adjective, individuals suffering from traumatic memories will report agreeing with the negative descriptions while expressing doubt and disbelief at the positive ones (Lanius et al., 2011).

To combat this, the Bikram Yoga mirror operates within the larger literature of self-referential techniques (such as journal writing and visualization techniques), allowing self-study to explore a loaded stimulus and then reframe it with positive images—literally powerful poses in this instance. As such, it seems probable that the mirror functions as a visual counterpart to the observational mindfulness previously discussed.

The extraordinary confidence of the instructor. Bikram Yoga is demarcated by the insistence that everything that happens during your yoga class is natural, normal, and part of your "yoga practice." (In a notable expression of this principle, founder Bikram Choudhury has said: "Whatever happens when you are in a posture, that is yoga. If you feel dizzy, nauseous, pain, you do very good! That is yoga. Even if you die in a posture, that is okay. It is yoga.")

Instructors passionately believe in the power of yoga to heal. While there are concrete, often troubling, reasons surrounding this confidence in Bikram Yoga (e.g., during Bikram Yoga teacher training, instructors are trained to recite from a script, force-fed testimonials of the yoga curing a wide variety of aliments, and repeatedly told the answer to any problem that occurs within the yoga room is . . . more yoga), for the purposes of this chapter, I think it is important to emphasize the manner in which this confidence can serve as a positive force—creating both a feeling of safety, and acceptance of the more extreme aspects of the self. Traditionally shameful experiences, such as collapsing in exhaustion, nausea, or the aforementioned avalanche of tears, are regarded without judgment or response—neither producing cooing positive judgments or doubt and worry. This confidence is rested on the bedrock that the human body is capable of tremendous growth and transformation, a point that is explicitly mentioned over the course of a typical class. Simply believing in this plasticity has been shown to create more positive therapeutic outcomes.

This confidence is of particular importance when it comes to the actual tears being shed. A 2008 study of 2,181 male and 2,915 female crying episodes found most crying does not actually leave participants feeling better (Bylsma, Vingerhoets, & Rottenberg, 2008). However, crying episodes which occurred in supportive environments, and which concluded with a positive emotion (like a blissful savasana), were far more likely to produce feelings of catharsis and benefit. Likewise, a second study noted that episodes that involve crying with great intensity (as opposed to great duration) were more likely to leave their participants feeling as if their crying was beneficial. Indicating that the intense physical sobbing of the yoga room is exactly the type of tears that lead to relief (Bylsma, Croon, Vingerhoets, & Rottenberg, 2011). Not surprisingly, contexts where individuals felt the urge to suppress their crying were negatively associated with catharsis, although as any long-term practitioner can attest, suppressing crying has nothing to do with Bikram Yoga.

Repetition. Bikram Yoga is exclusively offered as a single static series, meaning that for Bikram Yoga practitioners every class is identical—the same 26 postures and 2 breathing exercises, whether you come on a Monday or a Thursday, whether you have been practicing for twenty-five years or a single day. As discussed, it is common for practitioners with traumatic memories to feel afraid, even betrayed, by their bodies. Repetition offers a vehicle for control. Instead of approaching uncomfortable emotions unexpectedly, the series offers practitioners a chance to confront these emotions in a consistent manner and gradually achieve mastery. In this manner, there is a strong overlap with more conventional "exposure based treatments" currently used for treatment of patients with traumatic memory disorders.

Several clinical studies of these treatments suggest that, in the proper context, "repeatedly recalling past negative emotions leads to extinction of the negative thoughts and feelings associated with negative events" (Frattaroli, 2006). According to Frattaroli (2006), these repetitive processes have been compared to a neural "map updating" process, a reconstruction that allows individuals to integrate negative experiences into their present outlook. Bikram Yoga, with its strictly repetitive series, could serve as a full body counterpoint to these more traditional approaches.

Back to Tracey

Tracey Crosier, our bawling yogi from the beginning, did not have a clinically significant traumatic memory. She was not emotionally alienated from herself, nor did she perceive the memory of her hazing as haunting her. Instead, like many of us, Tracey had a traumatic experience buried within her past, an experience that she had "handled" on a conscious level and filed away. And so it is perhaps all the more remarkable that after her vivid recollection and uncontrollable sobbing, she felt the enormous relief she did.

After that breakdown in class, in addition to the pure visceral satisfaction of purging the tears, Tracey came to several new insights about her hazing. She realized that despite it being the work of a "few evil drunk cretins," she had felt lonely and hopeless throughout the event, abandoned by the bystanders who watched her personal horror unfold, and who not only didn't intervene but who regarded it with the nonchalance of a cocktail party. This new more complete understanding gave her an additional measure of peace. Despite many years more of intense yoga, she never cried about the hazing again.

Perhaps even more remarkable, however, was the manner her emotional relief paralleled physical change. Tracey never approached awkward posture with the same trepidation. Her anxiety was gone. It was as if the "icepick in her kneecap" had been removed, the pain suddenly much diminished.

Three Questions for Self-Inquiry for the Reader

The bulk of this chapter discusses ways in which re-experiencing traumatic memories in a safe and supportive environment can provide a path toward healing. However the chapter explicitly notes that in unsafe environments "repeated reoccurrences of the trauma can sink individuals into a 'black hole' re-enforcing the fragmentation and worsening their condition." In other words, it is critical to recognize a healing experience from one that is making things worse.

1. Based on the chapter and your own experience, what signs might you look for to distinguish between those two experiences? How might they *feel* different from a practitioner's standpoint? How might they *look* different from an instructor's? Similarly, in a proactive sense, what can you do to create an environment supportive to healing? What specific advice might you give to a beginning instructor on how to react to a student "crying her eyes out" in class?
2. Yoga practices and traditions are wildly diverse, and this chapter is explicitly rooted in the world of "Hot Yoga." Given that starting point, how well do you think the experiences related here translate? What variables might change? What might you have to be more mindful of if you are coming from a different tradition?
3. The author specifically notes that he is "not here to preach the benefits of Bikram Yoga, *especially as several of these aspects come complete with corresponding negative attributes.*" Given the list of characteristics in the chapter, which specifically do you think he is referring to? What other attributes conducive to eliciting and processing traumatic memories might have negative consequences in the larger context of a student's practice? After identifying at least one of these double-edged characteristics, what is one thing you can do to be mindful about its negative characteristics either in your personal practice or during instruction?

Author's Note

1. All description and quotes from T. Crosier are either direct correspondence between her and the author, via telephone and email, or extrapolations from excerpts of her (wonderful) memoir *Mighty Cobra and the Pink Rabbit* as selected by Tracey Crosier herself (Pink, 2006).

References

Buchanan, T. W. (2007). Retrieval of emotional memories. *Psychonomic Bulletin*, 133, 761–779.

Bylsma, L., Croon, M., Vingerhoets, A., & Rottenberg, J. (2011). When and for whom does crying improve mood? A daily diary study of 1004 crying episodes. *Journal of Research in Personality*, 45, 385–392.

Bylsma, L., Vingerhoets, A., & Rottenberg, J. (2008). When is crying cathartic? An international study. *Journal of Social and Clinical Pyschology*, 28, 1080–1102.

Dijkstra, K., Kaschak, M., & Zwaan, R. (2007). Body posture facilitates retrieval of autobiographical memories. *Cognition*, 102(1), 139–149.

Foa, E. B., Ehlers, A., Clark, D. M., Tolin, D. F., & Orsillo, S. M. (1999). The posttraumatic cognitions inventory (PTCI): Development and validation. *Psychological Assessment*, 303–314.

Frattaroli, J. (2006). Experimental disclosure and its moderators: A meta-analysis. *Psychological Bulletin*, 132, 823–865.

Freud, S. (1912). The psychical mechanism of hysterical phenomena. As quoted in van der Kolk, B. (2000). Posttraumatic stress disorder and the nature of trauma, *Dialogues in Clinical Neuroscience*, 2(1), 7–22.

Frewen, P. A., Dozois, D. J., & Neufield, R. W. (2010). Individual differences in trait mindfulness predict dorsal medial prefrontal and amygdala response during emotional imagery: An fMRI study. *Personality and Individual Differences*, 49, 479–484.

Frewen, P. A., Dozois, D. J., Neufield, R. W., & Densmore, M. (2011). Self-referential processing in women with PTSD: Affective and neural response. *Psychological Trauma*, 3, 318–325.

Herz R. (2004). A naturalistic analysis of autobiographical memories triggered by olfactory, visual, and auditory stimuli. *Chemical Senses*, 29(III), 217–224.

Holland, A., & Kensinger, E. (2010). Emotion and autobiographical memory. *Physics of Life Reviews*, 7, 88–131.

Kent, C., & Lamberts, K. (2008). The encoding-retrieval relationship: Retrieval as mental simulation. *Trends in Cognitive Science*, 12(III), 92–98.

Laird, J., Wagener, J., Halal, M., & Szegda, M. (1982). Remembering what you feel: Effects of memory on emotion. *Journal of Personality and Social Psychology*, 42(4), 646–657.

Lanius, R. A., Bluhm, R. L., & Frewen, P. A. (2011). How understanding the neurobiology of complex post-traumatic stress disorder can inform clinical practice: A social cognitive and affective neuroscience approach. *Acta Psychiatrica Scandinavica*, 124, 331–348.

Mircea, E. (1970). *Yoga: Immortality and freedom*. Princeton, NJ: Princeton University Press.

Pink, M. (2006). *Mighty cobra and the pink rabbit*. Booksurge.com.

Proust, M. (2013). *In search of lost time*. Amazon Digital Services: Centaur.

Riskind, J. H. (1983). Nonverbal expressions and the accessibility of life experience memories: A congruence hypothesis. *Social Cognition*, 2, 62–86.

Southwick, S. M., Krystal, J. H., Morgan, A., Johnson, D., Nagy, L., Nicolaou, A., Henninger, G. R,. & Charney, D. S. (1993). Abnormal Noradrenergic function in Post Traumatic Stress Disorder. *Archives of General Psychiatry*, 50, 266–274.

van de Kolk B. (1994) The body keeps the score: Memory and the evolving psychobiology of post-traumatic stress. *Trauma International*, 1(5), 253–265.

van de Kolk B. (2009). Yoga and Post-Traumatic Stress Disorder: An interview with Bessel van der Kolk, MD. *Integral Yoga Magazine*, 12–13.

7 Relaxing Into the Self

Why We All Need to Learn to Let Go

Judith Hanson Lasater

Some of us think holding on makes us strong; but sometimes it is letting go.
Hermann Hesse

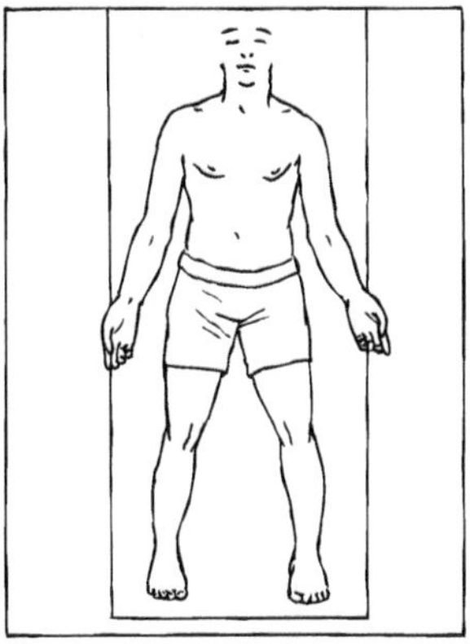

Figure 7.1

Beginnings

All I remember about my first yoga class is the ceilings. During the class, we lay down and rested between every pose for a minute or so. But at the end of class, we lay on the floor in formal relaxation for a much longer time, practicing a pose named *savasana.* I loved everything about the class but this last pose.

I simply abhorred lying there "wasting" all that time. Instead of the pose relaxing me, I felt agitated, even though I was seemingly lying still on the floor. My mind wanted me to get up and "be productive." In one of life's typical ironies, it was not long afterward that I became a yoga teacher myself, and eventually began to specialize in teaching restorative yoga, the entire focus of which is relaxation.

Savasana and Restorative Practice

While many are familiar with the health benefits of stress reduction and relaxation, how much a formal relaxation pose literally embodies the wider philosophy of yoga is not as well known an idea. The time spent in *savasana* gives us a chance to observe, not only any physical tension we may be experiencing, but more importantly, our mental tension, "the jumping bean" we call mind, the unrelenting stream of thoughts of judgment with which we are all familiar, and yet mostly try to avoid experiencing. This process of observing what is going on in the mind is the key to understanding all the practices of yoga.

Yoga is a variegated and richly sophisticated system developed in antiquity that attempts to address, to a depth which is profound, the major life questions of happiness, abiding and deep wellbeing, and true mental health. Most Westerners are only familiar with the most obvious techniques of yoga like postures, breathing, and meditation, but there is much more which underscores the teachings of yoga.

While we in the West know the famous line "mind over matter" the yogi (one who practices yoga) would no doubt smile at such a division. To a yogi, the mind is considered to be matter. To a yogi, if a division is to be made, the division is between the mind and the Self, a term meaning our personal connection with the consciousness that pervades all things.

This seeming individual Self, or *atman,* is immortal, permanent, and unchanging; it is what we are taught to identify with in yoga instead of identifying ourselves with the constantly changing world of mind and body. This Self is not personal like the "self" we think of when we think about ourselves, but something different. Variously called "the witness," "the observer," or simply "pure awareness," the Self is the ground out of which all existence grows (Tyberg, 1976).

The atman is our little piece of the whole. It is temporarily associated with our body–mind, yet is not considered to be separate from the whole of all existence. It is much like the air in the room in which I am writing. The air inside the room is like the atman. This air is temporarily seemingly held separately in this room, just like my atman is temporarily associated with me. Actually the atman is really not separate in any real way from the outside air. If the window were open, the oneness of the inside air and the outside air would be apparent. The outside air is called in Sanskrit *purusha.* Each atman is an individualization of the one purusha.

The texts and teachers of yoga offer this very important understanding of purusha because of the immense power such an understanding can bring, and the astounding effect this can have on our life and happiness. Yogis and others sometimes describe the experience of the atman/purusha as a sense of oneness, oceanic peace, or radical presence in the moment; it is most often called a state of enlightenment, or *samadhi.* Here again is a misunderstood word.

The common belief of samadhi is that it is a state of some form of trance. This is only partly true. While the states of samadhi have their own vocabulary that is beyond the scope of this chapter, samadhi is rarely understood to include a way to live *right now* in this life as most of us live it. However in some ways this "separateness" of the samadhi state from our normal life is true, and in others it is not.

On one hand, samadhi is a radical departure from the normal experience of reality, and on the other hand, *it may be the first sane and true experience of reality one has ever had.* The sages tell us there are many levels of samadhi, and that they each bring their own delights. The state of awareness discussed here is one that allows us to live our life without so much suffering, so much craving, so much longing and so much self-judgment and fear. These goals are the goals of all mental therapy in the West.

In savasana, many people may encounter for the first time that force, that energy, that mysterious thing we call mind. For something so ephemeral, this mind has almost unlimited power to create our own Heaven or Hell. During our normal waking life, the mind, which can also be described as a process or stream of thoughts rather than an entity, seems somehow to exist in the background of our awareness.

Our Thoughts Are Not Ourselves

Daily, we experience multitudinous thoughts. According to the Laboratory of Neuro Imaging (Department of Neurology – David Geffen School of Medicine UCLA, Los Angeles, CA), we have as many as 70,000, but mostly these thoughts stay in the unacknowledged background. That is until they erupt in emotions or choices. It is not unusual for these emotions and choices to startle us, amaze us, embarrass us, or lead us straight into difficulty by taking us far, far way from our own self-interest.

We are at the mercy of our unacknowledged thoughts. In fact, the more unconscious they are, the more powerful they are. In Jonathan Haidt's (2006) *The Happiness Hypothesis,* he uses the analogy of an elephant with a "driver" sitting on top, holding a bamboo pole. Of course it may appear to the casual observer that the elephant driver is in charge, but it is clear that whatever the elephant wants to do, regardless of the driver and his bamboo pole, the elephant is going to win. The elephant in Haidt's example represents the unconscious and the driver the conscious mind. Clearly there are so many forces at work that create our choices.

Some months after reading this book, I heard a story on the radio about a real elephant in India. A group of five elephants and their drivers were walking along a highway where the traffic was at a standstill. One of the male elephants looked across the road and spied a Volkswagen "beetle" automobile with its rounded shape. Instantly falling in love, the elephant thought this car was the most beautiful female elephant he had ever seen and lurched across the road, mounted the Volkswagen, and attempted to make mad passionate love to "her." In spite of the yells and other persuasions from all the elephant drivers and many car drivers who abandoned their cars and joined in to help, it was exceedingly difficult to detach the elephant from the object of his desire.

We are not unlike that elephant. The mind tells us something is valuable and we sometimes ignore reality and insist we must have the object of our desire at any cost. We lurch from one thing to another external thing, trying to gain our heart's desire. We repeatedly fixate on one thing, then another, on one accomplishment after another as the "solution" to our happiness. And we all know where that takes us. Yoga attempts to change this cycle by offering techniques for becoming aware of at least the surface of the stream of thoughts.

Normally during the day, we are moving the body and directing our attention externally. When we are in this state, the mind seems calm. This "calmness" is an illusion. The illusion becomes abundantly clear when we are lying still with the body in savasana, not sleeping and not daydreaming, but rather beginning to watch the stream of thoughts. Suddenly the mind, in contrast to the still body, seems to be very noisy and agitated.

Put another way, the body expresses "thoughts" through movement and the mind expresses "movement" through thoughts. When we are physically still and relaxed, the "movements" we call thoughts are, by contrast, quite apparent.

On Doing Nothing

Through my years of teaching, students have frequently complained to me "I can't just lie here, doing nothing. It agitates me." I react with the smile of recognition and empathy. That was my initial response as well. Obviously it is not savasana, or any other situation that agitates us. Truthfully, we are often already agitated, and yet we blame the external situation for our suffering, be it savasana, or another person or a task we do not favor.

Lying still is only the catalyst for becoming aware of the agitation that is lurking in the background of our consciousness all day long. This agitation is not usually apparent but becomes so when we are still. This agitation is the root of all suffering.

"Suffering" in this context is distinct from pain. Pain is inevitable in life, but suffering is not. Suffering is self-inflicted pain. Suffering is created by what we tell ourselves about the situation we are in at any given time. Making the distinction between pain and suffering is very important.

In savasana, the mind creates suffering by heaping judgments upon the situation. This is a typical response to difficulty. The student, instead of simply just lying on the floor and relaxing, spins out lots of thoughts about how the situation should be different. The very act of spinning the thoughts *is* the suffering.

The solution is both simple and difficult. The solution is to observe this mental process. By lying absolutely still with minimal external stimulation, the mental agitation is starkly apparent to the observer. Thoughts tumble and jump with no obvious reason. When we begin to observe what this process is it can be a bit of a shock. The mistake we often make next is to immediately try to "make" the mind be different.

This begins a process very akin to that of a dog chasing its own tail.

We hear our judging thoughts, we feel the agitation, and we create more agitation by telling ourselves not to be agitated. We can even go further by then telling ourselves to stop telling ourselves not to be agitated. Round and round the mind goes. It would be humorous if it weren't basically such a sad and impotent strategy for creating the happiness and mental health we seek.

Ultimately, the process of observing the thoughts must be just that, *simply observing the thoughts*. When we practice persistently with this level of letting go, over time, gradual but inexorably we have the proclivity to dance away with our thoughts less and less often.

This is not a process of "calming" the mind. The mind cannot be calm. Its business *is* to produce thoughts. Nothing wrong with that. The suffering comes when we believe them and let them carry us away from the present moment we are experiencing. In fact, it could be said that all the practices of yoga lead to this one thing: being radically present.

Here is an example of how can one be radically present with the thoughts without changing them. I was recently on a phone call in which the three parties were at an impasse. We went over and over the possible solutions and no one was willing to compromise. While it doesn't often happen any more, I became very triggered, very angry. In common parlance, I lost it.

But because of my training in savasana and its power to help me observe my mind, I immediately was aware of this very angry state. The image that my mind produced was of a dark room with a dusty weak light bulb hanging down in the center of the room, producing the paltriest light possible. I clung to that "light" of self-awareness and said the following: "Right now I am very angry and triggered and am sure I will not say what is consistent with my values or what will further this negotiation if I continue to speak. Therefore, I am going to get off the call and take a 10-minute break. Then I will come back and be ready and present to you two the possible resolution of this conflict."

I got off the phone and lay down on the floor in my yoga room and breathed slow long breaths and totally let myself be angry and irritated and impatient. All feelings were welcomed into my consciousness at that moment without judgment but with total awareness.

In a very few minutes, I was ready to return and I did. This time the call finally went well and a mutually agreeable solution did arise. Later that day, the mediator who had been on the call phoned me to say in all his years of mediation he had never seen such a triggered person do what I did and he wanted to know how I did it. I smiled as I told him it was decades of practice in observing my mind. Even the slightest space between my thoughts and my awareness had offered me a choice to act from my thoughts or to "step back" mentally and choose another way.

A great deal of our happiness and wellbeing is bound up in our relationships, the most important one being, of course, our relationship with ourselves. When we speak from the agitated mind we usually do not speak from our highest values. And certainly acting from the space of agitation is virtually guaranteed to create more suffering in self, in others, and in the wider world.

Let me be clear, I am not talking about "controlling" emotions. Rather, I speak of inviting all the emotions that arise in you into the tent of your being. The practice of yoga is not about transformation as much as it is integration, the integration of all aspects of you into the whole human you are. It is a bit like weaving disparate and myriad-colored threads into a coherent cloth that is both beautiful and strong because of its variation.

To be human is to have every possible emotion, sometimes seemingly all at once. Dissonance and suffering arise when we are unaware of what is alive in us and then we act without awareness of what we are choosing. We then become the "elephant" and are driven by a part of ourselves that usually will not help us make the best choices.

When one creates the habit of relaxing for 20 minutes every day, day after day, part of what that process is all about is to create a certain state of dis-identification in us. By this, I mean a dis-identification from our thoughts. Normally, we instantly identify with our thoughts.

We say, "I am angry" instead of "I am having an angry thought." There is a huge difference in the way we think about our anger, or any other emotion. Does our language reinforce that idea that our anger and self are one, or does it more truthfully express the fact that anger or irritation is what is arising in us at that particular moment?

Of course we cannot choose what emotion will arise, but we can practice savasana, and in a simple and relaxed way, we begin to understand that thoughts are like waves that rise and fall on the ocean. Thoughts arise; thoughts subside. We watch our thoughts like the visitor stands on the beach and watches the ocean's process, wave rising, wave falling.

Hopefully, we begin to realize in a consistent way that we *have* thoughts but we are *not our thoughts*. Thoughts are just neurotransmitters locking into receptor sites in the brain (Breazeale, 2012). We can be with this process without having to believe that *all we are is this process of thoughts*. And here is the most radical and paradoxical thought of all: whether this philosophical idea is true or not is actually not important. Regardless, it remains *life's most useful thought* to "choose" to use the thought that "*I am not just my thoughts*" to get something different in our interactions in the world. This understanding is at the heart of the deeply pragmatic tools we can learn from yoga. We can use this mega-thought as a *tool* to make our lives better, happier and less stressful.

The paradox is that even if the thought "I am not only my thoughts" cannot be proven scientifically, having this thought stimulates behavior and words which will be more likely to get us what we want in our relationships. It will be more likely to get us what we want in the world. Perhaps the strategy of choosing the thought "*I am not just my thoughts*" is a way to create a bigger perspective than just the perspective offered by the limited ego.

One way I think of "ego" is that it is a process that is very tied to one specific location, i.e. the location of my body/mind. When I see things only from my own "location" or ego, I have little empathy, little connection with myself, and little flexibility in my dealings with others. When I "act as if" I am more than my thoughts, that my thoughts are only one part of me, then I am more likely to soften toward the human being I am with and listen more from my heart. This does not mean I give up my values or my position on the issue at hand. Rather it does mean I can now see that the other person is just as attached to his beliefs about reality as I am to mine, and then perhaps an opening can come between us.

How Relaxation Works

How does the relaxation process provoke this miracle-like change in perception? In part, it is basic physiology. Many of us live in a state of constant stress. We are overfed, under rested, and just too busy all the time. We don't sleep enough, and when we do sleep, it is frequently disturbed and often not long enough. It is not unusual for busy adults to feel tired many days, and some even report feeling tired all the time. We hype ourselves up on sugar and coffee and push the limits of our mental, physical, and emotional resources to the breaking point. We are in a state of excitation of the sympathetic nervous system; we are not at ease within ourselves and we feel simultaneously agitated and depleted.

It is an established fact that it is very difficult, (if not impossible), to feel compassionate if one is exhausted. And the experience of compassion is the key to deep health and wellbeing: compassion first for self, then others, and then the world in general. When we act from compassion we not only help ourselves, but also help those with whom we come into contact. Dr. Dean Ornish (1999) reports in his book, *Love and Survival: 8 Pathways to Intimacy and Health,* that when one is in a loving compassionate state, the heart's coronary arteries actually measurably open; they close when one is angry. Compassion is good medicine.

What happens in savasana is that the state of sympathetic nervous system dominance begins to reverse. There are three stages to the state of deep relaxation one will encounter in savasana. First is the state of simple and deep physiologic relaxation. This state can be verified by measuring basic physiological processes. Heart rate and blood pressure drop, as does the respiratory rate. Muscles let go, the chemicals in the body associated with stress are no longer being produced, and the ones that are produced begin to be catabolized. Galvanic skin response changes, brain waves change, and one experiences a general sense of letting go and well being.

Physiologists would tell us that what has happened is that the parasympathetic nervous system is now activated and the sympathetic nervous system is dialed down. It usually takes the average person about 15 minutes to reach this state. Since the parasympathetic nervous system controls all long-term functions in the body, all kinds of healthy things are happening when the PNS is activated. Some of these long-term functions are digestion, assimilation, elimination, growth, repair, increased immune function, and fertility.

All these functions take time to proceed and succeed, from hours to months to years. Interestingly, these functions are interfered with or inhibited greatly by stress, and thus the body can be dominated by the SNS for long periods of time, much longer than nature intended. Interestingly, if one watches television for a while, it is likely that commercials advertising cures for headache, insomnia, and the all-important GI tract maladies of constipation, diarrhea, and upsets like too much stomach acid will be seen. All these functions are interfered with by an overactive SNS that seems to be common in Western culture particularly. Road rage is a perfect example of a reaction to a stimulus that is usually not worthy of such rage.

Recent research has found that the state of the gut, or GI Tract, is connected to our sense of wellbeing by direct neurological impulses that tell the brain "all is well" when the gut is functioning well. Apparently when we say, "my guts were in a uproar about that decision" we are speaking more than metaphor.

Relaxation is the antidote. Relaxation is a state that promotes the opposite of all these conditions. Remember, it is not stress that causes many of these maladies, but rather the unremitting nature of that stress which does not abate for days, weeks, or years. For example, stress negatively affects digestive functions; removing stress goes a very long way to re-establishing them (APA, 2014).

Not only does relaxation help to balance us physically. It has mental effects as well. The second stage of savasana is what I call *pratyahara.* This means "conscious withdrawal from the input of the senses." After the physiological relaxation of stage one is complete, one enters another state. This is a state in which one hears ambient noise, for example, but is not disturbed by it. There is sensibility but much less reaction. It feels like all sound is very far away and one loses the ambition to move, or act or control the environment. One feels deeply rooted in the present moment and content. I believe that this second stage of savasana is where the most healing, both physical and mental, occurs.

For example, it is a physiological fact that one cannot be both anxious and relaxed at the same time. One must be one or the other. All the physiological parameters that are increased in the state of anxiety are reduced in the state of relaxation, or PNS (parasympathetic nervous system) dominance. Practicing savasana, the pose of deeply letting go, is a way to reduce one's anxiety in the short term, and may have the possibility to reduce it in the long-term as well.

In a study conducted for the NIH (National Institute of Health), students who practice three 45 minutes of relaxation poses a week had reductions in serum levels of LDL cholesterol and triglycerides, and an increase in HDL cholesterol, "the good one." Some even could reduce their insulin as blood sugar levels began to stabilize (Cohen, Chang, Grady, & Kanaya, 2008).

I believe that it wasn't directly the relaxation that caused these benefits. Rather the process of deep relaxation took the "weight" off the body so it could more easily settle into its own equilibrium or homeostasis. When we remove the stress, in other words, the body is more likely to find balance or homeostasis.

This is what the body is always "seeking." There are other factors to health, of course, but relaxation is one of the simplest, least expensive and most effective of all the factors.

The final and third stage of savasana is ashunya, or non-emptiness. This is a state that is only known by its absence and one only realizes one was there when one returns from it. It is a very deep state of surrender.

Savasana is a process of consciously choosing to let go. And letting go is the highest form of spiritual practice and is the key to living well. Don't confuse letting go with giving in. They are not the same thing. Giving in is a response to difficulty that comes from weakness. Nothing takes more mental clarity and discipline than that of choosing to let go of one's attachment to how it should be, so that one can accept the ways things actually are.

Letting go requires a deep willingness to shift one's perspective on even the most important things. This ability to shift requires a flexible and adaptable mind, one that can act, then reflect, then act, then reflect again, and adjust to what has been experienced and learned. And the ability to adapt is both the hallmark of health and intelligence.

Practicing Savasana

To practice savasana, you need to remember these four requirements: still, quiet, dark, and warm. You want to facilitate all these four to attract the state of relaxation.

Now assemble the following props: a pillow for your head, a firm thick pillow or rolled blanket for the back of your knees, a soft cloth to cover your eyes, and a blanket to spread over you to keep you warm.

You may also like to have a timer; set it for 20 minutes. Turn off your cell phone and don't play music. Remember, you are trying to reduce input to your brain, not increase it. You are trying to reduce distractions, not create them.

Lie down on your back in a quiet safe place, place the pillow under the back of your knees, lie back and support your head and neck, cover your body with the blanket, and cover your eyes.

Take ten slow and long inhalations and exhalations. Count each one.

Then let the breath find its own rhythm. Watch it but don't change it.

Let yourself sink down into the props, sink into the floor, sink into the moment. Watch your thoughts. When your thoughts keep spinning, try this: pay attention instead to the sensations of your breath, not the breath itself, but rather how the ribs feel when they lift, how the belly moves, how the pressure alternates between the chest and belly with inhalation and exhalation. Focusing on the sensation will help you because sensation always exists in the present moment, never in the past or future. And you want to be in the radical present.

Don't worry if some days you fall asleep; everyone who practices this pose falls asleep sometimes. But if you fall asleep every time, try going to bed 30 minutes earlier every night. You are falling asleep because you are sleep deprived, and the only cure for that is to sleep.

When the timer rings, take a big inhalation, and while you exhale, bring your lower back to the floor, holding it there, bend one knee toward the chest and then the other, finally rolling softly and easily onto your side. Lie there for a couple of minutes before using your arms to help you sit up. Allow yourself the luxury of sitting quietly for a bit before you get up and proceed with the rest of your day.

Practice at least once a day for 20 minutes; you can do as many savasana practices a day, as you want. All side effects are salutary.

Remember, a quiet and settled person is more creative, more present, and simply more pleasant to be around. You will change your world, improve your health and increase your joy when you are connected with yourself. Remember this practice is magic; the magic is that it doesn't work if you don't do it.

Questions for the Reader

1. What is the simplest way to de-stress during my day if I can't lie down and do a formal relaxation practice?
2. We have thoughts, but we are not our thoughts. What is the most effective technique for remembering this all day?
3. What is the most important technique I can employ to allow equal acceptance of all my emotions as they arise?
4. What happens when I practice a regular 20-minute relaxation every day?

References

American Psychological Association, (2014). Five tips to help manage stress. Retrieved September 2, 2014 from http://www.apa.org/helpcenter/manage-stress.aspx.

Breazeale, R. (2012). Thoughts, neurotransmitters, body-mind connection: Our thoughts influence our bodies directly, and vice versa. July 17. Retrieved September 2, 2014 from http://www.psychologytoday.com/blog/in-the-face-adversity/201207/thoughts-neurotransmitters-and-the-body-mind-connection

Cohen, B. E., Chang, A. A., Grady, D., & Kanaya, A. M. (2008). Restorative yoga in adults with metabolic syndrome: A randomized, controlled pilot trial. *Metabolic Syndrome Related Disorders*, 6(3), 223–229.

Haidt, J. (2006). *The happiness hypothesis: Finding modern truth in ancient wisdom.* New York, NY: Basic Books.

Ornish, D. (1999). *Love and survival: 8 pathways to intimacy and health.* New York, NY: Harper Collins.

Tyberg, J. M. (1976). *The language of the Gods.* Los Angeles, CA: East-West Cultural Center.

8 How the Yoga Lifestyle Transforms Stress

Robert Butera and Erin Byron

All the suffering, stress and addiction come from not realizing you already are what you are looking for.

Jon Kabat-Zinn

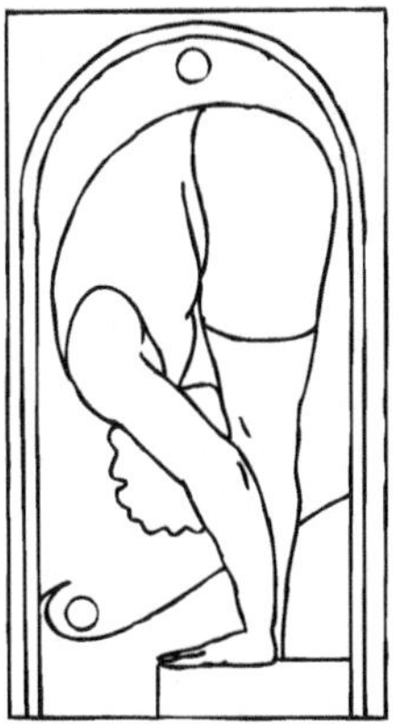

Figure 8.1

Imagine yourself eighty years from now, sitting at the dinner table with a group of friends. As you reminisce about the turn of the century, you reflect upon the many technological and scientific changes you witnessed through the course of your long lives. The topic shifts to health and you debate the issues facing developed nations in the early 21st century. The expected diseases come up: cancer, Type II diabetes, heart disease, and so on. One thing you all agree upon is that the ultimate source of the diseases, thus the number one health challenge facing the early-21st century populace was "stress."

One definition of stress is: a reaction of the autonomic nervous system to a stimulus, whether real or imagined, resulting in physical, emotional, and behavioral symptoms. Yogis have their own language for describing stress. In yoga philosophy, "stress" arises from a separation of the self from the unchanging reality. The *Yoga Sutras,* a fundamental text of yoga practice, teaches that we may completely eradicate stress by following a few simple lifestyle habits. This philosophy of internal (thinking) and external (lifestyle) endeavors guides us to replace the illusion of separateness (stress), with the reality of unity (peace of mind). The *Bhagavad Gita,* another core treatise of yoga practice, offers practical wisdom suited to a variety of people regarding yoga and the issues of separateness. Yoga philosophy acknowledges that no one path can possibly suit every individual; thus, there must be several paths to the same truth. The key point is: all sincere efforts in the direction of cohesion will remove beliefs that create stress. In other words, by applying the yogic lifestyle recommendations, anyone can transform stress into peace.

Epidemic: The Stress Generation

When we look beyond the diagnoses of specific diseases over the last 10 or 20 years, we see that stress is this century's epidemic. A simple statistic to support this is that cardiovascular conditions such as heart disease and stroke, which often are caused by stress, are the leading killers worldwide (WHO, 2007). High blood pressure plays an important part in the development of cardiovascular conditions, and stress reduction has proven to decrease blood pressure and preserve the integrity of the arterial wall thereby improving the health of the cardiovascular system. It is estimated that up to 75–90% of all doctors' visits are stress-related, and that the top three killers in first world nations (cardiovascular diseases, lung disease, and cancer) are all exacerbated by stress (Cohen, Doyle, & Skoner, 1999; Reiche, Nunes, & Morimoto, 2004; WHO, 2007; Yan, Liu, Matthews, Daviglus, Ferguson, & Kiefe, 2002). When the ancient oral tradition of yoga was being recorded into written word, 2500 years ago, they did not have a general concept for "stress" the way we do in modern society. Life in those times remained simple and slow-paced. Certainly, along the human timeline there has been pressure of survival, interpersonal relationships, and other obligations; however, the intense, continual strain on the nervous system that causes stress has reached an unprecedented height in human history. We gain perspective on illness after years of study – not only of the microbes and physiology around the illness, but also on the cultural conditions that create or support the problem.

If we could go back in time with the health information we have now and offer valuable precautions to our parents and grandparents: we could warn homeowners of the 1940s not to use poisonous lead paints, advise folks in the 1950s that their fashionable cigarettes are killers, inform the 1960s subculture that recreational drug use leads to brain damage, and 1970s musicians that if they don't turn their rock 'n' roll music down they may soon go deaf. What would we say to ourselves now, if we could visit the present with knowledge from the future? Although that may be impossible, if we look to the past instead of the future we will find advice that could serve the same purpose as a message from the future would. The yogis of ancient times knew that a simple, balanced, connected lifestyle was required to maintain peace of mind, and peace of mind is needed to reduce our stress levels. When we look at our lives objectively, we clearly see that they are out of balance. Our ancestors did not live with constant technological interference and continual, internal stress/pressure. Most of our daily habits support the exacerbation, rather than the obliteration, of stress; hence, the growth, rather than the reduction of stress and illness in modern society.

The presence of stress in our lives is no secret, yet it behaves like an invisible disruptor. Stress is an unseen force, like a stormy wind: it has no physical shape we can resist, yet we feel stress and know it is blowing destruction all around us. Even young children and the elderly report the negative impacts of stress in their lives (APA, 2009). Perhaps one of the reasons we allow stress to affect our bodies is that it doesn't cause a particular disease. For some diseases we can find a direct cause-and-effect relationship, but stress is a more subtle menace. Stress infiltrates the physiological landscape and alters our cellular and systemic functions, directly or indirectly leading to a myriad of health problems. Without obvious direct relationships between lifestyle choices and disease, it is challenging to convince people of the dangers of their current lifestyle choices. Plus there are perceived benefits to living a busy, stressful lifestyle, such as earning more money, having more things, the immediate gratification of sugar, alcohol, drugs, and so on. In the long run we often see those same immediate perceived benefits become attachments and causes of stress, but it is challenging to make that connection through the pressure of a busy lifestyle. The overload on the nervous system is so insidious that it is difficult to clearly observe the symptoms that the overload causes, until a disease makes itself present. Because stress breaks us down slowly, we do not necessarily equate the cancer diagnosis to losing a large business account three years earlier. More immediate consequences, such as a heart attack upon receiving bad news, are more easily integrated as stress-related health problems.

Nonetheless, the research speaks for itself. The American Psychological Association reported that in 2010 the majority of Americans are living with moderate levels of stress, rating themselves between four and seven on a scale out of ten. Statistics Canada (2010) indicates that up to one-third of Canadians aged 15 and older report that "most days are 'quite a bit' to 'extremely' stressful," with the highest and most consistent stress levels reported in those between the ages of 35 and 54. This report raised strong concerns about the rising stress levels in children, as parents lacking their own stress management skills are unable to teach their children how to deal with or transform stress. A Gallup Poll conducted in 2001 revealed that 80% of workers experience stress, with almost half of them claiming they require help coping with that stress. Similar statistics are repeated across numerous studies from universities, employment research boards, and the like. All these reports taken together make it abundantly clear that stress is the major health epidemic facing society today.

Stress is Separation

In each generation of humanity, there were herbalists, healers, and shamans who understood the imbalances that were occurring in their era. Not everyone smoked cigarettes in the 1950s and not everyone today sits in front of a computer or television monitor for ten hours each day. Those who understand the relevant lifestyle concerns of the day have the duty to share this information with individuals and the community at large. Yet how do we in the "stress generation" retrain ourselves and teach our children? To retrain ourselves requires lengthy personal observations, if we are to note the detrimental effects of prolonged technological use on our peace of mind. Some things are even less notable than technological use by ordinary means, such as the impact of artificial light and electronic images on the brain. We don't notice how gazing at small keys, characters, and screens activates the sympathetic nervous response. Most of us don't consider where our food comes from and how it was treated or grown before it came to our stores, even though the energy of that food is assimilated into our own. Since stress is invisible and pervasive, and because we have re-set our stress tolerance and baseline relaxation, it is a challenge to convince people that our lifestyles are contributing to the pervasive sense of pressure and fear we feel, even though there is some evidence about the above factors and their effects on our stress levels

Have you ever noticed the feeling you have after a long Interstate drive? When you first come off the highway and drive through city streets, the speed seems intolerably slow because you are accustomed to the prolonged feeling of faster movement. However, it is not safe to navigate your neighborhood at highway speeds and if you tried, inevitably, someone would get hurt. So it is with our fast-paced lives: they continue to accelerate with each technological upgrade, fuelled by stress, until it seems we are careening towards our own health crisis.

Many subjects in various studies indicated that they had sought both medical and professional counseling support for their stress. Employee Assistance Programs indicate that the top three presenting issues of clients are stress, anxiety, and depression—all of which can be reduced by yoga principles and practices (Homewood Employee Health, 2007). It is of note that of the other main presenting issues in Employee Assistance Programs (relationship, conflict at work, grief, health issue), stress was listed as the secondary counseling issue. After years of personal experience, anecdotal evidence, and targeted research, it is evident that yoga helps practitioners manage their stress. What is also evident is that stress "management" is not enough for most people. We must transform our relationship with the stress and eradicate its pervasive, detrimental effects on our lives. In most cases, living a comprehensive yoga lifestyle minimizes or even eliminates stress.

The *Yoga Sutras*, one of the fundamental texts of yoga, teaches us simple, practical ways of incorporating anti-stress strategies into everyday life. Yoga techniques support us in finding harmony in all aspects of ourselves throughout all stages of life. Many students of yoga consider yogasana as the objective of yoga, when truly self-realization or moksa is the objective of yoga. *Yoga Sutras*, and before them Samkhya philosophy, teach that all suffering in life arises from a sense of separation. Samkhya philosophy predates religion, teaches that everythi (prakriti) and is subject to the ever- humans possess an innate sense of long changing material world. We are natura ineffable, and beautiful. Purusa, another conc is that which is permanent, pure, and transcen purusa even when we don't realize that is what all forms of creation—art, dance, gardening, ra others—can be understood as attempts to realize unity all forms of despair—disappointment, rejection, lonelines result from a sense of separateness. When we connec unchanging, we experience deeper meaning in life and a grea who we really are.

The word "yoga" translates as "union" and is the path of remov through uniting, or having a relationship with that which is uncha divine. Yoga psychology teaches us to distinguish between the pure and the authentic, peaceful self and the self-centered, stressed self. We often co the stressed self, the "ego," to be fraught with attachments and lack of c vision and the loving, true Self to have realized union (yoga) with somethin greater than ourselves.

Preliminary scientific inquiry indicates that a relationship exists between people who do *not* have problems with stress and their spiritual practice of yoga, religion, or meditation. A lifestyle steeped in meaningful philosophy, regular practice, like-minded community, and a quest for peace alters our internal relationship with stress. The major stressors in life—personal finances, relationships/family, work, and the economy—are put in a different perspective when we establish ourselves in regular spiritual practice. Our entire point of view of what matters in everyday life shifts from the ever changing to the transcendent. Since finances, relationships, jobs, and the economy are ever changing, they will create highs and lows in us if we cling to them. We cannot depend on external conditions to create peace of mind. Yoga practice reminds us to seek peace in what is constant. Establishing ourselves in a yoga lifestyle strums this rhythm of constancy and peace throughout every day.

Yoga as a Remedy for Stress

According to Statistics Canada (2010), at any given time 20% of the population is suffering from a stress-related psychological disorder. Stress is reported from all walks of life, including business executives, stay-at-home parents, teachers, entrepreneurs, and those in the service industry (APA, 2010). Many people are medicated with SSRI (Selective Serotonin Uptake Inhibitors) medication for stress related conditions, but the risk of suicide attempt for people on SSRIs is double that of those not on SSRI medication. Instead of relying ion as a way of coping with stress-related psychological disorders, o find permanent, internal means of coping. As people continue ever-increasing levels of stress and pressure, the time has come to n our view of and relationship with stress. Stress is a special concern ple in the helping professions, such as nurses, therapists, and emergency s professionals, all of whom report extremely high job stress levels (APA,). Yoga can guide people in these professions to transform their stresses ugh healthy lifestyle choices, and after establishing their own healthy style choices they can pass on this knowledge and techniques to patients, nployees, children, and students.

Consider how three different people, the average person, the aspirant, and the long-time student of yoga, might handle a short deadline at work. The average person might face the stress of the situation with resentment and worry. He or she sacrifices self-care in the interests of work, multitask in interest of efficiency (even though time and again studies have shown multitasking makes us inefficient), and may be fearful of the outcome, which further reduces productivity. Those who have studied stress-management and personal growth may employ positive self-talk and deep breathing exercises to battle the edginess, but may also employ unhealthy coping strategies. Students of yoga continue their practice of concentration and holding a higher perspective. They apply these practices from the yoga mat to their work, preventing an internal stress reaction and maintaining a healthy perception regarding the long-term impacts of a single work deadline. Yoga practice infuses one's life with a perspective of peace.

Over years of practice, yoga aspirants create small, measurable changes in their daily routines. Through commitment to health, a steady mind, and the removal of stress, people find themselves choosing more whole foods, a regular movement regimen, reasonable bedtime, and closer connections with family and like-minded friends. Leisure time is spent less with technology and more with other people and in nature, sharing meaningful, joyful experiences. A yoga lifestyle revolves around simplicity, is guided by contentment, and supports a life free from stress.

Paths of Yoga

Stress arises from a sense of separation from meaning in our lives, from which we really are, from purusa. Historically, yoga has offered a path to freedom for each aspirant. Yoga addresses individual differences in inclination, learning styles, obligations, and interests. Not all people will be inspired to practice in the same way; yet all people will benefit from some form of practice. These practices/paths are addressed in the *Bhagavad Gita* and the *Hatha Yoga Pradipika* by teaching five paths to union with purusa: for those who follow energetics (tantra), those who work (karma), those who love (bhakti), those who know (jnana), and those who practice (raja). Most of us follow all of these five paths—

tantra (hatha), karma, bhakti, jnana, and raja—in varying degree. different phases of our lives.

The word "tantra" has acquired some notoriety in pop culture; however, what the average person might think of when they encounter "tantra" is only a small aspect of this path of subtle energies. We could think of tantra as a Hatha Yoga path, where physical health and connection to subtle energetic anatomy lead the aspirant to unity. To alleviate stress on the tantric path, we may begin by tuning more deeply to the breath. We know that balanced, deep breathing oxygenates and detoxifies the body, which in turn uplifts mood and clarifies thought. Proper nutrition, including what we take in emotionally, intellectually, and spiritually, also supports our intention to remove stress. On the other hand, rapid, shallow breaths activate our stress hormones and empty-calorie foods create a biological state of deprivation and alert the nervous system that something is fundamentally wrong. When the body is cared for, it rests in a sense of safety: spiritual needs move to the foreground. The tantric aspirant pursues moksa through connection with subtle energies and a union with the source of the subtle energies.

An example of the tantra yogi is the person who cooks a nutritious meal, cognizant of the life-building nutrients, minerals, and prana in the food. While eating the meal, this person breathes deeply and through a relaxed nervous system and energetically mindful state assimilates the benefits of the food on all levels.

Those who tread the karma yoga path experience freedom from stress as they work. Another way to think of Karma Yoga is selfless service or work as worship. It is union in action. In today's overscheduled, achievement-oriented world, Karma Yoga offers an extremely valuable awareness. For the karma yogi, the benefits of work are in the efforts themselves, rather than the outcomes. In other words, peace of mind remains the guide through all tasks, and all the actions are directed towards union with purusa instead of towards specific outcomes. When a karma yogi cooks a nutritious meal, the action of preparation and offering the fruits of labor are a means of enlightenment.

Bhakti Yoga is for the devotee. Love is the motivation, and the uplifting feeling of loving connection carries one on the bhakti path through all the trials and challenges in life. Unity is achieved through devotion to moksa, loved ones, or a Higher Power or religion. Yoga is not a religion but its philosophy offers a grammar for religious living, to those who feel devotion to God. Agnostic bhaktas love what they are doing, or the people they are doing it for, and free themselves from busyness and stress as a sense of devotion and caring overcomes them. The bhakti yogi cooks for the care of him or herself and family, imbuing that love into the food. Bhakti Yoga is the path of devotion.

The intellectual, or jnana yogi, discerns purusa and prakriti. For one on the jnana path, the power of the mind illuminates. Jnana is "realized wisdom," or that which is known through direct experience; thus, the jnana yogis understand union on a deep level, through svadhyaya, or self-study. Reading spiritual works, living the philosophies, and observing oneself in relation to that wisdom are means of applying the intellect to moksa. For those on the path of jnana, the thinking mind steers away from stress as wisdom reminds the aspirant that all is purusa and that peace and enlightenment live in the potential of each moment. A lifestyle example of Jnana Yoga is the cook who understands the importance of well-balanced, fresh meals and partakes in them as part of the rhythm of each day. Jnana yogis carry deep understanding of practice.

Raja Yoga, translated as "the royal path," is the path of practice. Patanjali outlines the eight-fold raja path in *The Yoga Sutras*. Enlightenment is achieved through meditation, which is supported by concentration, mastery of sensory input, proper breathing, physical balance, ethics, and morality. The raja yogi in the kitchen may use the act of meal preparation as an active, or mindfulness, meditation practice. All aspects of life are opportunities to practice a meditative mind.

Yoga is a philosophy and practice that guides us to replace this illusion of separation with the reality of unity. No matter a person's personality, learning style, or approach to yoga, there is a path for everyone. What is important is that we practice, that we traverse the path, and that each of us—and our students and clients—is offered the opportunity to employ these simple, ancient traditions and eradicate the unseen disease of stress from our lives.

Stress Transformation

Chronic stress has arisen from the current technological age and it has shaped our habits of recreation, communication, and work-life balance. Hand-held electronic devices, e-mail, and television, to name a few, have redefined our relationships with one another, nature, and our understanding of relaxation. Historically, we defined "stress" as some kind of despair. Now it is a constant sense of pressure and worry that is unnatural, no matter how normal it seems in modern life. Yoga teaches us to turn away from this illusion of fear and pressure and offers us a systematic means of rebuilding a healthy lifestyle and connecting to a peaceful reality beyond our everyday concerns. People of any personality or inclination may increase their peace of mind through the Yoga path, whether they are committed to physical health, work, relationships, wisdom, meditation, or a combination of these. Any effort in the direction of unity, the action away from the separation of stress, is worthwhile. Through small, practical, measurable lifestyle changes, guided by Yoga philosophy and a pure teacher, anyone may remove the habits and beliefs that create stress, transform the stress, and heal oneself of this generation's health epidemic.

Questions for the Reader

1. Samkhya philosophy teaches that all suffering in life arises from a sense of separation. How can you feel less "separate" in your life and more "connected" to that which brings you joy?
2. The word "yoga" translates as "union" and is the path of removing suffering through uniting, or having a relationship with that which is unchanging and divine. Since life situations are ever changing, how can you create a sense of peace and eliminate stress from such factors in your life?
3. Yoga teaches us to reject stress, rebuild a healthy lifestyle and connect to a peaceful reality beyond our everyday concerns. Can you list at least three ways that you can begin to employ this lifestyle in your life?

References

American Psychological Association. (2009). Stress in America. Retrieved February 29, 2012 from www.apa.org/news/press/releases/stress-exec-summary.pdf.

American Psychological Association (2010). Stress in America findings. Retrieved February 29, 2012 from www.apa.org/news/press/releases/stress/national-report.pdf.

Cohen, S., Doyle, W., & Skoner, D. (1999). Psychological stress, cytokine production, and severity of upper respiratory illness. *Psychosomatic Medicine*, 61(2), 175–180.

Gallup (2001). Attitudes in the American workplace VII. Retrieved February 29, 2012 from www.stress.org/2001Harris.pdf.

Homewood Employee Health (2007). *Counselling statistics*. Guelph: Homewood Employee Health.

Reiche, E. M., Nunes, S. O., & Morimoto, H. K. (2004). Stress, depression, the immune system, and cancer. *The Lancet Oncology*, 5(10), 617–625.

Statistics Canada (2010). Table 105-0501 Health indicator profile, annual estimates, by age group and sex, Canada, provinces, territories, health regions (2011 boundaries) and peer groups, occasional. *CANSIM (database)*. Retrieved February 29, 2012 from www5.statcan.gc.ca/cansim/a05?lang=eng&id=1050501.

World Health Organization. (2007). *Fact sheet: The top ten causes of death*. Retrieved February 29, 2012 from www.who.int/mediacentre/factsheets/fs310.pdf.

Yan, L. L., Liu, K., Matthews, K. A., Daviglus, M. L., Ferguson, T. F., & Kiefe, C. (2002). Time urgency/impatience (TUI) predicts incident hypertension 13 years later. *Circulation* 106(2), 755.

9 Yoga Therapy for Our Healers

How to Give to Self to Give to Others

Joanne Wu

Yoga is like music: the rhythm of the body, the melody of the mind, and the harmony of the soul create the symphony of life.

B. K. S. Iyengar

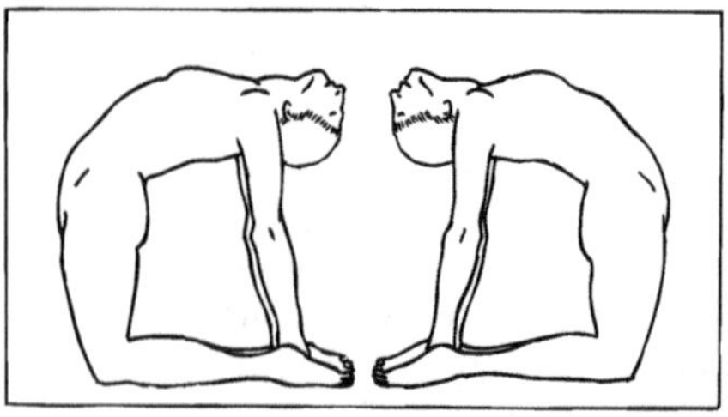

Figure 9.1

Introduction

According to medical research, more than two-thirds of physicians have experienced symptoms of emotional, mental, and physical exhaustion characterized as burnout. Healthcare providers who have burnout are at higher risk for health problems, tend to make more medical errors, and lose their sense of empathy for others. Furthermore, they are more prone to leave clinical practice. Unfortunately, this leads to a domino effect in our already critical state of healthcare, where there continues to be soaring illness burden and higher volume of patients. Latest research has started to point towards increasing mindfulness amongst care providers. Yoga has long been a totem in mind–body medicine but little is studied formally on how it can serve as therapy for our healers. In this chapter, we will explore current research in this arena, review the prevention strategies for burnout, and consider a mindfulness-filled stress reduction focused yoga program that will not only restore our ability to heal healers, but that will translate to better healthcare for our patients.

Healthcare Evolution: Background and History

There is no doubt medicine in the United States has changed over time. However, the evolution of healthcare in America had its beginnings long before the topic of reform and the establishment of the healthcare reform act, otherwise known as "Obama-Care" or the Affordable Care Act (ACA). Zinner & Loughlin (2009) once described six key periods: (1) the charitable era, (2) the origins of medical education era, (3) the insurance era, (4) the government era, (5) the managed care era, and (6) the consumerism era.

Prior to doctors, nurses and care teams, there was "family" medicine (Randolph, 2001). Early medical practice was mostly driven by the dedication, compassion, and love of the women for the home and their family. Outside of home concoctions and remedies, when serious life illnesses demanded, traveling doctors practiced their little credentialed expertise with great expectations and the warmest intentions of healing the sick. Many of them had performed such acts out of kindness and charity, in exchange for trade and appreciation. Then in 1765, the University of Pennsylvania opened its first medical school. Medical education later then became a focus of physicians, with the goal of raising the profession to a higher status and prestige similar to European counterparts through scientific foundation, research, and promise. With more formal and rigorous training and experience, doctors became entrepreneurs initiating a fee for service programs. As cities became more urbanized in the mid 1800s, doctors decreased home visits and patient care became more focused within hospitals. Doctors and nurses had firm support of the government in this era: public health focused on sanitation, hygiene, and dispensaries of medicine for control of epidemics of diseases such as cholera and tuberculosis. During that time, private insurances were slow to grow, but had much greater popularity compared to the concept of a National Health Insurance phenomenon, which was associated with socialism. This eventually led to the birth of Blue Cross towards the end of the 1920s, the country's first large insurance company. (Randolph, 2001)

Throughout the 1930s, the rise of the insurance era began. The capitalism of this change led to soaring healthcare costs. Medical advances in diagnostic and treatment techniques also played a role in the explosion of healthcare spending, along with workforce expansion and the start of the baby boomer generation. This led to further need of recruitment and training of care providers. Providers eventually formed care teams: nurses, therapists, technicians, and specialization of physicians. Government institutions, agencies, and social programs (such as National Institutes of Health (NIH), Centers for Disease Control (CDC), Food and Drug Administration (FDA), and Medicare and Medicaid) were established (Randolph, 2001). During this era, the government had desires to contribute to Americans' health. However, there was hesitation in any universal, nationalized healthcare such as those in collegial counterparts such as Europe, United Kingdom, and Canada. Many continued to fear socialism. The push for organized structure led to a revolution of insurances and birthed umbrella Health Maintenance Organizations (HMOs). These mammoth management services often required authorizations and approvals prior to diagnostics or treatments of patients, in attempts to streamline healthcare delivery and curb costs. These careful restrictions of services, some evidence based and others purely from insurance-set guidelines, often increased administrative demands of the physicians, and required increases in non-clinical staff to help care for patients.

This tortuous journey continues into the twenty-first century, which has no shortage of medical complexity and costs of care. The boom of the World Wide Web spawned consumerism of health care. Many are seeking opinions before going to see their doctors. There is interest in multiple physician consultations. There is also a greater range of treatment options, from vaccines and biologics, to minimally invasive surgeries and early screening of devastating diseases. Consumers are also starting to explore complementary and alternative medicines such as acupuncture, chiropractic care, and herbal supplements. Despite such advances, there are ongoing differences in care that are barriers to the satisfaction of patients and care providers to the healthcare industry. In fact, research shows dissatisfaction amongst U.S. doctors rising.

According to Forbes Magazine in 2012, in an online questionnaire of 24,000 doctors representing 25 specialties, only 54% said they would choose medicine again as a career, down from 69% in 2011. Unfortunately, just 41% would choose the same specialty again. Worse off, only a quarter of doctors said they would choose the same practice setting (Adams, 2012).

Beyond job satisfaction, there is a continued decline in primary care physicians (PCP), or otherwise known as a general practitioner. A PCP typically provides both the first contact for a person with an undiagnosed health concern, as well as continued care for stable medical conditions. The PCP generally emphasizes the importance of preventative care and coordinates screening for diseases such as cancer and diabetes. The continued decline of primary care is often underreported as complex in etiology. This down slope perpetuates uncontrollable inflation of healthcare spending, decreased access to necessary care, and increased fragmentation of care. Furthermore, as healthcare costs spiral out of control, this devastating trend, unless reversed, can eventually bankrupt our healthcare system, and perhaps even our country.

Burnout and Compassion Fatigue

It has been hypothesized that caring too much, whether it is too deeply, or for too long, can cause ailments. A heightened sense of vulnerability can result from repeated exposure to pain and suffering and as well can lessen trust (Herman, 1997; Portnoy 2011). When caregivers focus on others without retreat to self-care, negative behaviors can surface. This suffering can impact personally and minimally, but often turns toward serious pathology that can domino to other aspects of relationships. This is often referred to as secondary traumatic stress disorder, otherwise known as compassion fatigue. It can encourage destructive apathy, isolation, and substance abuse. A separate but parallel concept is burnout. This state can be in conjunction with or exists independently from compassion fatigue. According to Portnoy (2011): "Psychologists Pines and Aronson [1989] describe burnout as a state of physical, emotional and mental exhaustion caused by long-term involvement in emotionally demanding situations. It is accompanied by disillusionment and negative feelings" (p. 47).

Professional caregivers, and their employers, need to recognize signs of burnout and compassion fatigue, because people in helping roles are at great risk, and may put lives in jeopardy. Direct patient care can impact workers through constant exposure to negativity. As they face increasing demands of a healthcare workplace, many do not have a break at home. From managing family demands to juggling personal goals and interests, workers have little time to genuinely self-care for preventative or acute medical needs. Focus on quality, compassionate care for patients, in an efficient and low cost method, often takes precedence over empathy for healthcare workers themselves. This trend does not show signs of slowdown with the development of accountable care models in medical delivery.

In fact, in May 2014, the nationally renowned Cleveland Clinic explored the concept of "interdisciplinary empathy," as it held the first Empathy Innovation Summit. This implies compassion and empathy for not only patients, but also for healthcare workers. Earlier in the same year, Cleveland Clinic released a video named "Empathy: The Human Connection to Patient Care." This display emphasizes the need of understanding the human spirit, and how all our emotions are interconnected in meaningful and effective delivery of care for patients.

Pattern Recognition

In the early stages, burnout and compassion fatigue symptoms can include frequent colds, reduced sense of accomplishment, headaches, and fatigue. This, in turn, can lower resiliency, decrease immune protection, resulting in higher rates of infection. Moodiness and increased interpersonal conflicts can also arise. If not recognized or treated, burnout gradually moves into an advanced stage displaying symptoms of somatic complaints. Social withdrawal, depersonalization, cynicism, irritability often start to impact one's interpersonal relationships. This leads to a feeling of being underappreciated and overworked. In time, the care provider becomes numb, disillusioned, and hardened. This overwhelming sense of burden mushrooms and anxiety with or without depression starts to develop. Often, caregivers don't realize the negative effects until they experience a health crisis of their own, or the impact of their human errors become devastating.

The Professional Quality of Life measure (ProQOL) is a commonly used tool and applied theory of the negative and positive effects of helping others who experience suffering and trauma. The ProQOL has sub-scales for compassion satisfaction, burnout, and compassion fatigue. The measure has been in use since 1995. It was developed by Beth Hudnall Stamm. There have been several revisions and it has proven to be a valid measure of compassion satisfaction and fatigue. The ProQOL 5 is the current version and is widely available online.

It is not a medical or psychological test. It is not to be used in isolation, but as part of a bigger picture (Smith, 2012).

Professional Quality of Life is built on extremely complex relationships (Figure 9.2). It is not simply from the work environment, but also personal environment. Care providers bring a past and a present to everything they approach. This can include but is not limited to cultural beliefs, personal beliefs, social support systems, economic situation, past trauma, and illness. The ProQOL is a 30-question test that uses a Likert scale with a range of statements such as "I am happy" to "My work makes me feel satisfied" and "I believe I can make a difference with my work."[1]

Stress Response

Stress can be defined as a nonspecific response to perceived environmental threats, otherwise known as stressors. However, despite common triggers of stress, there are differences amongst people. While a particular demand or event may be perceived by one person as a stressor, another person may view it as benign. The generalized feeling of fear and apprehension associated with a stressor often leads to anxiety. Anxiety is typically accompanied by activation of the sympathetic nervous system and increased physiological arousal. This can present with symptoms of rapid breathing, increased heart rate, sweating, and dilation of the pupils.

In the 1920s, Walter Cannon recognized that the autonomic nervous system was activated in response to stress and suggested that stress mobilized the body's responses in readiness for either attacking or fleeing from a threatening situation. (This is popularly known as "Fight or Flight" theory.) Although such responses may have promoted survival in acute states, they are not productive given the longer periods of stress exposure.

Hans Selye (1950) is credited with identifying the body's reaction to stress with a syndrome he called the general adaptation syndrome, which has three phases, as evidenced by the level of stress hormones. The three phases are broken down into:

1. **Alarm**: The body first recognizes threat. It organizes physiological responses.
2. **Resistance**: Stress-activated responses continue. It stabilizes the body's adaptations to stress.
3. **Exhaustion**: The body has depleted its reserves. It can no longer maintain responses to the stressors.

During the alarm phase, the hypothalamus sends signals to the pituitary gland. This endocrine gland in turn secretes Adrenalcorticotropic Hormone (ACTH). This travels into the bloodstream to the cortex outer layer of the adrenal glands, where endogenous corticosteroids are secreted. The hypothalamus also activates the central part of the adrenal gland, which causes

PROFESSIONAL QUALITY OF LIFE SCALE (PROQOL)

COMPASSION SATISFACTION AND COMPASSION FATIGUE
(PROQOL) VERSION 5 (2009)

When you *[help]* people you have direct contact with their lives. As you may have found, your compassion for those you *[help]* can affect you in positive and negative ways. Below are some questions about your experiences, both positive and negative, as a *[helper]*. Consider each of the following questions about you and your current work situation. Select the number that honestly reflects how frequently you experienced these things in the <u>*last 30 days*</u>.

1=Never **2=Rarely** **3=Sometimes** **4=Often** **5=Very Often**

_____ 1. I am happy.
_____ 2. I am preoccupied with more than one person I *[help]*.
_____ 3. I get satisfaction from being able to *[help]* people.
_____ 4. I feel connected to others.
_____ 5. I jump or am startled by unexpected sounds.
_____ 6. I feel invigorated after working with those I *[help]*.
_____ 7. I find it difficult to separate my personal life from my life as a *[helper]*.
_____ 8. I am not as productive at work because I am losing sleep over traumatic experiences of a person I *[help]*.
_____ 9. I think that I might have been affected by the traumatic stress of those I *[help]*.
_____ 10. I feel trapped by my job as a *[helper]*.
_____ 11. Because of my *[helping]*, I have felt "on edge" about various things.
_____ 12. I like my work as a *[helper]*.
_____ 13. I feel depressed because of the traumatic experiences of the people I *[help]*.
_____ 14. I feel as though I am experiencing the trauma of someone I have *[helped]*.
_____ 15. I have beliefs that sustain me.
_____ 16. I am pleased with how I am able to keep up with *[helping]* techniques and protocols.
_____ 17. I am the person I always wanted to be.
_____ 18. My work makes me feel satisfied.
_____ 19. I feel worn out because of my work as a *[helper]*.
_____ 20. I have happy thoughts and feelings about those I *[help]* and how I could help them.
_____ 21. I feel overwhelmed because my case [work] load seems endless.
_____ 22. I believe I can make a difference through my work.
_____ 23. I avoid certain activities or situations because they remind me of frightening experiences of the people I *[help]*.
_____ 24. I am proud of what I can do to *[help]*.
_____ 25. As a result of my *[helping]*, I have intrusive, frightening thoughts.
_____ 26. I feel "bogged down" by the system.
_____ 27. I have thoughts that I am a "success" as a *[helper]*.
_____ 28. I can't recall important parts of my work with trauma victims.
_____ 29. I am a very caring person.
_____ 30. I am happy that I chose to do this work.

Figure 9.2 Beth Hudnall Stamm, 2009; www.ProQOL.org

epinephrine to be released. This activates the sympathetic nervous system, the "adrenaline" response. After maintaining high levels of the hormones for a long time, the body exhausts its resources.

Evidence has demonstrated that prolonged stress affects the ability of the immune system to function adequately and can affect the release of other neurotransmitters such as serotonin. Stress may also affect the release of natural endorphins, chemicals similar in structure to drugs used in the modulation of pain. The long-term activation of the stress-response system and its subsequent overexposure to stress hormones can interrupt a body's homeostasis. Numerous health problems have been related to chronic stress. These include:

- anxiety
- depression
- digestive problems
- heart disease
- sleep problems
- weight gain
- memory and concentration impairment
- chronic pain.

However, not all stress is bad. A cardiologist, Peter Nixon, MD, described what is known as "The Human Function Curve" (Nixon, 1982). This is a concept that illustrated the effects of long-term stress. Nixon (1982) showed that performance increases under stress initially. But over the long term, fatigue and exhaustion introduces decline in performance. According to Nixon, this decline is predicted to lead to illness. Nixon also demonstrated that long-term stress often produced unawareness of this shift in health and the breakdown process. This lack of mindfulness gradually became a focus of research and the process of healing.

Impact

In 2012, Shanafelt et al. published a study of burnout and job satisfaction on a large sample of United States physicians of varying specialties. There were substantial differences in burnout observed by specialty. Emergency medicine, general internal medicine, neurology, and family medicine had the highest rates of burnout. (These are typically physicians who had to care for a large volume of patients and who were at the front lines of care.) Pathology, dermatology, general pediatrics, and preventative medicine received the lowest rates of burnout. These differences were noticed even after adjusting for age, sex, call schedule, relationship status, hours worked per week, and years since graduation from medical school. Despite the fluctuations, the estimated overall burnout rate of physicians remained sadly at 35%.

Job dissatisfaction among healthcare workers contributes to costly labor disputes, turnover, and risk to patients. And doctors are not the only ones vulnerable. Survey data found much higher job dissatisfaction and burnout among nurses who were directly caring for patients in hospitals and nursing homes than among nurses working in other jobs or settings, such as the pharmaceutical industry (McHugh, Kutney-Lee, Cimiotti, Sloane, & Aiken, 2011). Patient satisfaction levels are lower in hospitals with more nurses who are dissatisfied or burned out. With all the attention to quality and safety of delivery of care, this trend signals problems. Researchers have described how burnout among nurses affects the quality of treatment for patients, lowers morale, and increases absenteeism, with an accompanying financial impact on the hospital. Nurse turnover due to stress takes a financial toll, as well.

Turnover is a major issue impacting the performance of healthcare organizations. Health systems require a stable, educated, and fully engaged nursing staff to provide effective levels of patient care (Alexander, Bloom, & Nuchols, 1994). The financial cost of losing a single nurse has been calculated to equal about twice the nurse's annual salary (Atencio, Cohen, & Gorenberg, 2007). The average hospital is estimated to lose about $300,000 per year for each percentage increase in annual nurse turnover. According to Atencio et al. (2007), losing these critical employees negatively impacts the bottom line of healthcare organizations in a variety of ways including:

- decreased quality of patient care
- increased medical errors
- increased contingent staff costs
- increased nurse and medical staff turnover
- increased staffing costs
- increased absenteeism and disability rates
- decreased engagement and "presentee-ism."

With the booming generation and the higher complexity of diseases, there has been focus of hospitals to curtail the problem of job dissatisfaction, burnout, and compassion fatigue dilemma with wellness programs that can be effective in helping the healthcare force stay strong, focus, and persevere. In recent years, wellness has shifted its focus towards mindfulness.

Mindfulness Based Stress Reduction (MBSR)

According to the Merriam-Webster dictionary, mindfulness is defined as a state of being aware. Mindfulness as a psychological concept is the focusing of attention to the present moment, thus achieving awareness (Chiesa, Calati, & Serretti, A. 2011). It is based on the concept of mindfulness in Buddhist studies. The eight fold path is one of such principle teachings that emphasize mindfulness in the path of enlightenment.

In 1979, Dr. Jon Kabat-Zinn developed the Mindfulness Based Stress Reduction (MBSR) program at the University of Massachusetts Medical Center. Since its inception, MBSR has evolved into a common form of complementary medicine that integrates with traditional, Western, allopathic modalities to address a variety of health problems. It is a structured group program that employs mindfulness meditation to alleviate suffering associated with physical, psychosomatic, and psychiatric disorders. MBSR is based upon a systematic procedure to develop enhanced awareness of moment-to-moment experience of perceptible mental processes (Grossman, Niedman, Schmidt, & Walach,

2004). The approach predicts that greater awareness will provide more honest perception, reduce negative effect, and improve vitality, resiliency, and coping strategies. In the last two decades, a number of research reports have appeared that seem to support many of these claims.

According to National Institutes of Health's Center for Complementary Medicine (NCCAM), MBSR has been shown to have a positive impact on a variety of health conditions. From Irritable Bowel Syndrome (IBS) and chronic pain, to stress management and infections, this program is showing benefits in quality of life improvement and symptom control. Research demonstrates that mindfulness interventions can effectively reduce stress, anxiety, and depression in both clinical and nonclinical populations (Shapiro, Schwartz, & Bonner, 1998). For healthcare professionals, Dr. Shauna L Shapiro has demonstrated MBSR can have beneficial effects on health. In 1998, she and her colleagues published a randomized control trial of MBSR for medical and premedical students. Her findings noted significant decreases in depression and anxiety while demonstrating significant increases in empathy in the MBSR intervention group compared with controls. In 2005, Shapiro, Astin, Bishop, & Cordova published a pilot study completed for healthcare professionals. She compared an experimental and a wait-list control group from baseline to post-treatment. She designed an 8-week education focused program that taught participants to become more aware of their thoughts, feelings, and body sensations on a moment-to-moment basis. This "carpe diem" or "seize the day" approach to stress allowed for better acceptance and more honest adaptation to the stress.

Barriers to Application: Case Example

Thirty-two-year-old PM is a family medicine doctor in Rochester, NY. She runs a small private practice. Her staff includes a nurse and a secretary. To save on overhead costs, she does her own billing. She is a sole income provider for the family. This includes herself, her husband, and her 3-year-old child. Her dream was to have a practice where she could save on overheads so she could spend more quality time caring for patients. This included longer than average visits and telemedicine where she interacted with patients online and via email. She started her day with caring for her child around 6 in the morning and despite her husband helping with child care, she became increasingly worried about getting home on time to spend quality time with her young child before bedtime. With federal regulations changing, insurance patterns shifting, and continuing medical education demands, she found herself spending more time doing administrative work and more preoccupied with work when not working. She was also on call daily since she cared for patients by herself. Vacation time was difficult. Outside of medicine, she enjoyed yoga but struggled to attend classes due to her schedule. She noticed more daytime fatigue, headaches, frustration, and dissatisfaction with her job. She worried about her patients, many of whom remained noncompliant with recommended treatment options. After five years in practice, she sadly decided to close her practice.

Time is a common trigger of stress amongst healthcare workers, such as the case of this young doctor. With increasing clinical demand along with administrative work that is falling on the shoulders of care providers, there is little time spent with the patients in a typical clinical encounter. Aside from time needed to practice mindfulness, it takes effort. Mindfulness is no small feat. It requires the commitment. It requires honesty. It requires an open mind and a brave heart to face all of the deep-rooted emotions that have been buried for many years. The practice of mindfulness asks the practitioner to not only observe all these emotions but to examine it: Observe the stress of caring for people, digest the fear of failure or disappointment, release the expectation to never make an error, and resolve the pressure to always have an answer. This assessment process is not just about time, it is about being able to face the feelings that come rushing with "taking a pause."

Beyond Mindfulness: Yoga Roots and Philosophy

Yoga often translates to "yoke, join, or concentrate." Yoga describes a means of uniting mind, body, and spirit through the use of intentional breath. The Indian sage, Patanjali has been credited with the collation of the tradition of passing yogic teaching directly to student, into his classical work, the *Yoga Sutra.* It is a 1700-year-old treatise on yogic philosophy. A collection of just under 200 wise statements, the *Yoga Sutra* is a philosophical guide for dealing with the challenges of humanity. The *Yoga Sutra,* split into four chapters, or *padas*, helps provide a framework upon which all yoga practiced today (Iyengar, 1995). In the second chapter of Iyangar's book, he presents five specific ethical precepts called *yamas*. These serve as basic guidelines for living a life of personal fulfillment. Patanjali noted if not fulfilled, suffering might be the end result. Yamas address "the whole" of our lives, not just physical health or solitary.

When many people think of yoga, the thought of physical postures, or *asanas*, that promote flexibility and strength often comes to mind. In addition to the practice of such postures, meditation, or *dhyana*, is often the secondary image to what yoga is all about. However, these are simply a few aspects to Patanjali'*s* eight limbed system. For an in-depth account of this system, the reader is referred to Iyengar's treatise (1995). However the yama is perhaps the most easily relatable to healthcare providers: *ahimsa* usually translated as "to not injure." This parallels the Hippocratic Oath, which emphasizes "to abstain from doing harm," that is historically taken by physicians. To practice ahimsa is to be constantly perceptive, to observe and be aware ourselves in interaction with others, and to notice our thoughts and intentions.

The *Yoga Sutra* does not imply that humans are "bad" or "good" based upon behavior, but rather that *behavior is by choice*, and the end result should be accountable to oneself. Beyond the fundamental yamas, there are *niyamas*. These are the observances or attitudes we have toward things and people, as well as how we relate to ourselves. It is with understanding niyamas we are able to better understand the relationship we hold with the rest of the world. As

Iyengar has been oft quoted, "When we free ourselves from physical disabilities, emotional disturbances, and mental distractions, we open the gates to our soul."

Any activity that cultivates self-reflective consciousness can be considered svadhyaya (one of the niyamas). Beyond mindfulness, this awareness teaches us to be centered and non-reactive to the dualities. Similar to traditional Chinese medicine, there is no single existence of black and white, there is balance and interdependence. This dynamic concept is ever evolving, but despite constant change, there is peace with each present moment (Kaptchuk, 2000).

Diving beyond yamas and niyamas, we revisit the limb that is familiar and has popular association with yoga: *asana*. Asana is the practice of physical postures. Similar to other types of exercise, the practice of moving the body into postures has widespread benefits. On a deeper level the practice of asana, which means "staying" in Sanskrit, is used often as a tool to calm the mind so to find a connection to our true essence. The poses help explore the unity between the physical and the ethereal body. It helps teach us our responses to the physical world. Practicing asanas can toughen mental attitudes and strengthen our will while quieting the mind. Sweating through postures has a profound grounding energy in the body and fosters an expansion of awareness with the control of breath. This is the fourth limb of Patanjali's *ashtanga: pranayama*.

Pranayama is very important in yoga. It goes hand in hand with asana. It is the process of purification, and calms the nervous system. Patanjali suggested the control of breath and bodily posture would harmonize the flow of energy, thus preparing the body for control of the senses. According to Iyengar (1995), "The needs of the body are the needs of the divine spirit which lives through the body."

Pratyahara, the retreat of the senses from attachment to external objects, severs this link between mind and senses. No longer functioning in their norm, the senses sharpen, similar to a hearing impaired individual who learns to read lips or feels the vibration of the music to understand its meaning. To tune in, to be mindful, is to tune out external excess. A person who is influenced by outside events and sensations can never be tranquil in inner peace. Energy is exhausted in trying to suppress unwanted sensations. This will eventually result in a physical or mental imbalance, thus dampening the immune system, resulting in illness. This model is similar to the previously mentioned, scientifically noted, Human Function Curve (Nixon, 1982). When one is able to retreat and stop engaging with external stimuli, one can recognize dharana, the sixth limb of Patanjali. This is concentration or focus of attention in one direction. The mind finds power in stillness and full absorption. Deep contemplation and reflection can be intense. It encourages us to face satya, our truth. The objective is to steady the mind in the chaos that exists around us. Through this practice, we can begin to unleash potential for inner healing, leading to dhyana, meditation or contemplation. When one focuses for an extended period of time, one becomes more reflective of one's objective. During this practice, layers of keen perception further unify the consciousness.

As the ripples fade, and a glass of water settles, the mind reflects clarity. This state of freedom, or Moksha, is the liberation of this journey.

The final step in Patanjali's eight-fold path of yoga is *samadhi*. In this state, the body and senses are at rest, but not asleep. There is alertness beyond consciousness. During samadhi, we realize how a freed soul can enjoy awareness of one's true identity and purpose. It is a state often sought but *never fully achieved*. This process of the yogic journey is what distinguishes itself from simply being an exercise or a mindfulness practice. Patanjali's eight limbs are *not* what defines yoga: they help form the essence of its roots and can be a pathway that leads to the attainment of *biopsychosocial wellbeing*. Yoga does not seek to change the individual: it is unraveling who the individual truly is.

Yoga Therapy

Despite the influence of Patanjali, not all ways to explore the practice of yoga are created equal. There are many schools that have various crossovers, but there also exists much diversity. From Iyengar to Kundalini and Viniyoga, there have been no studies directly comparing one yoga school to the other. This makes sense. Yoga nurtures the individual. All individuals are unique. In addition, despite therapeutic benefits of practicing yoga in a fitness setting, it does not define yoga therapy. Over the years, there have been many definitions but not a large consensus. According to Judith Lasater, PhD, expert and author of restorative yoga, yoga therapy is "the use of techniques of yoga to create, stimulate, and maintain an optimum state of physical, emotional, mental, and spiritual health." Each year, organizations such as the International Association of Yoga Therapy (IAYT) strive to work towards the mission of establishing yoga as a recognized and respected therapy. And nationally, people are taking notice.

Yoga is one of the top 10 complementary health approaches as noted by the National Health Interview Survey. According to Centers for Disease Control (CDC), thirteen million adults in the U.S. practice yoga (Barnes, Bloom, & Nahin, 2008). The survey noted 58% use yoga for therapy to maintain wellbeing and good health, 10% use it for treatment of musculoskeletal conditions, 16% use it for treatment of other health conditions.

The term "yoga as medicine" was coined by Dr. Timothy McCall in his 2007 book on prescribing yoga with intent to heal. According to NCCAM, 22% of people who practice yoga noted it was recommended by a doctor. Yoga strengthens different systems in the body, including the heart and cardiovascular system, the lungs, muscles, and the nervous system. It can improve function of the digestive system while improving oxygen delivery to tissues. Yoga also can help the body more efficiently remove waste products, carcinogens, and cellular toxins. Through a healthy body, the feeling of wellbeing is often described by those who practice yoga.

Most people live stressful lives. As previously stated, stress has been linked to a wide variety of medical problems, from migraine headaches, insomnia, chronic pain, and irritable bowel syndrome to potentially life-threatening conditions such as diabetes and heart disease. Since persistently high levels of stress hormones, particularly cortisol, can impair function of the immune system, yoga can also help with infection control and prevent flares of rheumatologic conditions such as arthritis. According to Dr. McCall, studies suggest yoga can even lessen the side effects of chemotherapy and radiation treatments for cancer. In clinical trials, many patients with asthma and high blood pressure who began a regular practice of yoga were able to either lower their drug dosage or eliminate drug therapy entirely. This not only improves quality of life, but also decreases healthcare spending. It is no wonder over 90% of Integrative Medicine Centers offer yoga as part of their healing services (McCall, 2007)

There are currently 74 open clinical trials for yoga for health. This spans from yoga for chronic pain, smoking cessation, hypertension, post-traumatic stress disorder, to substance abuse, cancer care, and eating disorders. A barrier to more research in this arena is partly funding, but to create scientific protocols around yoga, which emphasizes individuality. Yoga therapy, despite its popularity and benefits, has its risks if not delivered in an incremental approach. It is best to begin yoga as medicine slowly and ramp up the intensity and duration of practice only if it feels good and without contraindications. For example, students with blood pressure issues should not practice regular heated yoga or extended inversion poses. There is not one pose or sequence that will promote healing. We are unique by nature. Yoga practice is an art. Many people have more than one medical condition and what gets one person excited to practice, may not bring joy to another. It is important to evaluate the individual in front of them and decide what is best on a case-by-case basis, on a day-to-day basis. We are constantly growing, evolving—and so does a solid yoga practice. The realization that change is constant and inevitable, so adaptation is expected and embraced, is the key to success of a mindful, healthful lifelong journey.

The Giver Receives: Yoga for Healers

A survey for nurses asking what they do to take care of themselves has noted exercise is, not surprisingly, a very common self-care activity (Walker, 2012). Out of that small pool of those who move, few respondents reported regularly practicing yoga. Doctors fared no better. Despite an increasing popularity to prescribe yoga and exercise (Ross & Thomas, 2010) for patients due to dangers of inactivity, many doctors didn't exercise enough (Gupta & Lampson 2009). British researchers (Gupta & Lampson, 2009), in a study that queried 61 hospital physicians, found that only 21% get the recommended 30 minutes of moderate exercise at least five days a week. Barriers included lack of time, lack of motivation, or lack of workout facilities. It is no wonder healthcare providers are at high risk of burnout. While mindfulness has a growing base of research for benefits for doctors, yoga has yet to be studied on a large scale. It is hypothesized that yoga, with mindfulness being a part of the foundation, may provide similar if not additive positive effects. As more health centers are noticing the need to improve wellness amongst employees, yoga may help not only enhance wellbeing and happiness while decreasing burnout, but breed a more empathetic, warm, and caring environment.

Off the Mat

Love is a great healing power in the yogic world, but not always realized or practiced off the yoga mat. It also roots a therapeutic connection between healthcare providers and patient. But how can one give what one does not feel? There are many ways to experience, to share, to learn love. Yoga can help you appreciate it practically and meaningfully, every day. Begin with yourself. This starts with engaging in learning patterns of your mind and cultivating new positive ways of being. Consider beginning with a loving-kindness meditation, called Metta Bhavana.

Below is an adapted guide inspired by my yoga journey to help bring Metta Bhavana into your daily life. This is a reflection of my love for my yoga, my support system, and my patients to help ignite your unconditional love for yourself, and may you spread this power to all around you.

Suggestion for the reader: try this daily for a week and note changes in your life.

1. Sit comfortably
2. Close your eyes
3. Reflect on your own goodness by thinking of a time when you showed kindness, compassion to others. Bring attention to one of your strengths that you appreciate. Smile.
4. Take a deep breath and notice how you feel. Really notice.
5. Begin to repeat these phrases, loud enough for you to hear the words:
   May I be safe from inner and outer harm.
   May I be happy and peaceful.
   May I be healthy and strong.
   May I be able to take care of myself with joy.
6. Take another deep breath and notice how you feel. Yes, again. Really notice.
7. Repeat as often as you feel. It may be different each time. Say it with authenticity.

Practice is the key. There is no magic. There is no destination for completion. Let the love sink in. You might get bored, or feel undeserved at times, but don't give up. You are never too old or too young to begin this practice. Everyone deserves self-love to receive never-ending love. And in order to provide care for others, you must first feel love. You don't need a month, a day, or an expensive gift, to remind you of the importance of that. You are worth it. As Gautama Buddha said, "In the end these things matter most: How well did you love? How fully did you live? How deeply did you let go?" (Brekke, 1999).

Editors' Note

1. The ProQOL is free and available for download in order to continue the research of Beth Hudnall Stamm. For more information the reader is directed directly to the website: www.proqol.org/.

Additional Resources

www.cdc.gov History of healthcare
www.compassionfatigue.org Information for caregivers
www.cultureofempathy.com Information for caregivers
www.clevelandclinic.org "Empathy: The Human Connection to Patient Care"
www.clinicaltrials.gov Clinical trial information for yoga as therapy
www.iayt.org Yoga therapy science and research
www.Fit2bWell.com Information about the author and her blog
www.myselfcare.org Self-care quiz, articles
www.nccam.nih.gov/health/yoga Information about yoga and National Institutes of Health support
www.proqol.org Professional Quality of Life Scale self-test; professional quality of life information

References

Adams, S. (2012). Why do so many doctors regret their job choice? *Forbes Magazine*, April.

Alexander, J. A., Bloom, J. R., & Nuchols, B. A. (1994). Nursing turnover and hospital efficiency: An organizational-level analysis. *Industrial Relations*, 33, 505–520.

Atencio, B., Cohen, J., & Gorenberg, B. (2007). Nurse retention: is it worth it? *Nursing Economics*, 21.

Barnes, P. M., Bloom, B., & Nahin, R. L. (2008). Complementary and alternative medicine use among adults and children: United States. *National Health Statistics Reports*, 12, pp 1–24. Hyattsville, MD: Center for Disease Control and Prevention.

Brekke, T. (1999). The religious motivation of the early Buddhists. *Journal of the American Academy of Religion*, 67(4), 860.

Chiesa, A., Calati, R., & Serretti, A. (2011). Does mindfulness training improve cognitive abilities? A systematic review of neuropsychological findings. *Clinical Psychology Review*, 31(3), 449–464.

Grossman, P., Niedman, L., Schmidt, S., & Walach, H. (2004). Mindfulness-based stress reduction and health benefits: A meta-analysis. *Journal of Psychosomatic Research*, 1, 35–43.

Gupta, K., & Lampson, F. (2009). Doctors: Fighting fit or couch potatoes. *British Journal of Sports Medicine*, 43, 153–154.

Herman, J (1997). *Trauma and recovery: The aftermath of violence—from domestic abuse to political terror.* New York: Basic Books.

Iyengar, B. K. S. (1995). *Light on yoga: Yoga Dipika.* New York: Schocken.

Kaptchuk, T. (2000). *The web has no weaver* (2nd Edn). New York: RosettaBooks, LLC.

McCall, T. (2007). *Yoga as medicine.* New York: Bantam.

McHugh, M., Kutney-Lee, A., Cimiotti, J., Sloane, D., & Aiken, L. H. (2011). Nurses' widespread job dissatisfaction, burnout, and frustration with health benefits signal problems for patient care. *Health Aff (Millwood)*, 30(2), 202–210.

Nixon, P. (1982). The human function curve—a paradigm for our times. *Act Nerv Super (Praha)*, Suppl 3(Pt 1), 130–133.

Pines, A., & Aronson, E. (1989). *Career burnout: Causes and cures.* New York: Free Press.

Portnoy, D. (2011). Burnout and compassion fatigue: Watch for the signs. *Health Progress*, July–August, 47–50.

Randolph, F. (2001). The evolution of the U.S. healthcare system. Science and its times. Tampa, FL: Gale Publishing.

Ross, A., & Thomas, S. (2010). The health benefits of yoga and exercise: a review of comparison studies. *Journal of Alternative and Complementary Medicine*, 16(1), 3–12.

Selye, H. (1950). Stress and the general adaptation syndrome. *British Medical Journal*, 1(4667), 1383–1392.

Shanafelt, T., Boone, S., Litjen, T., Dyrbye, L., Sotile, W., Satele, B., West, C., Sloan, J. & Oreskovich, M. (2012). Burnout and satisfaction with work-life balance among US physicians relative to the general US population. *Archives of Internal Medicine*, 172(18), 1377–1385.

Shapiro, S., Astin, J., Bishop, S., & Cordova, M (2005). Mindfulness-based stress reduction for health care professionals: results from a randomized trial. *International Journal of Stress Management*, 12(2), 164–176.

Shapiro, S., Schwartz, G., & Bonner, G. (1998). Effects of mindfulness-based stress reduction on medical and premedical students. *Journal of Behavioral Medicine*, 21(6).

Smith, P. (2012). *Compassion satisfaction: 50 steps to healthy caregiving.* Amazon: CreateSpace Independent Publishing.

Walker, M. (2012). Surprising health benefits of yoga. *NursingDegree.net.* December 19.

Zinner, M., & Loughlin, M. (2009). The evolution of health care in America. *Urologic Clinics of North America*, 36(1), 1–10.

10 Yoga, Is It Learning or Therapy?

Comparing Medical and Educational Models

Staffan Elgelid

Take care of your body. It is the only place you have to live.

Jim Rohn

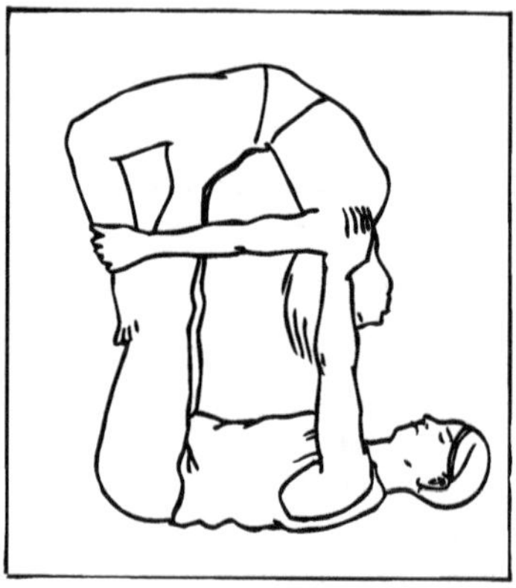

Figure 10.1

Introduction

In the last three decades, the number of people going to yoga to improve their health and wellbeing has increased dramatically. According to research, many people attending yoga studios have some form of physical or emotional medical condition, and are seeking out yoga as a solution to their health problems (Fishman 2009). Whatever the reason is, the number of people that are looking for yoga as a solution to their health problems is growing. But what model of care are we working with as yoga therapists? Are we working with the medical model, or educational model? Before we go any further we need to take a look at and define the differences between the medical and educational model.

Medical Model—Therapy

The medical model is based on the idea that medical care is given for an illness or injury. The medical practitioner administers the treatment to the patient.

The illness or injury will be cured/healed and the patient will be declared well. In medical rehabilitation there will be an educational component. The educational component often consists of the therapist instructing the patient in certain exercises. The patient demonstrates an understanding of the exercises and will continue to perform the exercises until full, or optimal health is reached. The patient will leave the medical model with better health status on the measures that relates to the illness or injury, but the patient does not have a deeper knowledge of his or her self and usually acts, feels, and thinks the same way as he did before the illness. The interaction between the therapist and patient in the medical model is often prescriptive and directed from the medical practitioner to the patient.

Educational Model—Education Draw Out

Education comes from the word Educere—to bring out or draw out. A good education "draws out" what is already there. From a yoga perspective it is about helping the client draw out information/knowledge that is already present in the client. The goal is to get the client to mobilize his or her own resources. The yoga therapist can guide and facilitate the process, but the client is using the resources that are already present in him or her. The educational model is an interactive approach and both the practitioner and client stand to benefit and learn from the interaction.

Included in the educational model, and more relevant to yoga, is the field of somatic education. What then is somatic education and how does somatic education relate to the field of yoga?

Somatic Education Model

Somatic education could be considered a subset of the field of Somatics. Thomas Hanna introduced the term Somatics in 1986 in four articles under the title "What is Somatics?" Hanna defined Somatics as "the art and science of the inter relational process between awareness, biological functioning and the environment, all three factors being identified as a synergestic whole" (1986, p.39). Why did Hanna use the word soma instead of body? According to Hanna, the term body tends to be something very fixed and static in most people's minds, while *soma* implies the *living body* as an *ever-changing process.* A body can be dead or alive but soma, as defined in Somatics and somatic education, indicates a *living body.* Joly (2001) defined the soma as the sum total of the body's subjective (First person, I) lived experience. This includes our thoughts, emotions, and fantasies; the totality of our biological and neurological processes. Here again the emphasis is on the lived experiences, and not a body as a third person object to be probed and examined. How then is somatic education different from Somatics?

Somatic Education

Somatic education, according to Joly (2001), "is the art and science of a variety of methods interested in the learning of awareness of the living body (the soma) in the environment" (p.18). Here again the *living body* (the soma) is mentioned, but in addition, the environment augments the concept of soma. More specifically, it could be stated that Somatic education *addresses* one's relationship with the environment. Somatic education is not therapy, or health care (allopathic or complementary), but is a learning process. A somatic education practitioner does not necessarily work with a specific problem such as pain relief, nor does the practitioner diagnose specific illnesses or dysfunctions. Instead the somatic educator tries to provide the student with an environment where he or she can observe/become aware of his/ her habits and actions. By observing his/her own habits and actions the student gains a better understanding of him or herself and can then move towards better health, emotional stability, spiritual growth, or whatever the student wants to improve. The environment where the student's actions take place may include family, society, relationships, work, and any other atmosphere that is significant to the student.

Joly (2001) outlined four central aspects of somatic education:

1. *Movement.* According to Hanna (1980, 1986), Feldenkrais (1972), and Maisel (1990), movement equals life which equates to vitality in all functions. Movement, gross muscular movement as well as visceral and cellular movements, can be considered the basis of life. Movement is necessary for the development of the body, brain, and nervous system. Movement can and has been studied from the viewpoint of many disciplines including anatomy, physiology, biomechanics, kinesiology, neurology, etc. All these disciplines look at movement from a third person perspective. Somatic educators study movement from a first person, subjective experience.
2. *Awareness of the living body from the inside.* "Awareness refers to the skill with which the living systems regulate their behavior in response to the feedback produced by their own actions" (Joly, 2011, p.19). Here we are dealing with awareness as a biological phenomena. Damasio (1999), Easwaran (2007), and Maturana and Varela (1987) have popularized a view of awareness as a biological phenomena. Organisms (living beings) self-regulate and self-organize in a way so that the organism perceives itself to be in balance and homeostasis. If the organism's (client's/student's) awareness of its own functioning has gotten used to a "faulty" input, then the somatic educator's role is to give the organism new information so that it can recalibrate itself utilizing the new awareness information to create a more efficient pattern of action.
3. *Learning.* Learning refers to a change in neural connections leading to a change in self-regulation, actions and behavior. Both Feldenkrais (1972) and Hanna (1980, 1986) believed that most diseases are caused by learned behavior, and are not a result of aging. They further believed that these

diseases were the result of *cultural conditioning*. (Here, it is worth repeating that somatic education is a *learning paradigm* and *not* a form of therapy.)

4. *Space*. The last of the four aspects of somatic education is space or environment. The context of the student's everyday environment such as family, culture, society, etc. is considered by somatic educators to be an *extension* of the student. A person embodies in his soma his actions in the environment. The somatic educator can affect the way the student acts in the environment through increasing the student's awareness of his actions, himself, and others. If one takes the view that the self stops at the skin, then increased awareness of the self is not changing one's interactions with the environment. If we believe as somatic educators do, that we embody our environment, then our perception and awareness of the soma influences how we act in the world. How do the four components of somatic education translate to yoga?

Yoga and Somatic Education

1. *Movement*. Much of modern day yoga is built around gross movement such as what is performed in asanas and pranayama, but even in apparent stillness, as is experienced in meditation, there is subtle movement in the cells, organs, and mind. Both the educational and medical model acknowledges that life is movement, and without gross and subtle movements there is no life. While the medical model tends to disregard or downplay the subjective experience, both yoga and somatic education are interested in the experiences of the person performing the movements. What memories, experiences, thoughts, etc. are coming up when performing movements, asanas, pranayama, meditation, and like experiences?
2. *Awareness of the living body from the inside*. The somatic educator would say, "Awareness refers to the skill with which the living systems regulate their behavior in response to the feedback produced by their own actions." In the *Bhagavad Gita* (Easwaran, 2007), Chapter 2:50, it is stated "yoga is skill in action" (p.95). To be skillful in action we first need awareness of our actions. We need to get new information from the internal senses so that we can identify habits and become more skillful in actions. Without awareness in action, we tend to do the same actions, based on the same input, with the same level of skill over and over again (Butera, 2009). Yoga attempts to identify the habits of the mind (*samskaras*) to reveal the larger consciousness (*brahman*) that is behind the habits of the mind. (It should be noted here that the feedback that is being discussed is internal feedback. While humankind is conditioned to look for external input, approval, and rewards as feedback for one's actions, in yoga and somatic education the goal is to increase and trust the internal feedback.)
3. *Learning*. For the somatic educator, learning implies a change in self-regulation, actions and behaviors. Yoga is also looking for changes in behaviors and actions. The first two petals of the eight petals of yoga are

yamas (restraints) and niyamas (observances). The five yamas are non-violence, truthfulness, non-stealing, moderation, and non-attachment. The five niyamas are purity, contentment, discipline, study of self and surrender to infinity. As the student continues on the road of yoga, observable behaviors will change and be more in line with the yamas and niyamas. So both the somatic educator and yoga therapist will look for how the student's actions and behaviors change. Change in action and behavior are signs that learning is taking place.

4. *Space.* For the somatic educator, the space or environment is considered an extension of our environment and influences our movements. In yoga, the third kosha, the mind, colours our actions. The mind is made up of our habits, culture, family etc. So yoga acknowledges that the environment affects our actions, and that we embody our environment. Yoga is a way to become aware of that embodiment and, through the 4th and 5th koshas, free ourselves from actions that are habitual and influenced by our environment, so that we can act with freedom.

While it might seem to the reader that I favor the somatic education model over the medical model based on the amount of space i have used to describe the somatic education model, I have indeed spent more space describing the somatic education model since many people are *not* as familiar with the somatic education model as they are with the medical model. The reader should be aware that there is space for both models, and that we need to be aware of both models and consciously choose the model that is applicable to the patient. Many use one model habitually and will therefore only be able to help a certain type of client. But yoga is skill in action and as yoga therapists we need to skillfully apply the model that is right for the situation. So when do we chose one model over the other?

When Do We Do What? A Case Study

AB is a 48-year-old male who has had back pain for the last 10 years. The original injury happened while AB was lifting at work. AB bent down to lift up a 15 lb. box and twisted to the right at the same time. After the injury AB went to see an MD, who ordered pain medication and muscle relaxers, and scheduled AB for a follow up visit in two weeks. AB returned to work after two weeks, but continued to have pain with lifting and any forward bending or twisting of the spine. Since the original injury, AB had been working intermittently and had seen physical therapists, chiropractors, pain specialists, personal trainers, and massage therapists, but the pain relief had only been temporary. (Note: AB uses a lumbar roll for sitting to make sure that the spine is held in extension, and is aware of his lumbar lordosis at all times). AB reported that he has a continuous ache and stiffness in his low back. He feels that the pain is limiting his exercise ability as well as his social life, and the pain and stiffness is getting worse. AB denies any radiating pain down either leg. AB walks using hip flexion and extension with very little movement in the spine. X-rays and MRIs of the low back were negative and AB denies taking any medications at the present time.

Medical Model

On the first visit, AB went through a complete evaluation that included mobility, strength, and range of motion (ROM) testing. AB also filled out a Visual Analog pain scale, a depression scale, and the OSWESTRY Disability Index. AB was informed that he suffered decreased movement of his lumbar spine, and decreased strength of the lumbar stabilization muscles. He also experienced a mild-moderate depression, and a disability score of 47% on the OSWESTRY, which indicated a "severe disability." AB was informed about the results of the testing and was given three exercises to do at home.

On follow up visits, AB progressed through Dr. White's Lumbar Stabilization program, a strength and flexibility program for spinal mobility, and instructions on correct lifting technique. AB was also referred to a psychologist who prescribed medication for his depression.

Upon discharge, after five visits, AB felt that he could return to previous work and felt that the exercise instructions and anti-depression medication had helped him. AB was discharged and did not have any more problems with his back.

Somatic Education Model

On the first visit, AB talked to the Somatic Education Practitioner (SEP) about how he experienced his pain, what situations caused his pain to increase, what he thought about his job, personal relationships, etc. After that, he was then asked to walk across the room using his normal gait. The SEP noticed that AB used hip flexion and extension to walk and hold his spine aloft. The SEP asked AB if he noticed these aspects of his gait. AB said that he was not aware of that. The SEP then asked AB to walk across the room again with exaggerated hip flexion and extension movements, and then with exaggerated stiffness in the spine. This was done so that AB could get the kinesthetic sense of how he uses his hips and spine. The rest of the session was spent on having AB sense the differences between different amounts of movements in his hips and spine. This was done in laying down, in sitting, and in walking. The reason for the exaggerated movements was to get AB to be aware of what he was doing. For a SEP the first step is for the client to realize what movements he repeatedly performs. Only after the client recognizes what he is doing are new movements and actions introduced. The client learns to sense the differences between old, habitual movements and new movement options. The client explores movements under the guidance of the SEP. At the end of the session AB again walked across the room and was asked to compare his walk at the end of the session to the beginning of the session. Somatic learning has taken place if the client can notice changes in his movements, actions, and behaviors. It is not about removing an old habitual movement, but to add movement options.

At the beginning of the second session AB was asked to walk across the room paying attention to any sensations in his spine, legs, or feet. AB was then asked to lay down on the treatment table on his back and asked to pay attention to how he was resting on the table, especially to the space between the lumbar spine and the table. He was asked to compare the size of the space between the lumbar spine and the table, to the space between the cervical spine and the table. Was the area in the lumbar spine that did not touch the table larger or smaller than the area of the cervical spine that did not touch the table? Again, the reason for comparing is so that the client can differentiate movements and holding patterns in different areas of the body. The more the client can differentiate, the more aware he becomes of his body, and the more options of moving in different environments he will have available to him.

It was clear when AB lay down that the area under the lumbar spine that did not touch the table was quite large. This could be an indication that his lumbar muscles did not let go of the tension, even when AB was resting on his back. This is fairly common in a person with chronic back pain. The muscles are constantly being held in a contracted state to guard against the pain. After a period of time this becomes so normal to the client that his nervous system re-calibrates this as the new normal.

After the body scan AB was asked to bend his legs and arch his low back from the table and then to push his low back into the table. As he was doing this he was also asked to pay attention to what happened to the space between the lumbar spine and the table, and his cervical spine and the table. Did the space increase or decrease in size? This comparison was performed to give AB a sense of the whole spine and how movement travels throughout the spine. The next movement variation AB performed was to arch and flatten the low back while alternatively paying attention to the pressure under his feet as he was arching and flattening his back, then arching and flattening his back while pushing the front or heel of his feet into the table. This was done so that AB could get a sense of how using the feet can help the movement of the spine. After the client went through several variations of the above he did similar variations in sitting with his feet on the floor, then standing and then walking. Since while lying on his back AB had his knees bent and feet standing, the brain got feedback from the changing pressure under his feet with the various movements. Therefore AB's nervous system could recognize the movements in the back based on the feedback from the changing pressure under the feet while eventually performing the same movements in sitting and standing.

In the third session the focus was on side bending of the spine. Side bending is a component of rotation of the spine and therefore side bending was introduced before rotation of the spine. As during the other sessions AB was asked to walk across the room before any movement explorations were started. Most of AB's movements in walking came from flexion and extension of the hips, with minimal side bending or rotation of the spine. The SEP therefore asked AB to lie on his side. The SEP then used his hands to introduce small movements of the shoulder toward and away from the hip. These movement explorations introduced the concept of side bending to AB in a non-threatening manner. The SEP then introduced the same kind of movements, but now from the clavicle to get the spine more involved. Eventually the SEP moved to the pelvis/greater trochanter of the femur to move the hip towards the shoulder. Instead of touching the spine, which might have set off a fear/avoidance reaction in AB, all side bending was introduced by pushing on the shoulder, clavicle, and pelvis without touching the spine. After AB passively sensed the movements, AB then performed the movements in an active assistive and then active manner. AB was then asked to lie on his back and sense the differences between the side where he had performed the movements and the side he had been resting on. AB was then asked to perform the same movements in sitting and standing and then walk across the room to sense the differences between the two sides. During the session AB did not perform the movements on the other side. It was important that AB could feel the difference in the two sides of himself.

The fourth session was similar to the third, but instead of side bending the focus was on rotation, with the pelvis and shoulder moving forwards, backwards, together and apart, while AB was in various positions such as laying on his back, sitting, standing, and walking.

AB was discharged after the fifth session. He still had minor back pain but reported that he could feel when his pain was about to increase and could then reverse the onset by doing some gentle movements of the spine. He also reported that he could tell what situations, environments, and reactions, physical and emotional, caused his back pain to increase. By being aware of these situations and his reactions to them, he reported that he could then avoid those situations or change the way he reacted to the situation and thereby avoid an increase in back pain. In this case, the SEP guided AB so that on a biomechanical level he had movement options in his spine, but at another level it gave him increased awareness of his environment and his emotional reactions to the environment. During the fifth session the SEP also had AB perform his exercise program, and showed him how to incorporate the different movement explorations into the exercise program.

Where To Start?

From the above hypothetical case it should be clear that AB's back pain would have subsided with the introduction of either the medical or educational model. So does it matter which model we use? If we again go back to the statement in the *Bhagavad Gita* 2:50 that "Yoga is skill in action," then if we are skillful we will apply the model that is most appropriate for our client at the stage they are at in the present moment. To be skillful we need to listen to what our clients say. More than likely they will point us to the right model for them. They will point us towards the right model to start with, but after a few sessions it is quite likely that a mixed model will be used or that there might be a shift to another model. Below are two medical histories that the fictional AB might give on his initial visit to his yoga therapist. One will indicate that the medical model is the best model to start with and one will indicate that he is more receptive to the educational model.

AB—Medical Model

I hurt my back many years ago. I have been through many kinds of therapy and exercise. During acute episodes I have received massage, ultrasound, and electrical stimulation to my back and that seemed to decrease the pain. It seems like they help as long as I do the exercises, but the exercises are too time-consuming. Right now I need something to decrease the pain and then be shown some exercises that don't take too much time. I am wide open to any techniques that you have that might help me.

AB—Education Model

I hurt my back many years ago. I have been through many kinds of therapy and exercises, but it seems like I only get temporary relief. I feel like my back gets worse in certain situations. It seems like my back first stiffens up and then starts aching. By then it is too late for me to reverse the pain, and I end up having to take sick days and have to go get help to decrease the pain. I am doing the exercises I got when I first started having pain, but they really don't seem to be too effective anymore.

The way AB explains his problem in the first scenario is very different than AB in the second scenario, and the approach taken needs to be different. In the first scenario AB is interested in being "prescribed" something that he can do to get rid of the pain. The medical model works well as a starting point in this case. To suggest that AB should feel and explore movements would more than likely not be successful, and AB would not return to the yoga therapist. Instead he would more than likely go back to a medical/rehabilitation expert that speaks the same language as him and would give him the prescribed exercises.

AB in the second scenario is at a different place in his journey. The yoga therapist can introduce ways that AB can explore and increase his awareness of the situations and reactions that lead to increased back pain, including how before the back starts aching he stiffens up his spine. If AB became aware of how to stop the cycle when he first noticed that his spine stiffened up he could then stop the rest of his reactions/behaviors before he has to see a medical/rehabilitation expert. Instead he could do some simple movements of his spine and avoid the stiffening up of the spine that leads to increased back pain. To show AB how to move his spine in different directions *without increasing* his awareness of when and in what situations the spine stiffens up would not have been effective since AB wanted to be able to stop the cycle of stiffness and pain before he had to seek help. To demonstrate to AB how to move the spine in different directions would have fit better with AB who wanted someone to "fix" him (e.g., the medical model).

To prescribe the medical model for someone who is looking for the educational model or vice versa will not lead to good outcomes. More than likely, a patient whose worldview fits one model will not be successful if the yoga therapy model aligns with a different worldview. Much research uses a standardized treatment for all patients without taking the patient into account. Yoga therapy must take the patient's expectations into account.

Implications for Research

Sackett, Straus, Richardson, Rosenberg, and Haynes' (2000) original model for evidence based medicine, introduced in the early 1980s, was composed of three different components: the components were research, clinical expertise, and patient values. Each component was weighted the same. But perhaps treatments will only show to be effective if the treatment is coupled with the patient who has the same value/belief system as the treatment that is being offered. Therefore the value/belief system of the patient must be taken into account for clinical treatment as well as in research. For the outcome to be successful, the intervention must be coupled with the appropriate approach for that client. Randomized controlled trials (RCT) are considered to be the "gold standard" for research studies. Subjects in an RCT are randomly assigned to either the experimental group or the control group, but that does not take into account that subjects will react differently to different models of care. An RCT will more than likely indicate little significance since it does not take into account the subject's orientation regarding the educational versus the medical model. But there is one more component, which needs to be considered when investigating the evidence based model, the clinician's expertise.

The Yoga Therapist/Educator

Our worldview is to a large extent shaped by our family, cultural background, education, and lived experiences. This is true for yoga therapists and teachers too. Many yoga therapists start out as yoga teachers. If their education was mostly focused on asanas and not much time was spent on physical, emotional, spiritual, and philosophical aspects of yoga, then their clinical expertise will be strongest in the asana aspect of yoga. One would therefore expect that for a yoga therapist to be more successful with a client who expects an intervention based on the medical model; the yoga therapist would be effective applying treatments similar to the medical model. Many yoga therapists are trained in medical professions such as nursing, physical therapy, occupational therapy, etc. When previous training has focused on the medical model (and is a model that works for specific clients), then the yoga therapist would be more comfortable in that model.

So what yoga therapists would be more comfortable and inclined to use the educational model? The training of such a yoga therapist might have started with meditation, or a degree in Psychology or Divinity. The therapist tends to ask open-ended questions and trust that with the right guidance the client will find the answers within himself. The therapist who tends to apply the educational model is comfortable with allowing the client to find the answers and allow the client to feel what sensations emerges from within himself during the sessions.

Usually, a well-trained yoga therapist will mix and match models according to what works. It is important that we are aware of what model we habitually use, what model we are more comfortable with, and what model might work best for our clients. If as a yoga therapists we are not comfortable with applying one of the above models, or we feel like we do not have the expertise in one of the models, it is our duty to refer the client to a yoga therapist that is more skilled in what the client needs. Yoga is "skill in action." Part of that skill is to be able to notice when a referral to another yoga therapist or healthcare professional is appropriate because our skill set might not match with the needs of our client.

What Is Most Effective Long Term?

Long term, the educational model is probably more effective, since the client is increasing his or her self-awareness. The client learns to notice and trust the sensations from the body and the environment. That means the client should be able to notice small changes in pain levels and be able to self-treat before the problem gets to the level where he or she has to see a yoga therapist or a medical practitioner. Also the ultimate goal of yoga is to still the fluctuations of the mind. By doing that we need to raise our self-awareness so that we can notice the fluctuations of the mind. A strict medical model does not help the client with that. The medical model will be very helpful for clients that want someone to "fix" their problem, but if the client's problem resurfaces in the future then the client will have to see the practitioner again.

Or Maybe It Is Guidance From Where The Client Is

The bottom line is that we need to meet our clients where they are, where we are, and provide them with the guidance that they need for a successful outcome. If the medical model is an appropriate starting point, then that is where we start but we can gently guide our clients towards the educational model so that in the future they will have more self-awareness and will be less likely to have the same problem again. If the educational model is the starting point, then that is where we start and we guide the client towards where they need to go from there. Even for a client that starts with the medical model, it is possible that the client needs to learn something from the medical model, so we cannot close the door to either the medical or educational model. If yoga therapists are more comfortable with one model or the other, it might help stimulate learning and moving towards the other model so that we can guide our clients from their starting point, and not from our starting point. Yoga therapy is "skill in action." For a skillful outcome it takes the skill of the therapist to find the starting point of the client, guide him or her towards the desired outcome, as well as knowing where our biases are so that we can be trustworthy guides for our clients and ourselves.

Questions for the Reader

1. How do you determine if your work with clients is therapy or somatic education?
2. How do you determine if your client needs a more therapeutic approach or a more educational approach?
3. At what point in your sequence of sessions do you evaluate if your approach (therapeutic or educational) is the right one, and if you have to change your approach mid-stream how do you do that?
4. If you change your approach mid-stream, how do you explain the switch in approach to your client?

References

Butera, B. (2009) *The pure heart of yoga: Ten essential steps for personal transformation.* Woodbury, MN: Llewellyn Worldwide.

Damasio, A. (1999). *The feeling of what happens: Body and emotion in the making of consciousness.* New York, NY: Harcourt Brace.

Easwaran, E. (2007). *The Bhagavad Gita.* Tomales, CA: Nilgiri Press.

Feldenkrais, M. (1972). *Awareness through movement.* San Francisco, CA: Harper and Row.

Fishman, L. (2009). Understanding and preventing yoga injuries. *International Journal of Yoga Therapy*, 19, 47–54.

Hanna, T. (1980). *The body of life. Creating new pathways for sensory awareness and fluid movement.* Rochester, VT: Healing Arts Press.

Hanna, T. (1986). What is somatic education? *Somatics*, 6(1).

Hannaford, C. (1995). *Smart moves: Why learning is not all in your head.* Arlington, VA: Great Ocean Publishers.

Joly, Y. (2001). The Feldenkrais method of somatic education. *International Feldenkrais Federation Newsletter.* January, 17–20.

Maisel, E. (1990) *The essential writings of F. Matthias Alexander: The Alexander Technique.* New York, NY: Carol Publishing Group.

Maturana, H.R., & Varela, F.J. (1987). *The tree of knowledge: The biological roots of human understanding.* Boston, MA: Shambala Publications.

Sackett, D. L., Straus, S. E., Richardson, W. S., Rosenberg, W., & Haynes, R. B. (2000). *Evidence based medicine. How to practice and teach EBM* (2nd Edition). London: Churchill Livingstone.

11 Family Yoga Therapy and Art Therapy

New Models of Treatment

Ellen G. Horovitz

> The greatest discovery of my generation is that a human being can alter his life by altering his attitudes of mind.
>
> William James

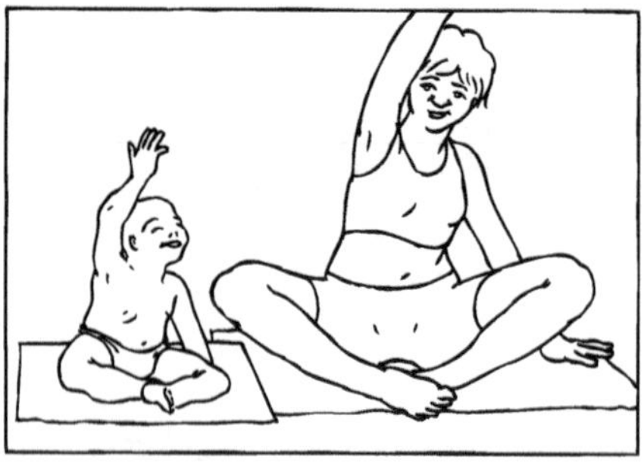

Figure 11.1

Epigenetics and then some

What you do changes you. Fundamentally, what you resolve, how you approach it, and what you come to value are of great consequence. Such interaction defines us. In life, we are in relationship with *everything*: the dirt on the floor, the humidity in the clouds, the parched, dusty cornfields, the sweat trickling down our brow, the reverberation of a piano's key, even the words on the paper from which we read.

The above quote by William James was prophecy. In essence, James, the prominent nineteenth-century American psychologist, was talking about epigenetics, the study of heritable changes in the gene activity which are not caused by changes in the DNA sequence; in effect these changes in gene expression (or cellular phenotype) evolve from other causes. Epigenetics renders our brains (and bodies) as flexible, capable of adapting, evolving, and change. Given how important mapping out the psychosocial background of our clients is in understanding their psychodynamics and life story, at intake, I create a three-generation genogram (using the software program Genogram Analytics). The reason is simple: we do not exist in isolation from one another. We are a product of not just our genetics but also our upbringing (McCartney, Harris, & Bernieri, 1990). A genogram is a three-generation (minimum) visual map of an identified patient's (IP) family system. According to Butler (2008), Jolly, Froom, and Rosen (1980), and Wikipedia (2014):

> A genogram (also known as a McGoldrick-Gerson study, a Lapidus Schematic or a Family Diagram) is a pictorial display of a person's family relationships and medical history. It goes beyond a traditional family tree by allowing the user to visualize hereditary patterns and psychological factors that punctuate relationships. It can be used to identify repetitive patterns of behavior and to recognize hereditary tendencies.

Moreover, this construct can include psychological scores (intelligence quotient scores such as a WISC-R), strengths and weaknesses, DSM-V information from an attending psychiatrist, and visual symbols that help track conflicts handed down from generation-to-generation. (Therapists who function from a family systems platform routinely use genograms.)

In addition, a chronological time-line can be created which maps out any nodal events that have influenced the client's history. So in yoga therapy, whenever possible, I invite the nuclear family system. Not everyone can and does participate, but conducting yoga therapy from a family systems perspective is a novel concept. Adding art therapy to the mixture makes this form of therapy unique.

Some Definitions: Art Therapy, Family Therapy, and Yoga Therapy

Art therapy: So, what exactly *is* art therapy? In a nutshell, art therapy is a mental health profession in which clients create artwork in order to explore their feelings and express emotions surrounding conflicts (such as: dysfunctional behaviors, addictions, stress, trauma, etc.) and foster self-awareness and healthy coping strategies (Nainis, Paice, Ratner, Wirth, Lai, & Shott, 2006). In addition, art therapy helps the client increase self-esteem in order to restore his or her level of functioning and sense of personal wellbeing. (For more information, see www.arttherapy.org).

Family therapy: According to Sluzki (1983), family therapy represents an entirely new paradigm in conceptualizing human problems, understanding behavior, the development of symptoms and their resolution. Looking at a family from these perspectives allows for a wholly different method of collecting and interpreting information and data. The family as a functioning (or dysfunctional) transactional system and entity in and of itself, more than the sum of its individual components, provides the context for individual functioning.

While often someone is considered the IP (Identified Patient), if one views an individual in relation to his/her family system, then the person is seen in a much fuller context. Since we do not operate in isolation from others and are a product of genetics, psychosocial systems, culture, belief systems, and our environs, to view someone in isolation from these different systems is indeed a mistake. Figure 11.2 is a map of how to view someone in relation to the chronosystem patterning that effects our functioning. (A chronosystem links individual and families by social interdependence, sociohistorical influences, environmental events and transitions over the life course.) Figure 11.2 is based on Bronfenbrenner's Ecological Theory of Development (Bronfenbrenner, 1994).

Salvador Minuchin (1974), a pioneer of structural family therapy, theorized that families could be categorized into two distinct patterns: "enmeshed" (chaotically intertwined) and "disengaged" (isolated and ostensibly unrelated). Yet according to Minuchin and Nichols (1993), enmeshment and engagement tend to be reciprocal. Indeed, structural family therapy gave rise to mapping out the chaotic interactions of the family system in order to more visually delineate interactions and the objectives and goals for the therapist. This allows the therapist to visualize both cutoffs and conflicts within the family system. As well, it offers the therapist a visual map from which to operate.[1] Thus after conducting an intake and generating a family genogram the formula below can aptly aid the yoga therapist:

- joining and accommodating (getting the therapist into the system);
- enactment (positioning and creating awareness amongst members);

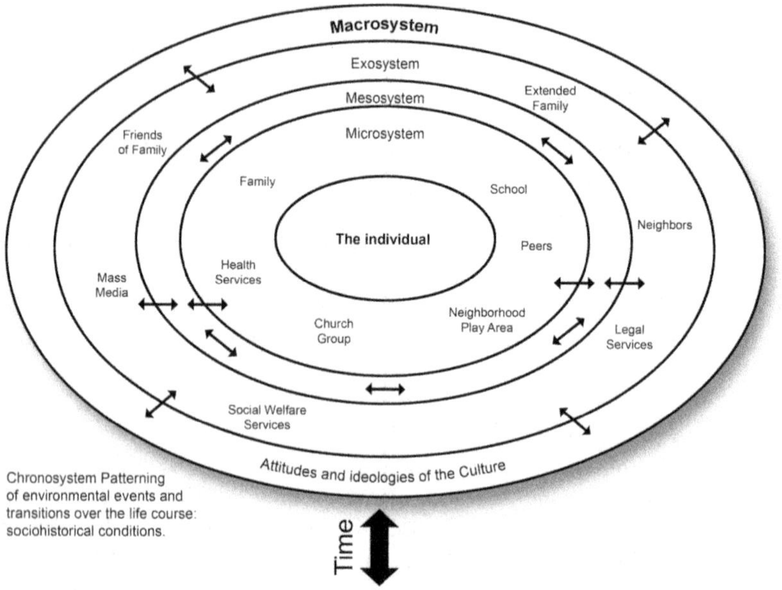

Figure 11.2 Chronosystem patterns of the individual

- structural mapping (accounting for problems and dynamics);
- highlighting and modifying interactions (focusing on process not content);
- boundary making (realigning relationships between subsystems);
- unbalancing (changing relationships within subsystems);
- challenging unproductive assumptions (relating and viewing the system differently) (Nichols, 2007, pp. 135–141).

In essence the features described above by Nichols replicate what occurs in a "yogic" situation when acting as a (family) yoga/art therapist and how I operated in the case to be presented:

- Perforce, the (yoga/art) therapist has to *join* and *accommodat*e one's client.
- The (yoga/art) therapist, through structural remapping, repositions the client via bhavana (Weintraub, 2012), meditation (Rosen, 2002), asana, and/or emotive issues (Horovitz, 2011a, 2013) and *enacts* structural changes.
- The (yoga/art) therapist *remaps* the emotional, physical and spiritual systems, and identifies /recreates new structure via co- creation (Boscolo & Bertrando, 2004; Horovitz; 2002).
- The (yoga/art) therapist *realigns* the subsystems within the family (either by example or restructuring boundaries) and therefore reinstates a healthier system.
- By *unbalancing* the homeostasis in the family system, the (yoga/art) therapist shakes up dysfunction and opens up the family system to change.
- The (yoga/art) therapist *challenges unproductive assumptions* through his or her zeitgeist and co-creates (Boscolo & Bertrando, 2004; Horovitz; 2002) a new reality system with the client.

Yoga therapy: while definitions abound by many respected yoga practitioners, and can be found in Chapter 2 of this book, this one below by my friend and colleague, Judith Lasater (2014), most appeals to me since I feel it *simply* captures the spirit of how I operate:

> [Yoga therapy is] the use of the techniques of Yoga to create, stimulate, and maintain an optimum state of physical, emotional, mental, and spiritual health.

The Sanskrit word *yoga* has the literal meaning of "yoke," from a root *yuj* meaning to join, to unite, or to attach. And the case to be presented is all about attachment. (Move over Sir John Bowlby, the pioneer of attachment theory.) According to Simpkins and Simpkins (2011):

> Yoga offers distinctive methods to address deficits and build fundamental skills. . . . (It also offers) specific mental techniques and diverse meditative methods for cognition and emotions (to) develop a reflective ability, where consciousness becomes capable of observing itself objectively.

I urge the reader to peruse the website (www.iyat.org) and resources in this book to ascertain what fits for your individual practice. It is widely recognized that yoga can enhance physical and emotional wellbeing. Furthermore, if yoga therapy is practiced from the seat of *intention*, it can help prevent and aid recovery from physical and mental ailments, enlist transformation, and thereby result in an epigenetic shift (Horovitz, 2011a). There are many that espouse a variety of theories as to why this occurs. Personally, I think this therapeutic change is enhanced by pratyahara, Sanskrit for withdrawing from the external and diving deeply within one's senses. When one reaches this place of withdrawing into the senses, the change is at the deepest cellular level. As a therapist and yoga practitioner, I aspire towards pratyahra as a way of deeply honoring the self/Self.

A Life-changing Experience

Because of yoga, I attached, coupled, mended, fixed, and restored myself. In essence, this sashay into a yogic lifestyle altered me, radically: I transmuted. Yoga changed my life and caused a ripple effect in aiding me to transfigure the life of others. I started incorporating yoga therapy in my work with stroke survivors, cancer survivors, people with physiological issues (for example: Rheumatoid Arthritis, eating disorders) and emotional and psychological issues.

It so happened that in 2008, I decided to take a sabbatical. While I accomplished my sabbatical aim (Horovitz & Eksten, 2009; Horovitz, 2011b), something unplanned and unexpected happened: I entered an Iyengar Yoga teacher training under Francois Raoult and also acquired additional yoga therapy training through Phoenix Rising Yoga Therapy and Amy Weintraub's Yoga for Mood Management training. Historically, my body had been unfolding to this metamorphosis for some time but the sabbatical offered up the luxury of time for this eruption to complete itself. You see, a secondary gain occurred every time I practiced yoga: I entered what Csikszentmihalyi (1996) coined a "flow" state and I literally transformed. The more I became in touch with this part of myself, the sharper my interoceptive (gut feeling) became.

Sommer Anderson (2008) amassed countless analysts who relayed stories about this "subsymbolic and nonverbal symbolic mode" of processing information. This is truly the language of art therapy and yoga therapy: it is the interoceptive, proprioceptive, and kinesthetic experience of being with another human being—it is that "felt" experience when you "know" something immediately in your body, even if you cannot verbally articulate it in the speech center of your brain. I have come to rely on this second brain, this visceral patch, housed in the stomach organ. This has served me well as after thirty-five years as a clinician, I often "thin slice" (Gladwell, 2005) accurately when analyzing client facial and body language. Thin slicing is accepting our first impressions seriously: according to Gladwell (2005), "sometimes we can know more about someone in a blink of the eye than we can after months of study" (p. 76).

Sommer Anderson (2008) in discussing this technical term of interoception compared it to being paralyzed with writer's block (something every writer experiences at one point or another). She likened that block to a closed peony. (That's what she coined the opposite of "letting go.") Its opposite (a voluptuous 13-inch peony, in a full-bloomed self-state) was how she described yoga and meditation.

A report in the *New York Times* (Reynolds, 2012), confirmed this: "Exercise, the latest neuroscience suggests, does more to bolster thinking than thinking does." In a laboratory setting, Justin S. Rhodes, a psychology professor at the Beckman Institute for Advanced Science and Technology at the University of Illinois, gathered four groups of mice and set them into four distinct living arrangements. The animals completed a series of cognitive tests at the start of the study and were injected with a substance that allowed the scientists to track changes in their brain structures. Then they ran, played, or, if their environment was unenriched, lolled about in their cages for several months. It turned out that the toys and tastes, no matter how stimulating, had not improved the animals' brains. *Only one thing mattered and that was whether they had a running wheel.* Animals that exercised (whether or not they had any other enrichment in their cages) had *healthier brains* and performed *significantly better* on cognitive tests than the other mice. Animals that didn't run, *no matter* how enriched their world was otherwise, did *not* improve their brainpower in the complex, lasting ways that Rhodes's team was studying. Since then, there have been numerous publications on exercise and its ability to maintain the brain in its plastic, ever-evolving development. Somehow, my interoceptive, proprioceptive, kinesthetic self knew this for a very long time. Forget Sudoku, this was the mother lode.

Recently, the well-known psychologist Daniel Goleman wrote a piece for *The New York Times* entitled "Exercising the mind to treat attention disorders" (2014). According to this article, experts claimed that " there are no long-term, lasting benefits" from taking medications to alter attention disorders and furthermore it was suggested that "mindfulness seems to be training the same areas in the brain that have reduced activity" in attention disorders. According to this latest research the singular mental ability of mindfulness training predicted success in school and in work life: "specialists are now suggesting this might be particularly effective in treating ADHD and ADD" (Attention Deficit Hyperactivity Disorder and Attention Deficit Disorder). Indeed, according to a recent report in *Clinical Neurophysiology* mindfulness based cognitive therapy led to improved inhibitory regulation (Schoenberg, Hepark, Can, Berendregt, Buitelarr, & Speckens, 2013).

While yoga has been practiced for over 5,000 years to improve physical and emotional wellbeing, empirical research has only been ongoing for several decades. However, coupling yoga therapy with art therapy, family therapy and/or psycho-spiritual treatment is a relatively new approach (Horovitz, 2002, 2011a; Franklin, 2001). As a result, I developed intake forms to gather pertinent information. This combined approach was unlike any therapy I had previously conducted and so I needed a new toolbox. (My intake form is available in the Appendix section of this book.)

The Case: An Amalgamation of Art/Yoga/Family Therapy

Intake Interview, Initial Assessment and the Sessions

Initially, I met with the mother (Elizabeth) in order to obtain a detailed 3-generation genogram and medical history on Elvira, then aged 9 (see Figure 11.3 and timeline). (Elvira was the referred client.) However, what became clear during both the intake and the first session was that treating as much of the nuclear family system as possible would be the optimal course of action. Post the initial yoga session with Elvira, I decided to conduct the Kinetic Family Drawing (KFD) assessment in order to ascertain psychosocial familial issues, cognitive and developmental functioning, and analyze the artwork in terms of the FEATS (Formal Element Art Therapy Scale; Gantt & Tabone 1998). Moreover, because Elvira was only 9 years old when treatment began, I ascertained, post her initial yoga therapy assessment, that Elvira might be more comfortable *if* her mother were present for some of the sessions. Since the mother joined the combined yoga/art therapy sessions (during session 2), occasionally, I have checked in with Elvira to determine whether or not she was interested in individual, weekly sessions. But she continued on from session 2 with her mother joining all sessions for the next year. Occasionally, her brother, Moriarty, joined sessions but mostly the focus was on the mother/daughter dyad. (To date, due to work obligations and Moriarty's activities, the father did not attend any family sessions. While this might not be uncommon in family systems therapy, it is possible that his "questioning his sexuality" may have influenced his decision not to join in family therapy and affect the family dynamics.)

Elvira's Timeline:

Talked Early (big words)
Allergies—placed on Soy Formula—colicky
Age 4–5 years in Kindergarten—day dreamed in school.
Made Few Friends
Age 7—appeared to have anxiety
Age 6–7 placed on Metaline (experienced "zombie" like effects, taken off meds)
Age 8—met with audiologist to screen for Auditory Processing deficits
Age 7 on placed on Adderall—M–F only (for school)
Age 9–10/2012—taken off meds completely; 1/13 placed on no preservatives; no additives/coloring , dairy free/sugar free diet; positive feedback from teacher—30–50% improved. 5/13 gluten free—Feingold Diet. Testing for celiac disease yielded negative results.

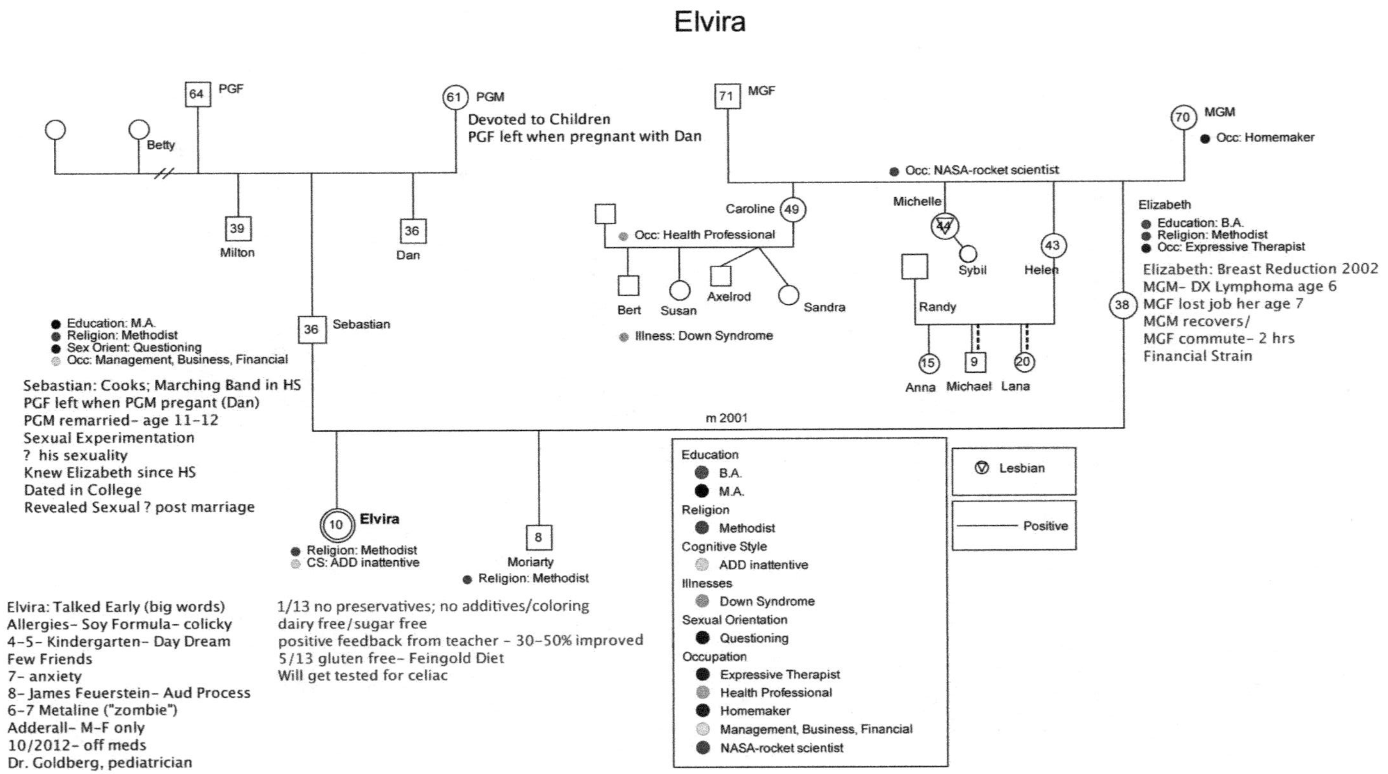

Figure 11.3 Genogram of Elvira's family system

Elizabeth's Timeline (Mother—Significant Events):

MGM—Diagnosed with Lymphoma, Elizabeth's age 6
MGF lost job; Elizabeth's age 7
MGM recovers from Lymphoma, Elizabeth's age 7
MGF commute—2 hours to work—financial strain on family
Married—2001
Breast Reduction 2002

Sebastian Timeline (Father—Significant Events):

PGF left when PGM pregnant with his brother
PGM remarried—age 11–12
Sexual Experimentation began in high school
Likes to cook; was in a Marching Band in high school
Around college, he questioned his sexuality (knew Elizabeth since high school; dated in College)
He revealed sexual orientation questionings post marriage (2001).

Session 1 with Elvira—Yoga Therapy and KFD Assessment

I wanted to gauge Elvira's breathing and pranayama capacity. I demonstrated how to hold one hand to the stomach area, the other to the chest, in order to inform her of the differences in breathing. She admitted her difficulty with sitting still. Clearly, she struggled with this. While yoga was new for her, she persevered. Her ability to make eye contact and conversation increased as the session wore on with statements like, "I don't like my brother—he is annoying, he is always repeating others' jokes." Nevertheless, her mood was depressed, her balance was off (even though she was proficient at ice skating, winning competitions), and her energy level was clearly low. All of this was palpable during the yoga therapy assessment and caused me to conduct a preliminary art therapy assessment to corroborate what I was witnessing in the yoga therapy session.

As a result, I conducted the KFD (Kinetic Family Drawing, e.g., the instruction is to "draw yourself and your family doing something"). While Elvira was able to engage and seemingly relax, her drawing (see Figure 11.4) was surprisingly disconnected and reflected her diagnosis of ADD—Inattentive type, and general dissociation from her body. All family members were depicted as floating heads: mother was drawn first, then father and finally her brother between them. (Brother's placement in and of itself (between the parents) was revealing regarding Elivira's perception of the parental system.) Next, she inquired whether or not she should add herself, clearly suggesting feelings of displacement with the family system. (While Elvira eventually drew her head larger than the other family members, this may reflect her escape into fantasy

Figure 11.4 Elvira's KFD: (upper left), mother, (center left) Moriarty, (upper right) father, (lower figure center) Elvira

and dissociation (yet none of the family members sported bodies)). When I asked what they were doing, she explained that they "watch(ed) movies together" but that is the extent to which they "d(id) things together." As the sessions progressed, a different story unfolded.

While one can interpret the KFD for its symbolic elements, standardized analysis using the Formal Art Therapy Elements Scale (FEATS) (Gantt & Tabone, 1998; Gantt & Anderson, 2009; Horovitz, 2014), confirmed the symbolic findings of the art therapy and yoga therapy interaction. The FEATS analysis of the art product confirmed the depressed mood that had been obviated during the yoga therapy portion of the first session (see Table 11.1). Elvira would have received a total tally of 30/60. (Each scale (0–5) is worth 5 points; since 2 scales were not applicable the total would be 60.)

Elivra's KFD score suggested cognitive and developmental delays for her age of 9.8 years. Identifying features that stood out were lack of space, integration, detail, problem solving and perseveration in her response. While linking artwork with "diagnostic categories" has been considered "reductionistic" by some art therapists, according to Gantt (2004), doing so, accomplishes "separating fact from clinical myth, developing more precise definitions, building a better theoretical foundation, and, most of all, pointing the way to more precise treatment plans" (Gantt & Tabone, 1998, pp. 2–3). Gannt and Tabone (1998) found "observations in the art therapy literature" that they could relate to DSM (Diagnostic and Statistical Manual of Mental Disorders) symptoms and then

Table 11.1 Elvira's FEATS Analysis

Scale	*Rating*	*Comment*
Scale 1—Prominence of Color	N/A	
Scale 2—Color Fit	N/A	
Scale 3—Implied Energy	2	The drawing appears to be done with an excessive amount of energy.
Scale 4—Space	2	25% of the space is used.
Scale 5—Integration	2	The composition is not well integrated nor balanced.
Scale 6—Logic	2	There are bizarre or illogical elements in the picture.
Scale 7—Realism	3	The items are drawn with a minimal realism.
Scale 8—Problem Solving	2	The family is depicted but not "doing something."
Scale 9—Developmental Level	2	The drawing is at the schematic level (age 7–9 years, Lowenfeld & Brittain, 1987).
Scale 10—Details of Objects & Environment	1	Little attention to detail and or objects.
Scale 11—Line Quality	5	The lines are quite fluid or flowing (even excessively so).
Scale 12—Person(s)	1	The person (s) are not drawn with articulated body parts.q
Scale 13—Rotation	5	There is no rotation.
Scale 14—Perseveration	3	Heavily shaded.
Total Tally:	*30/60*	

(Note: a total score of 60 would represent normalcy while 30 placed Elvira below her cognitive developmental age.)

adapted these observations to the distinctive points of the FEATS scale: for example depression, with its symptom of decreased mood, could be indexed as lack of color and detail. While the FEATS is *not* categorized for specific disorders such as ADD (Attention Deficit Disorder), Elvira's KFD results reflected possible depression and cognitive dysfunction (Gantt & Tabone, 1998).

The art therapy results mirrored Elvira's shallow breath regulation as demonstrated during her yoga therapy session. (While indeed, Elvira's lungs were not fully developed (since only age 9), her breath regulation was exceedingly shallow and her energy level during the yoga therapy component bordered on flat.) Both the yoga therapy and art therapy reflected the same results. Since Elvira's 9-year-old lungs (not yet fully developed) were incapable of deep pranayama, I employed coherent breathing regulation as outlined by Elliott (2005) who focuses on heart rate variability. According to Elliot, coherent breathing is a breathing modality that directly results in autonomic nervous system balance and cardiopulmonary resonance. Using this format with Elvira increased oxygenation, suppressed anxiety, and engaged parasympathetic nervous system functions.

The First Family Session—Dyadic Treatment with Elizabeth and Elvira

Because the sessions were limited to a full hour of treatment, generally the first 30 minutes was dedicated to yoga therapy. This often consisted of:

- coherent breath regulation/meditation;
- warm-ups using hula hoops;
- LFYP (Life Force Yoga Practitioner) warm-ups, bhavanas, specific asanas (often with mantras) depending on physiological/emotive factors that influenced which postures to employ; savasana and setting intentions.

While the above was a lot to pack in, it almost always preceded 30 minutes of art therapy. Suffice it to say, many sessions went beyond the therapeutic hour.

My initial intention was to aid Elvira in breath regulation (and eventual pranayama) and teach her how to incorporate meditation into her day-to-day functioning. Unknown was whether or not the mother would be joining the first session but she did.

Both Elizabeth (mother) and Elvira arrived on time. I was surprised that the mother did not let me know that she intended to join but instead made the decision for Elvira. This gave me some clue into the family dynamics and my need to "challenge unproductive assumptions" (Boscolo & Bertrando, 2004; Horovitz, 2002, 2011a, 2013). We started off with a bit of chitchat about the summer and what had occurred since our initial intake session. Elvira looked remarkably the same, and was still wearing the same boots as the session in May. (Due to Elvira's summer schedule, several months had elapsed between the yoga/art therapy intake and this first dyadic session.). Elvira appeared wan and lithe but remarkably taller. During the check-in time, when I asked if anything had been bothering her, Elvira quipped about her foot; her mother quickly chimed in that they had seen a podiatrist and it was unclear whether or not it was plantar fasciitis.

Here the first display of Elvira falling into the category of the IP (Identified Patient) reared its head and I witnessed a need to remap the emotional, physical and spiritual system (Boscolo & Betrando, 2004; Horovitz, 2002).

Since it was the first family session, we focused on stretches intended for plantar fasciitis and stretching the muscle between the toes and the heel. We did several exercises and mother joined in. (We also did some warm-ups à la LFYP (LifeForce Yoga Therapy Practitioner training—see www.yogafordepression.com for Amy Weintraubs's training, CDs, and DVDs and I joined them using hula hoops, which was great fun for both of them (Nichols, 2007.)) Here, Elvira soared with skill thus breaking the IP mode and realigning the subsystem within the family. Next, several yoga exercises were implemented to aid the plantar fasciitis, one in which they partnered together. During the ending stretches (supta padangusthasana, where they were supine on the floor and one leg stretched over the other as their arms were out at the shoulders (T-shaped), the mother jokingly tipped me off to her underlying passive aggression by kicking Elvira.

Later, it was clear during the art therapy component just how much frustration the mother harbored towards Elvira. I realized then that tiptoeing around the mother's passive aggressive actions would be pinnacle to the treatment in order to realign the family system and challenge unproductive assumptions (Boscolo & Bertrando, 2004; Horovitz, 2002, 2011a, 2013). Otherwise, the case would be lost.

The mother became increasingly tuckered during some of the poses and so savasana (corpse pose—where the body relaxes and restores itself) followed after about 25–30 minutes into the yoga session. Elvira, ever unable to relax, twitched and opened her eyes, while her mother was completely calmed by the restorative and healing qualities of the 5-minute savasana. When they finished, I asked them to silently head to the table and make a drawing together that communicated something to the other taken from their yogic practice and intention set during savasana. Figure 11.5 shows the artwork.

The mother worked on the left side of the page and took up approximately 66% of the space, a clear reflection of her need to dominate; colonized, Elvira worked in the upper right corner. Like Elvira's KFD, no bodies were present (save Elvira's thought bubble of a princess and a castle, clearly suggesting continual dissociation and retreat into fantasy, a factor that annoyed her mother). Yet, cognitive improvement was evident since Elvira's initial KFD drawing. (Here, Elvira was able to create an entire person (complete with body, in her thought bubble. Yet, interestingly enough, the princess in her thought person lacked formed feet suggesting her immobility to make change in her own life.) The upper left part was described by the mother as representing the calm feeling that resulted from the yoga and below the chaos. Elvira aptly pointed out that the image below looked like a tornado. Her mother explained that it was a tornado but it was below the calm and "dying out." Nevertheless, Elvira's ability to aptly point out the brewing storm reflected her ability to "thin-slice" (e.g., using our instincts and first impressions —Gladwell, 2005) her mother's emotive state.

Elvira drew her mother's head (elevated) above hers with butterflies coming out of the thought bubble. Her own head sported a princess and tower, more signs of need/desire to retreat into fantasy. She remarked that the princess in the tower reflected her desire to escape from her brother, Moriarty, who "annoyed" her on a "daily" basis. Once again, sibling rivalry rose to the surface and I was presented with a need to *remap* the system. While the mother

Figure 11.5 Dyadic communication

talked about the tornado, Elvira separated out their two respective spaces by drawing two black angled lines below her princess/tower in her head; she then created a tornado enclosed by a circle and placed a cross over it, as if to excise it from both mother and its effect on the family system, and possibly create a boundary for her self. This theme of setting boundaries with her mother became a precursor to the therapy ahead and spoke boatloads about Elvira's need to *unbalance* the homeostasis and *realign* the family system (Boscolo & Bertrando, 2004; Horovitz, 2002, 2011a, 2013).

That was my first window into their dyadic dance. Changing that tempo (Boscolo & Bertrando, 2004; Horovitz, 2002, 2011a, 2013; Nichols, 2007), while not unseating the mother's parental control, was a dance of two steps forward and two backward. In all therapy, but *always* when working with family systems, one has to be mindful of such progression. Homeostasis *always* rules the day. The adage is that it's easier to remain the same than walk towards a trajectory of wellness. One of my past family therapy supervisors, Sybil Baldwin, once told me, "It's easier to love a bad mother than none at all." Not that Elizabeth was bad; on the contrary. She was committed to getting her daughter the help she needed and recognized (in the process) that she, too, needed help with her own issues.

Had the yoga therapy component been absent from the dynamics of the family session, the mother's passive aggressive behavior might have been overlooked (when she jokingly kicked Elvira during suptha padangusthasna). But having that replicated in the same session through the artwork (vis à vis colonizing the space and creating her self-revealing tornado) triggered my need

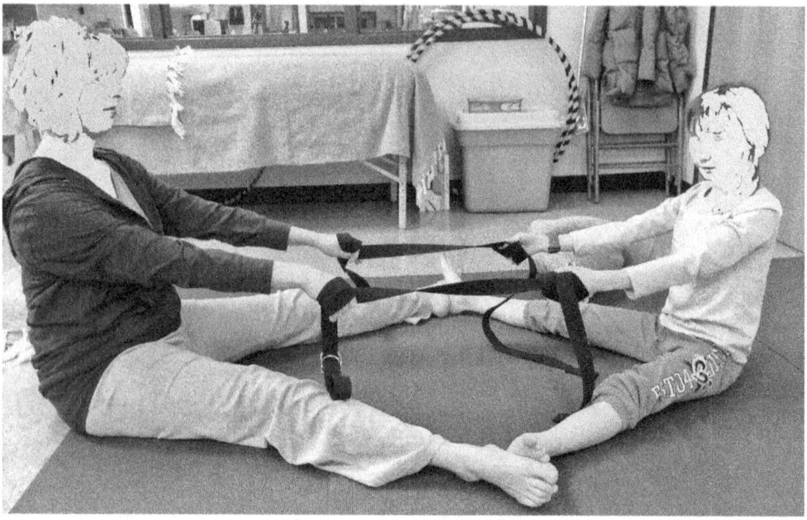

Figure 11.6 Mother and Elvira in dyadic yoga therapy (faces digitized to protect identities)

to be vigilant. When I coupled mother and Elvira through yoga therapy postures (see Figure 11.6), this enabled me to *challenge unproductive assumptions* and co-create (Boscolo & Bertrando, 2004; Horovitz; 2002, 2011a, 2013) a new reality system for the family.

Significant Family Sessions

So let's dance ahead into treatment since sessions ranged over a 12-month period. My yoga therapy direction in treating this family system was organized around coherent breathing and what I learned from my LFYP training with Amy Weintraub: setting intention through regulated coherent breathing, pranayama (for the mother), bhavana (Sanskrit for the development or cultivation of the heart/mind through a suggested story idea, meditation, sharing the intention, and making art). I always started with the body first: warm ups, hula hooping was the direction and then progressed to whatever seemed most pertinent at the time I checked in: meditation, coherent breathing, pranayama, asana, bhavana, savasana . . . there was no specific yogic recipe, save one: *always setting the intention.* The intention was what threaded the yoga into the art. Clues were always offered to me by "thin slicing" the family's facial and body gestures and verbal associates to the yoga therapy/body work. But it was the *intention* that enabled the body to chart its course through the art.

Several times post yoga therapy, Elizabeth and Elvira chose to work in clay. (Clay, being a most formidable medium, is extremely forgiving: undoing and redoing rules the day.) Even if "mistakes" were made, they could easily be "erased" and reshaped and molded anew. Clay was indubitably the ultimate mirror for forgiveness (Horovitz, 1999; Henley, 2002). And the medium itself could be used to reflect ambivalence in act and words. For example in one dyadic session below, which I videotaped, the mother created a "straight and narrow path" and talked easily about how it was "okay to fall off the path" but likened this passage to be lined with the possibility for growth, change, and acceptance of things that were not necessarily an exact recipe. Here the mother may have been self-projecting yet this verbal translation allowed Elvira to view herself as fallible yet *accepted* while simultaneously offering her mother a platform to air grievances about her daughter's "differences." Being authentically accepted despite her differences and limitations was liberating. Yet, Elvira's blackened heart, with three white protrusions, spoke of her inner self-struggles and darkness around feeling fully accepted and loved (Figure 11.7). Together they fashioned a "yogic bracelet," the arc fashioned by mother and the floating heads atop the circular construction created by Elvira. Once again, dissociative heads yoked Elvira both figuratively and symbolically (Figure 11.8).

As sessions progressed, so did Elvira's maturation: she relented to have Moriarty join thus *enacting structural change* (Nichols, 2007). Moriarty was often left in the waiting room until his father could pick him up and take him to another activity. On one session, when Moriarty joined, I had suggested in advance, that I could teach them how to make their own hula-hoops (decorating

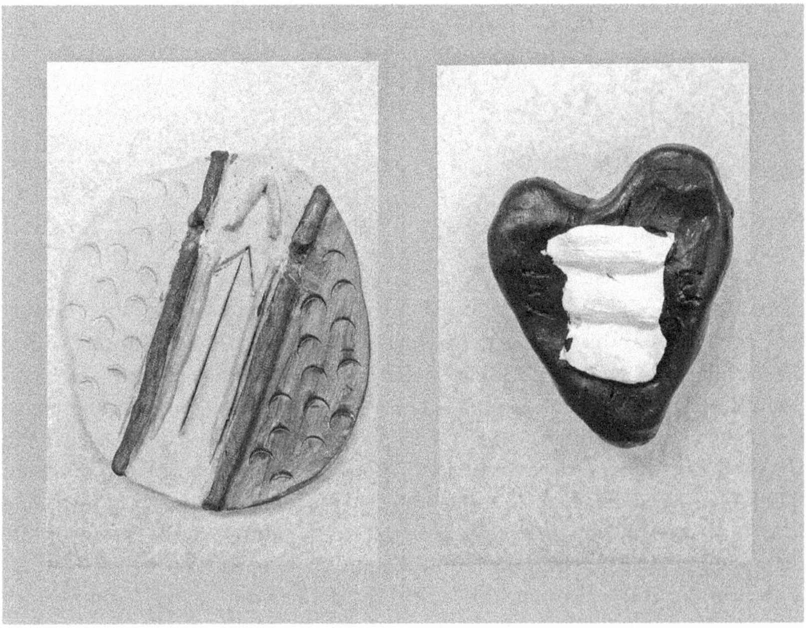

Figure 11.7 (Left) Elizabeth's straight and narrow path, (right) Elvira's black heart

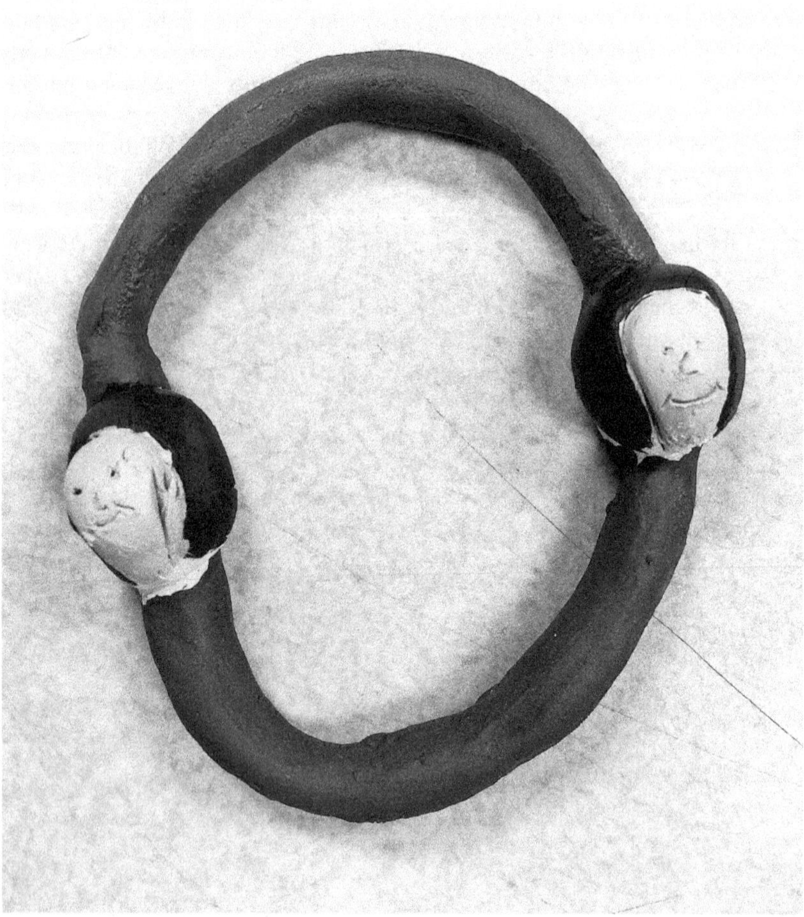

Figure 11.8 Mother and Elvira's combined yogic bracelet (clay)

them with different colored electrical tape). This was the *one time* where the art making preceded the yoga activity. Figure 11.9 shows Elvira, Moriarty, and the mother engaged in hula hooping as I filmed and then after the yoga therapy session ended in savasana. (During savasana, I anoint the temples of my clients with aromatic oil, such as lavender, and play bells to seal the chakras.) But before entering savasana, much to my surprise, Elvira requested that I allow *her* to use the bells to seal the chakras on her brother post savasana. I was touched by her desire to both attend to him as well as mirror the therapeutic stance, *rebalance* the family dynamics, and *remap* the system (Boscolo & Bertrando, 2004; Horovitz, 2002, 2011a, 2013; Nichols, 2007). Figure 11.9 is a picture of all three hula hooping with their products and in savasana before Elvira sealed her brother.

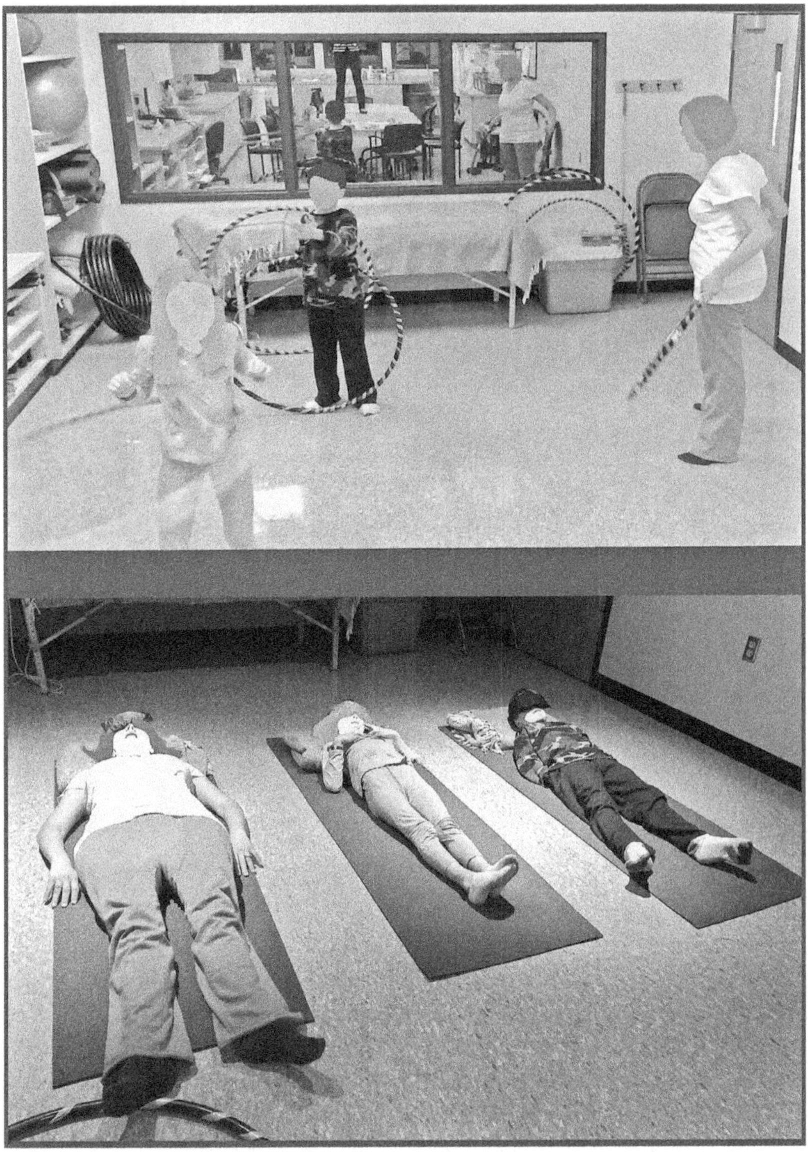

Figure 11.9 Top, Elvira, Moriarty, and Mother hula-hoop and below in savasana (faces have been digitized to protect identities)

Figure 11.10 Clay pinch pots by mother (bottom), Elvira (top left), and Moriarty (top right)

In later sessions, Elvira complained of "no longer wanting to be sick" (thus rejecting the IP notion and *realigning* the subsystems—Nichols, 2007). Much of the artwork post yoga flowed around those issues. While Elvira was struggling with flu-like symptoms, the metamessage was clear: she was also tired of being identified as the "patient" in the family system and was struggling to be viewed as healthy and thus recast the family system and *challenged unproductive assumptions* (Boscolo & Bertrando, 2007; Horovitz, 2002, 2011a, 2013; Nichols, 2007). In another session, mother, Moriarty, and Elvira engaged in creating clay pinch pots and the results of that session are shown in Figure 11.10.

Summary

As can be seen by the above significant sessions, combining the yoga therapy and art therapy with a family systems approach allowed me to *join* and *accommodate* my clients through *structural remapping*; using bhavana (Weintraub, 2012); meditation (Rosen, 2012); *remap* and *realign* the emotional, physical, and spiritual systems and co-create a new structure (Boscolo & Bertrando, 2007; Horovitz, 2004); *unbalance* the homeostasis in the family and *challenge unproductive assumptions* by co-creating a new reality system with my clients (Boscolo & Bertrando, 2007; Horovitz, 2004, 2011a, 2013).

Discussion

In sum, there had been a cognitive, emotional and developmental shift in Elvira as well as in her relationship with her mother and brother. After approximately one year of treatment, Elizabeth (the mother) had come to accept Elvira, was more accepting of her differences, and in fact had embraced those variances as can be seen in the asana where they coupled and trust was involved to support each other's weight (Figure 11.11). Here Elvira was most comfortable since the bodily activity allowed for the interaction and connection for which she so hungered. Elvira's attention was improving in all areas of her life: home, school, and her competition in ice-skating. While much work remains, there has been enormous progress and even though Elvira often complained about their "hectic schedule" (mother's choir practice, ice-skating practice/competitions, Moriarty's hockey and then some), she verbalized on more than one occasion both *in and out* of the therapeutic sessions that she did not want to "give up" the yoga/art therapy. Clearly the yoga/art therapy had "yoked" this family into a more healthy form of attachment.

To quote Mae Thompson, "Grace is how you look, when no one is looking." May I continue to be guided by those words, and those of my teachers. Namaste.

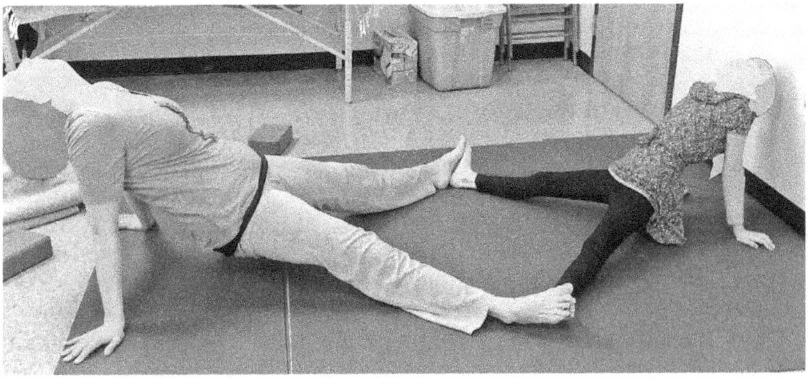

Figure 11.11 Mother and Elvira in coupled therapeutic activity

Questions for the Reader

1. In this case, there was a notable absence of the father. How would you have addressed this in the family yoga therapy/art therapy sessions?
2. Given the family issues, Elvira's diagnosis and health issues, how do you feel this case might have been affected if Elvira and the family embraced an Ayurvedic lifestyle?
3. Imagine yourself combining yoga therapy with expressive arts (art, dance, music, narrative, play, or like expressive art therapies). What expressive art would you use to aid this family into co-creation and healthy functioning?

Author's Note

1. For more on the symbols of family structure and explication see Minuchin (1974) and Nichols (2007).

References

Boscolo, L., & Bertrando, P. (1992). The reflexive loop of past, present, and future in systemic therapy and consultation. *Family Process*, 31(2), 119–130.

Bronfenbrenner, U. (1994). Ecological model of human development. In *International Encyclopedia of Education*. Vol. 3, 2nd Edn. London, England: Oxford Press: Elsevier.

Butler, J. (2008). The family diagram and genogram: Comparisons and contrasts. *American Journal of Family Therapy*, 36(3), 169–180.

Csikszentmihalyi, M. (1996). *Creativity: Flow and the psychology of discovery and invention.* New York: Harper Perennial.

Elliot, S. (2005) *The new science of breath: Coherent breathing for autonomic nervous system balance, health and well-being.* Allen, TX: Coherence Press, LLC.

Franklin, M. (2001). The yoga of art and the creative process: Listening to the divine. In M. Farrelly-Hanson (Ed.), *Spirituality and art therapy: Living the connection* (pp. 97–114). London and Philadelphia: Jessica Kingsley Publishers.

Gantt, L. M. (2004). The case for formal art therapy assessments. *Art Therapy: Journal of the American Art Therapy Association*, 21(1), 18–29.

Gantt, L., & Anderson, F. (2009). The formal elements art therapy scale: A measurement system for global variables in art. *Art Therapy: Journal of the American Art Therapy Association*, 26(3), 124–129.

Gantt, L., & Tabone, C. (1998). *Formal elements art therapy scale: The rating manual.* Morgantown, WV: Gargoyle Press.

Gladwell, M. (2005). *Blink: The power of thinking without thinking.* New York: Little Brown.

Goleman, D. (2014). Exercising the mind to treat attention disorders. *New York Times*, May 12. Retrieved October 18, 2014 from http://well.blogs.nytimes.com/2014/05/12/exercising-the-mind-to-treat-attention-deficits.

Henley, D. (2002). *Clayworks in art therapy: Plying the sacred circle.* London, England: Jessica Kingsley Publishers, Ltd.

Horovitz, E. G. (1999). A leap of faith: The call to art. Springfield, IL: Charles C Thomas, Ltd.

Horovitz, E. G. (2002). *Spiritual art therapy: An alternate path* (2nd Edn). Springfield. IL: Charles C Thomas.

Horovitz, E. G. (2011a). American Art Therapy Association 42nd Annual Conference, Washington, D.C. July 10. Advanced Practice Half-Day Workshop: *Healing Mind and Body: The Integration of Art Therapy and Yoga Therapy*.

Horovitz, E. G. (2011b). *Digital image transfer: Creating art with your photography*. New York: Sterling Publishers: Pixiq.

Horovitz, E. G. (2013). *Embracing the mind, body & spirit: Integrating art therapy & yoga therapy*. Georgia Art Therapy Association, April 5–6.

Horovitz, E. G. (2014). *The art therapists' primer: A clinical guide to assessment, diagnosis and treatment* (2nd Edn). Springfield, IL: Charles C Thomas.

Horovitz, E. G., & Eksten, S. L. (Eds). (2009). *The art therapists' primer: A clinical guide to assessment, diagnosis and treatment*. Springfield, IL: Charles C Thomas.

Jolly, W., Froom, J., & Rosen, M. G. (1980). The genogram. *Journal of Family Practice*, 10(2), 251–255.

Lasater, J. (2014). What is yoga therapy? Retrieved October 18, 2014 from www.yogatherapyconference.com/what_is_yoga_therapy.html

Lowenfeld, V., & Brittain, W. L. (1987). *Creative and mental growth* (8th edition). Upper Saddle, NJ: Prentice Hall.

McCartney, K., Harris, M., & Bernieri, F. (1990). Growing up and growing apart: A developmental meta-analysis of twin studies. *Psychological Bulletin*, 107(2), 226–237.

Minuchin, S. (1974). *Families and family therapy*. Cambridge, MA; Harvard University.

Minuchin, S., & Nichols, M. P. (1993). *Family healing: Tales of hope and renewal from family therapy*. New York: The Free Press.

Nainis, N., Paice, J. A., Ratner, J., Wirth, J. H., Lai, J., & Shott, S. (2006). Relieving symptoms in cancer: Innovative use of art therapy. *Journal of Pain and Symptom Management*, 31(2), 162–169.

Nichols, M. P. (2007). *The essentials of family therapy* (3rd edn). Boston, MA: Pearson, Allyn & Bacon.

Reynolds, G. (2012). How exercise could lead to a better brain. *New York Times*, April 18. Retreived October 18, 2014 from www.nytimes.com/2012/04/22/magazine/how-exercise-could-lead-to-a-better-brain.html?_r=1&emc=eta1.

Rosen, R. (2002). *The yoga of breath: A step-by-step guide to prananyama*. Boston, MA: Shambhala.

Schoenberg, P. L. A., Hepark, S., Can, C., Berendregt, H. P., Buitelarr, J., & Speckens, A. E. M. (2013). Effects of mindfulness-based cognitive therapy on neurophysiological correlates of performance montoring in adult attention-deficit/hyperactivity disorder. *Clinical Neurophysiology*, 26 December.

Simpkins, A. M., & Simpkins, C. A. (2011). *Meditation and yoga in psychotherapy: Techniques for clinical practice*. Hobokin: John Wiley & Sons, Inc.

Sluzki, C. E. (1983). Process, structure and world views: Toward an integrated view of systemic models in family therapy. *Family Process*, 22(4), 469–476.

Sommer Anderson, F. (Ed.) (2008). *Bodies in treatment, the unspoken dimension*. New York: Routledge Press.

Weintraub, A. (2012). *Yoga skills for therapists: Effective practices for mood management*. New York: W. W. Norton & Company.

Wikipedia (2014). Definition of a genogram. Retrieved October 18, 2014 from http://en.wikipedia.org/wiki/Genogram.

12 An Ayurvedic Lifestyle and Diet

An Internet-Based Study

Lisa Conboy, Hilary Garivaltis, Erin E. Casperson, and Scott Blossom

Because we cannot scrub our inner body we need to learn a few skills to help cleanse our tissues, organs, and mind. This is the art of Ayurveda.

Sebastian Pole

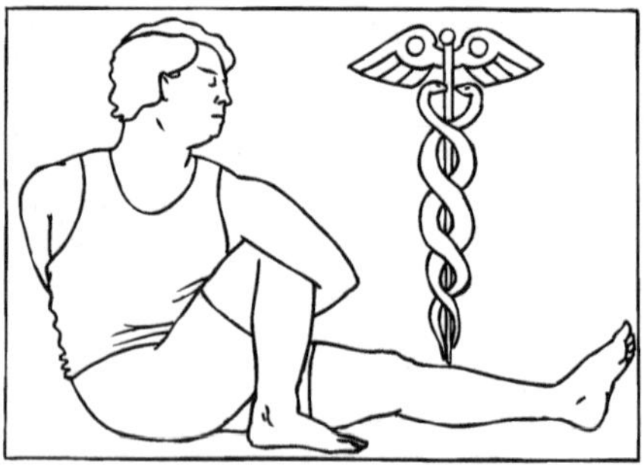

Figure 12.1

Introduction

From the Ayurvedic perspective the quest for good health, high quality of life, and prevention of illness requires daily and seasonal routines of purification and rejuvenation. Preventative medicine, which is tailored to individual needs and imbalances, is called in Ayurveda *svastha vritta,* "establishing oneself in good habits." This sentiment speaks to the fact that humans are creatures of habit who become easily accustomed, if not addicted, to unwholesome patterns of eating, resting, and exercising. It is for this reason that Ayurveda advocates temporarily changing your daily routines that you may open yourself to seeing and feeling from new perspectives and inquire into which habits are supporting your health and which are undermining it.

As the demographic profile of the United States shifts to more individuals enjoying a longer life span, health practices to improve vitality and avoid disease are gaining more attention. Ayurvedic medicine offers many affordable, clinically supported techniques that could be implemented more widely for an

American audience if scientifically proven. Below we report the results of a pilot study of one Ayurvedic program for which we found a number of promising results.

We studied an Ayurvedic cleansing and rejuvenation program that utilizes a whole food diet, yoga, meditation, and lifestyle regulations over a one-week period to promote health and wellbeing. Participants were assigned to slightly different regimens for the week based on the results of Ayurvedic diagnostic tests. With these tailored recommendations, we expected participants to come through the experience feeling stronger and more stable both physically and psychologically. Scientifically we found strong support that this cleanse program is helpful for a number of health outcomes. Future work should continue looking at other types of Ayurvedic practices, and at other types of outcomes such as biomarkers, and narratives of patient experiences.

Methods

The Himalayan Institute and Yoga International host an Ayurvedic Spring Renewal Challenge on their website (www.himalayaninstitute.org/yoga-international-magazine/cleanse/). This seven-day yoga and Ayurvedic spring cleanse offers participants daily diet, yoga, and lifestyle advice. All clinical elements of the study were designed by Scott Blossom L.Ac., RYT, CAS Dipl. C.H. The implementation of the study was a collaboration between Yoga International, Himalayan Institute, and Doctor Blossom Inc. This research project design and analysis were conducted by Dr. Lisa Conboy to evaluate improvements associated with cleanse participation from the point of view of participants.

Participants who signed up for the cleanse volunteered for additional measurement collection. Data was collected from volunteers participating between March 24 and May 21, 2012. Human subjects review and oversight was completed by the New England Institutional Review Board (www.neirb.com).

To evaluate changes following the cleanse we linked from the Himalayan Institute's Cleanse webpage to a research hosting page on the web-based survey interface Survey Monkey which included: 1) an informed consent form, 2) a demographic questionnaire, 3) health history questionnaire which included questions of relevance to yogic and Ayurvedic health sciences, 4) a number of Western health science validated and reliable measures of psychosocial health including the profile of mood states (Nyenhuis, Yamamoto, Luchetta, Terrien, & Parmentier, 1999), 5-factor mindfulness scale (Baer, Smith, Hopkins, Krietemeyer, & Toney, 2006), interpersonal reactivity index (Davis, 1983), self-efficacy scale (Bandura, 1977), perceived social support scale (Cohen, 1985; Cohen & Hoberman, (1983), positive and negative affective states (Watson & Clark, 1988), and the self-compassion scale (Neff, 2003).

To allow for comparison and communication between Western health and Ayurvedic sciences we also included two Ayurvedic questionnaires that are used clinically. Doctor Claudia Welch designed these latter forms. The first is current state of being, which evaluates dosha balance for the individual at the current time. A second scale evaluates base constitution. These latter two questionnaires are used clinically at the Kripalu School of Ayurveda in Lenox, Massachusetts.

Analysis

The SPSS data collection system was used for all data management and analysis (SPSS, 2006). Outcomes were calculated using paired students' t-tests of difference in group means testing the hypothesis that mean values were not significantly different per measure over time. Baseline responses were compared to outcomes after participation in the 7-day cleanse. Demographic information and other descriptive categories were tabulated and frequencies were conducted.

Results

Sample: Two hundred and twelve cleanse participants volunteered to complete pre-cleanse and post-cleanse measurements. The sample was 92% female and primarily White (93.55), non-Hispanic (95.1%) with English as a primary language (91.7%). Mean age of the sample was 47 years, with participants' ages ranging from 27 to 72 years. Participants represented 15 countries; with the majority being the USA (83.7%). Other countries included: Canada (6.2%), UK (2.8%), Australia (1.1%) and Austria, Bahrain, Denmark, Finland, France, Guatemala, India, Mexico, New Zealand, Taiwan, Turkey with less than 1% (representing 1 participant). Within the United States, 37 of the 50 states were represented. The state with the highest participation was CA (16.8%) followed by PA (10.7%), MA (8.1%), and NY (7.4%)

The sample overall had good pre-existing health habits; only 7.2% reported cigarette smoking; drinking was moderate with 7.5% reporting consuming more than one alcoholic drink per day. The most common drinking habit was less than one drink/week at 47.7%, followed by more than 1 drink/week but less than 1 drink/day at 44.7%. Sixty-one percent reported regular use of a neti pot (Himalayan Institute, 2014), 90.4% had a regular yoga practice, 59.8% had a regular meditation practice, and 81.3% regularly practiced yogic breathing.

The sample was highly educated with 53.1% having some professional training beyond college, 26.6% were college graduates, and 17.9% had some college or an associate's degree. Most were employed full-time (34%), 24.6% part-time, 3.4% were full-time homemakers, 9.9% were unemployed. About one quarter (22.2%) of the sample identified themselves as other in the employment category, and of these 67.7% gave the added detail that they were self-employed.

Most of the sample reported an average household income of $70,000 (45.9%). Only 14.9% reported a household income of $20,000 or less.

Pre-cleanse versus Post-cleanse Comparisons

Fifty-two subjects completed both the pre- and post-cleanse surveys; despite this small sample size interesting and predictable comparisons were found.

Average self-reported weight loss during the cleanse was 2.5 pounds, which is statistically significant using students' t-test ($p<0.001$). Most of the Western health science psychosocial measures showed positive trends but only a few of these changes reached statistical significance using students' t-test ($p<0.05$). Positive improvements included:

- 5-facet mindfulness scores of facets non-judgment and non-reactivity were statistically significantly higher post-cleanse compared to pre-cleanse.
- The profile of mood states scores for factor depression-dejection and confusion were both statistically significantly lower post-cleanse compared to pre-cleanse.
- Post-cleanse compared to pre-cleanse, there was a statistically significant change in current state of being scores. Table 12.1 illustrates the percentage of individuals reporting VATA symptoms fell by 50%, the sample percentage of individuals reporting mainly PITTA symptoms remained comparably constant between 55.5% and 60.5%. Percentage of individuals reporting mainly a KAPHA state increased more than threefold (5.3% to 18.4%).[1]

Students' t-test results indicate that the sample percentages of participants reporting the different types of energetic qualities changed significantly pre-post for current state of being ($p<0.005$), but not for constitutional type.

Discussion

Most of our scales of psychosocial health showed trending in the direction of improvement but few changes reached statistical significance. This finding was expected given our previous Ayurveda and yoga research in other healthy populations who were yoga and Ayurveda savvy (Conboy, Wilson, & Braun,

Table 12.1 The Outcomes of the Two Ayurvedic Questionnaires: 1) Current State of Being, 2) Base Constitution

N=38	*Vata (%)*	*Pitta (%)*	*Kapha (%)*	*Vata/Pitta (%)*	*Pitta/Kapha (%)*	*Vata/Pitta/Kapha (%)*
Constitutional type (p>0.1)						
Pre	31.6	50	10.5	2.6	5.3	0
Post	31.6	57.9	10.5	0	0	0
Current state of being (p<0.005)						
Pre	34.2	55.3	5.3	0	2.6	2.6
Post	15.8	60.5	18.4	5.3	0	0

2010). Individuals in this population are healthy and have little room for improvement on Western health science scales designed to differentiate illness from health. Thus work like ours looking at the positive effects of preventive health behaviors in non-ill populations should include measurement instruments that can record more subtle salutogentic changes. Toward this aim we included the scales of 5-facet mindfulness, and self-compassion; both of these scales showed significant improvements following the cleanse. More work in the area of measurement development can further elucidate the positive effects of these practices.

Although the more traditional Western measures of psychosocial health may generally not offer much information in measuring changes in healthy populations due to ceiling effects (i.e. subjects are healthy and have no latitude to improve on such scales), we did find a few theoretically interesting changes. The profile of mood states scores for the depression-dejection and confusion subscales were both statistically significantly lower post-cleanse compared to pre-cleanse. This latter result is particularly interesting as a traditional benefit of cleansing is mental clarity.

The inclusion of metrics that can record changes of importance in the language of the traditional system being studied—our example here Ayurvedic medicine and yoga—is necessary both for results to make sense to practitioners of these complementary sciences, and to further validate the effectiveness of these practices to a Western scientific audience.

For example, we included measures of Ayurvedic base constitution, on which scores should not change over time, as well as current state of being, which can change over time. Current state of being did show significant changes following the cleanse. This result makes sense as the cleansing process can be prescribed to help the body eliminate excess doshic energies to reduce signs and symptoms of pathology and promote a stable state of health and wellbeing.

Table 12.1 illustrates that the percentage of individuals reporting VATA symptoms fell by 50%, the sample percentage of individuals reporting mainly PITTA symptoms remained comparably constant between 55.5% and 60.5%. Percentage of individuals reporting mainly a KAPHA state increased more than threefold (5.3% to 18.4%). Further analyses are necessary to track how particular individuals changed due to the cleanse.

However, base constitution scores did not change significantly post-cleanse compared to pre-cleanse. This makes sense according to Ayurvedic theory, which considers base constitution to remain relatively static over one's lifetime. Western science values measurement devices that behave in a predictable manner. To our knowledge ours is the first report validating the consistency of self-reported base constitution in a Western sample. Further validation work is planned to better understand how reliable and valid such self-report measures are.

Our goal is to continue to find Western science-type evidence that these Ayurvedic concepts are reliable and valid to facilitate Western science's acceptance of these practices. Such validation work, coupled with evidence showing that the practices are effective on the biological, psychological, and experiential levels, create a strong framework to build increased appreciation and use for this medicine.

Data collection using the internet and a self-selected sample limits our ability to generalize our results to a larger population. However, we collected a rich description of our sample, including standard demographics as well as daily health behaviors in order to accurately describe our sample. Future work will consider the effects of yoga and Ayurvedic practices in more representative samples, as well as other specific populations. Further, Ayurveda and yoga offer many specific practices, which can be tailored for individuals with different health and wellness goals; our future work will include measurement of the effects of practices beyond self-administered, outpatient cleansing.

In this analysis our results were subtle; other work we have done with the more intensive in-patient Ayurvedic cleansing program Panchakarma (Conboy, Edshteyn, & Garivaltis, 2009) indicates that short yoga and Ayurveda interventions can show dramatic, significant changes using traditional Western science measures of psychosocial health and disease. Many other Ayurvedic and yogic therapeutic processes are yet to be scientifically evaluated for their positive effects; these promise better health for many different people in different health situations. This current project is a well-needed beginning point however, for such outpatient lifestyle practices are easy and inexpensive to administer. Finding effectiveness here will help support greater implementation of programs that can help more people with little expense. Subtle health improvements can go a long way toward health maintenance and disease prevention.

Questions for the Reader

1. How do you think outcomes might have been different if the participants had been more "mainstream" in terms of their dietary, exercise and lifestyle habits?
2. How does food affect your mood?
3. Have you compared the difference of how you feel when you practice yoga daily to how you feel when you practice more sporadically?

Editors' Note

1. VATA, PITTA, and KAPHA are the 3 different doshas.

References

Baer, R.A., Smith, G.T., Hopkins, J., Krietemeyer, J., & Toney, L. (2006). Using self-report assessment methods to explore facets of mindfulness. *Assessment*, 13, 27–45.

Bandura, A. (1977). Self-efficacy: Toward a unifying theory of behavioral change. *Psychology Review*, 84(2), 191–215.

Cohen, S. (1985). Measuring the functional components of social support. In I. G. Sarason, & B. R. Sarason (Eds.) *Social support: Theory, research, and application*. Martinus Nijoff, The Hague.

Cohen, S., & Hoberman, H. (1983). Positive events and social support as buffers of life change stress. *Journal of Applied Social Psychology*, 12, 99–125.

Conboy L., Edshteyn I., & Garivaltis, H. (2009). Ayurveda and panchakarma: Measuring the effects of a holistic health intervention. *The Scientific World Journal*, 9, 272–280.

Conboy L., Wilson A., & Braun, T. (2010). The salutogenic effects of a yoga teacher training program. *The Scientific World Journal*, 10, 788–795

Davis, M. H. (1983). Measuring individual differences in empathy: Evidence for a multidimensional approach. *Journal of Personality and Social Psychology*, 44, 113–126.

Himalayan Institute (2014). *The neti pot: The original since 1972*. Retrieved September 2, 2014 from http://www.himalayaninstitute.org/products-publications/neti-pot-products/.

Neff, K. D. (2003). The development and validation of a scale to measure self-compassion. *Self and Identity*, 2(3), 223–250.

Nyenhuis, D. L., Yamamoto, C., Luchetta, T., Terrien, A., & Parmentier, A. (1999). Adult and geriatric normative data and validation of the profile of mood states. *Journal of Clinical Psychology*, 55(1), 79–86.

SPSS (2006). *SPSS for Windows Rel. 15.0*. Chicago: SPSS Inc.

Watson, D., & Clark, L. (1988). Development and validation of brief measures of positive and negative affect: The PANAS scales. *Journal of Personality and Social Psychology*, 54(6), 1063–1070.

13 Yoga and Mental Health

The Crumbling Wall

Amy Weintraub

Yoga teaches us to cure what need not be endured and endure what cannot be cured.

B. K. S. Iyengar

Figure 13.1

Introduction

The gulf between yoga therapy and medical treatment is narrowing. Nowhere is this more in evidence than in the area of mental health. In my own training program, more than half of the LifeForce Yoga Practitioners have advanced degrees in mental health and many of them have become yoga teachers. This has not always been the case. Although there were plenty of pioneers like Eleanor Criswell, who began teaching the psychology of yoga at Sonoma State College in 1969, and a handful of mental health professionals who practiced and taught yoga, there was a reluctance to integrate the yoga practices into standard mental health treatment. "There were those of us," says psychologist and iRest founder Richard Miller (2011), "who were integrating somatic and spiritual elements into our psychotherapy practices back in the early 70s, but we were far and few between and definitely on the cutting edge." Until the 1990s, most training programs in mental health did not include a spiritual dimension or even reference to a body–mind connection. "We were taught," says a psychologist friend, "that if your patient talked about God, you should consider a diagnosis of psychosis."

The Body in Mental Health

In non-Western cultures, the blending of body, mind, and spirit has been assumed and not separated in healing practices. But since 1641 when René Descartes condemned Western science to a dualistic approach that essentially separates mind and body, the dominant treatment theories for mental and emotional disorders left the body out. With the advent of psychopharmacology in biomedicine, which considered the balance between mental illness and mental health as simply the proper mix of brain biochemistry, even psychotherapy was often left out of the equation. Still, the body has had a place on the fringes of Western psychology (somatic psychology). There were pioneers in mental health like Alexander Lowen, MD, who in the mid-1950s developed bioenergetics, a body-psychotherapy rooted in the earlier work of Wilhelm Reich, MD. Lowen understood that suppressed emotions, unhappiness, and anger can block energy flow and cause physical distress, and he encouraged his patients to practice yoga. For decades, somatic psychology was a fringe movement, outside regular academic programs. Still, many mental health professionals sought out mind–body trainings after they had fulfilled their academic studies and licensing requirements. They studied with pioneers in the field like Pat Ogden, PhD, founder of the Sensorimotor Psychotherapy Institute, or Peter Levine, PhD, the creator of Somatic Experiencing (SE), a body-awareness approach to trauma. Until the more recent advent of a few integrative graduate psychology programs, mental health professionals emerging from graduate schools supplemented their academic and clinical training with programs like Ogden's or Levine's.

Major innovators in the field of psychology, from Carl Jung to Stanislov Grof, have studied and integrated Eastern spiritual traditions, including yoga, into their treatment models for nearly one hundred years. For over forty years, psychiatrist Stanislov Grof, MD, his wife Christina, and their colleagues have been teaching healing professionals and anyone who comes to the Grof Transpersonal Training (GTT) an accelerated breathing practice called Holotropic Breathwork. This breathing practice is not unlike a vigorous form of yoga breathing.

Pioneers like Ogden, Levine, and Grof have since been joined by others in the field like psychiatrist Bessel van der Kolk, MD, who directs the Trauma Clinic in Brookline, Massachusetts. Van der Kolk is a pioneer in first identifiying post-traumatic stress disorder (PTSD) and second in recognizing the physiological components of a trauma response and the importance of including the body in treatment. He has often said that he won't treat a patient with a history of trauma unless they are practicing yoga (van der Kolk, 2007).

While there have always been innovators in mental health who have drawn on Eastern spiritual philosophy and practice, the traditional view has been dominated by the biomedical model, which posits that mental disorders are the result of a disordered biochemistry, and therefore the best way to treat them is with a chemical. This has given rise to the huge reliance of doctors and their patients on psychopharmacological agents. Despite recent evidence that in most cases the class of antidepressants known as selective serotonin re-uptake inhibitors (SSRIs) work no better than placebo and offer patients a wide range of side effects, prescriptions continue to be written in ever greater numbers. As Integrative medicine pioneer Andrew Weil, MD (2011) says, "consider the possibility that the basic assumptions of the mainstream psychiatric medicine are obsolete and no longer serve us well. Those assumptions constitute the biomedical model of mental health and dominate the whole field." Weil joins a small group of visionary psychiatrists, who, through their books and training programs, are leading the way into a new conception of mental health treatment that includes yoga. To name a few, see Emmons and Kranz (2006); Gordon (2008); Lake (2009); Brown, Gerbarg, and Muskin (2009).

Just as the Descartian separation of treatment between body and mind is dissolving in the light of recent scientific inquiry and a mounting body of evidence, so are boundaries falling between body and mind approaches in the treatment room. Now many psychotherapists and some yoga teachers have been trained to lead the evidence-based 8-week Mindfulness Based Stress Reduction (MBSR) program developed by Jon Kabat-Zinn. Included in the MBSR program is mindfulness meditation, a body scan, not unlike a basic yoga nidra practice, yoga movements, and breathing exercises. Currently, mental health CEU providers offer daylong seminars and webcasts where psychotherapists receive continuing education credit for learning yoga that they can apply in a clinical setting.

As a yoga professional and author involved in yoga and mental health research, I speak and teach at medical and mental health conferences, and while there, I go to as many seminars and workshops as I can. Since 2004, I have not attended a conference for medical professionals that did not include a workshop on breathing exercises or meditation or even yoga movement. Often, mental health professionals with little or no yoga training teach these workshops. They are teaching psychotherapists yoga or yoga-like practices that the clinicians can then begin integrating into their psychotherapy practices. I once watched a famous medical doctor and author teach over 300 medical professionals with no prior training in yoga a rapid breathing practice for the treatment of depression. No contraindications were offered, and there are many. I mention this trend as evidence of what is already happening in the mental health arena, not as endorsement of such offerings.

Mental Health in Yoga Practice

The *kosha* model by which many yoga professionals assess and offer support to their students has within it conscious attention to emotions, thoughts, and beliefs. (The kosha model consists of five sheaths representing the simultaneous aspects of human existence—physical, breath/energy, emotions, beliefs, and bliss or a sense of interconnectedness with all beings.) When we practice yoga, there is no mind–body split. We are whispering a soothing message of well-being to all the koshas. For thousands of years, yoga practice has supported practitioners in breaking through the framework of self-limiting emotions and beliefs. When we practice with attention to breath and sensation, we move into the present moment and a more spacious awareness that allows us to see how much more we are than our personal stories and dysregulated moods. However, the history of integrating *specific* Western psychological principles into yoga trainings is more recent and can be traced to 1986, when Michael Lee, MA led the first Phoenix Rising practitioner training. Since then, health professionals and yogis have been studying this unique blend of therapeutic and supported posture holding combined with Rogerian dialoguing, a technique that involves close listening and mirroring back the client's own words.

My own training program, LifeForce Yoga Practitioner Training for Anxiety and Depression, began at Kripalu Center in 2004, and offers specific yoga skills appropriate for use in yoga classes, yoga therapy, psychotherapy, and other healthcare settings. Richard Miller, PhD, began offering iRest (Integrative Restoration) Training for yoga and health professionals, as well as lay practitioners in 2006. iRest is a form of yoga nidra and meditative self-inquiry that he developed, which has been shown to benefit many mental health populations, including those suffering from combat related post-traumatic stress disorder (PTSD).

In the last two years, a number of training programs for yoga and mental health professionals have begun that offer yoga skills for specific populations with mood imbalances and trauma. These include Trauma Sensitive Yoga, Breath~Body~Mind, Yoga for the Mind, and shorter weekend trainings for special populations.

Both Breath~Body~Mind, developed by Richard Brown, MD and Patricia Gerbarg, MD, and Mind–Body Medicine training, developed by James Gordon, MD, include yoga components. These two programs train professionals as well as the survivors themselves at sites around the world in response to traumatic events like combat or natural disaster. Community leaders in places like Haiti, Rwanda, or Kosovo, who have experienced the disaster themselves, go through the program and then learn simple skills like yoga-based movement, breathing, and meditation practices so that they can continue to serve their traumatized communities. In a recent International Journal of Yoga Therapy, Gerbarg, Wallace, and Brown (2011) state,

> Mind–body programs . . . First, are adaptable to local needs, cultures, religions, and languages. Second, they are low-cost, requiring no equipment,

> electricity or specific spaces, and they involve fewer healthcare professionals. Third, through group programs, a few teachers can rapidly serve large numbers of survivors. Fourth, community leaders can be rapidly trained to teach simple techniques, extending the benefits to others and creating a sustainable resource for long-term treatment and support.

These training programs make movement, breathing, and meditation techniques accessible to as many disaster survivors and care-givers as possible by teaching the interventions in brief training periods to both professionals and non-professionals, who, after the experts leave, can then go on to serve their traumatized communities.

Yoga and the Emotions

Yoga practice itself can often be a cathartic experience. When I ask a group at the beginning of a workshop or training how many people have cried on their yoga mats, nearly everyone who practices yoga raises a hand. The tears we shed on the mat are most often not about the story, but rather are a release of a physiological or emotional constriction for which we may not have words. Even a simple breath may activate feelings. If a student who has been a shallow, upper chest breather is encouraged to breathe more deeply and slowly, the parasympathetic nervous system is activated on the extended exhalation, calming and soothing the body mind, and deactivating the limbic system. In such a relaxed state, the individual may feel safe enough for emotions to surface. If she has been tamping down her feelings, then the deeper breath may be all it takes to trigger a release. This may come as a surprise to both the student and the teacher or therapist. But if the safe container has been set, such a release can be an opportunity for therapy (be it yoga therapy or psychotherapy) to progress. Without the addition of the breath, such a client may be in psychotherapy for many sessions before authentic emotions rise to the surface. What better place for feelings to emerge than in sitting with a trusted mental health therapist with whom the client has established a safe and therapeutic bond?

In one case, I was working through the wisdom of yoga, not psychotherapy, with a client who had developed a strong asana based practice prior to our meeting, partially as a form of self-medication, and a way not to deal with an issue she was reluctant to take to therapy. When she began to breathe deeply in a supine position and tears erupted, she became aware of how much she was trying to repress and was finally receptive to a referral to a psychotherapist.

Yoga teachers need to be prepared for such occurrences, and be able to normalize the experience, as well as know when to refer. One LifeForce Yoga Practitioner tells of her surprise and dismay when during her first yoga class many years ago, tears unexpectedly erupted. What further disturbed her was her teacher's alarming advice when she spoke with her about it after class. Instead of normalizing the common occurrence, the teacher told her that her tears were an indication of her need for psychotherapy. As a beginning yoga student, she was confused and upset. She had been in psychotherapy for several years, and she felt the yoga teacher was saying that there was something wrong with her. Had the yoga teacher been trained in understanding yoga's potential for the release of repressed emotion, she would have been able to reassure her student in that regard. She could have let her student know that when tears come on the yoga mat, they often arise as a release as they might on the massage table or in an intimate embrace, usually without a story attached. If the student had then felt unsatisfied with the answer and had wanted to tell the teacher her story, that would have been the appropriate time to suggest a referral.

Yoga and Trauma

Because of the growing body of evidence that yoga can be an effective intervention for mood disorders and trauma, and new books popularizing the idea (Cope, 2000; Weintraub, 2004; Liebier & Moss, 2009; Forbes, 2011; Emerson & Hopper, 2011; Weintraub, 2012), students with mood issues and trauma histories are being referred by their health professionals and are showing up in larger numbers in regular yoga classes and calling for individual sessions. I had the privilege of working with Jacquelyn Jackson who was Congresswoman Gabrielle Giffords' former outreach director. Our sessions were paid for by the Pima County Victims Fund, because Jacquelyn was at the Safeway in Tucson on January 8, 2011 when Jared Loughner opened fire. Her life was spared in the shooting that took the lives of 6 people, many of them her friends, and critically wounded her former boss. A year after the event, Jacquelyn sat on the couch in my yoga therapy treatment room, because her beloved brother had suddenly died of a brain tumor at Christmas. Despite the good talk therapy she did with a grief counselor after the Tucson tragedy, many of her symptoms were back, including insomnia, anxiety, and binge-eating.

Through our deep attunement, I answered Jacquelyn's call with a response that was never calculated. That plan changed session to session, even moment to moment, in accordance with what she presented. In our initial session, Jacquelyn's breath was shallow and labored as she talked and her hands shook. It was clear that the trauma was still embodied, and that talking about it now was making her run "one more lap through hell." I suggested that we begin with the breath, breathing slowly through the nostrils with an emphasis on the exhalation. I asked her to place her hands on her lower belly and to notice them rising as the breath moved into her lower lungs. But her hands didn't move. Jacquelyn was unable to take a deep breath. So I invited her to stand. It was clear to me that Jacquelyn was tamping down a lot of emotion. Had I pushed my own agenda of helping her to breathe more deeply in that first session, we might have risked emotional flooding. Most of us have had such catharsis on the yoga mat, and it often facilitates a deep emotional and physical release, usually without a story attached. But this was our first session together,

Jacquelyn was suffering from trauma, and I wanted to make sure that she felt safe with me, so that her emotions might arise, without shame or blame. To do that, I first needed to meet her in that revved up, anxious place. In yoga, we might consider this state of mind and mood to be dominated by rajas, or the principle of excitement. Had I moved too quickly, she might have felt overwhelmed and scared. Instead, I offered a centering ritual of self-acceptance as we stood to create sacred space together.

First though, to get her moving and shaking out the tension I was still observing, we practiced a dance-like joint warm-up with lively kirtan music. Then we continued to stand as we centered with the ritual, using sound and a hand gesture, as I asked her to visualize her own soothing image of peace. I gave her the option of thinking the word "peace" if an image didn't readily come to mind. I asked her to set an intention for our work together. After we centered, she was visibly calmer but anxiety was still present, so we did a slow, brief round of prana pulling at one breath per second. Then I asked her to sense into her face, her hands, and her fingertips. This cueing to sensation calmed her further. Her breath was finally slow and even.

I could safely lead her through self-soothing practices that included bee breath (brahmari), cooling, calming mantra tones and mudras to calm and focus the mind. I stayed attuned to Jacquelyn, checking in with her at every stage of every practice. I led her through postures with an emphasis on forward bending to help with sleep and general limbic deactivation.

Yoga breathing and chanting with its known activation of the vagal nerve can actually reverse this process of limbic over activation by stimulating the parasympathetic nervous system, slowing heart rate, breath, pulse, and lowering body temperature. And that is how I worked with Jacquelyn. After every new element of our practice, I invited Jacquelyn to sense into her face, her hands, her fingertips. I didn't say, "Feel the sensations in your body," which is too vague and actually anxiety-producing in some trauma survivors. In this direct cueing to sensation, I was offering her a window through the agitated mood. In the moments of noticing specific sensation in her body, she was totally present, not gripped by her story. Since her brother's recent death, Jacquelyn had avoided her emotions. It wasn't even safe to feel her body sensations, because staying present to them evoked too much feeling. Many who have experienced trauma feel this way. Some, especially those who have been physically abused or sexually traumatized, will tell you that they are living from the neck up.

To keep from feeling, trauma survivors find ways to numb out—food, drugs, sex, alcohol, gambling, work—whatever it takes. Even yoga can be practiced in a numbed out, disconnected, and driven way so as not to feel. Yoga without attention to body sensations and breath is simply exercise. It's good for you as exercise, but as research has shown, there are many more benefits when the attention is inwardly focused (Telles, Nagarathna, Nagendra, & Desiraju, 1993). Many practitioners think of yoga as postures only, and use it as a distraction from what they are feeling. It's a healthy distraction, as compared to drugs or alcohol, but it's still a distraction that can become an addiction. But when yoga is practiced with a more mindful inward focus that includes pranayama breathing and other timeless yoga practices, in addition to postures, yoga can be the portal into a deeper healing for the trauma survivor.

When the yoga teacher moves slowly and gently while cueing to sensation, she is offering her numbed-out, hyper-vigilant student a small window into feeling, first the body, and then, as the window opens wider, the emotions. This window into the body-centered moment can facilitate a "reoccupation" of the body as a safe place. This can be yoga's greatest gift to a trauma survivor.

On that first day with Jacquelyn, I concluded our session with a yoga nidra, and then I gave her a yoga nidra CD with some simple suggestions for home practice. Between our first two sessions, she practiced the CD every evening before bed and bee breath regularly and, by the second session, she was able to give up the sleep medication she had been using since the shooting.

During our second session, Jacquelyn paraphrased the language I use on the LifeForce Yoga Nidra CD with which she had been practicing. She told me that she felt her spaciousness "so much more than the story." Aside from a calmer demeanor, Jacquelyn's abdomen was now expanding during inhalation and she was able to lengthen her exhalation. She had come to this on her own, simply through a daily home practice.

Let me make it clear that I am not suggesting that yoga teachers should hang out a shingle to treat trauma survivors. In fact, I carry business cards for two psychotherapists so I am always ready to refer. Yoga professionals need to understand their limitations and know when to refer. But trauma survivors are already coming to yoga classes and calling for private sessions. It's vital that yoga professionals know how to help.

Yoga in Clinical Practice

In the lexicon of yoga, there are simple calming (*langhana*) and stimulating (*brahmana*) practices not regularly taught in posture-based yoga classes or in most 200-hour basic yoga teacher training programs. Yoga and mental health professionals can learn these skills to empower their students and clients to manage their moods. There are now specialized training programs led by experienced yoga and yoga-trained mental health professionals that offer these practices and their contraindications, and that cover scope of practice issues so that professionals can appropriately refer to each other.

Psychotherapists who have not completed a 200-hour yoga teacher training do not teach yoga postures or some of the specialized yoga breathing practices that may have strong effects and numerous contraindications for certain individuals may benefit from the aforementioned trainings/workshops. However, shorter trainings can offer medical professionals skills that are appropriate in clinical settings like 1:2 breathing, alternate nostril breathing, simple meditation techniques that rely upon breath, mudra, mantra, or imagery (bhavana), finding authentic sankalpa (intention or resolve), and nondual self-inquiry practices that allow the client to experience herself as more than her story.

Deborah Lubetkin, PsyD, a clinical psychologist in northern New Jersey, who is trained as a LifeForce Yoga Practitioner, says, "My patients are grateful for this work. It adds to their therapy, and provides relief in shorter time frames." So how might this look in clinical treatment? Lubetkin, who learned yoga strategies in two seven-day trainings for yoga and mental health professionals, with mentoring sessions with a yoga professional and psychotherapist, used a very simple breathing exercise to begin her work with Suzanne, a 40-year-old client with a severe eating disorder who presented her problem as "wanting to control what is sometimes uncontrollable." Suzanne was so anxious at the start of treatment that Lubetkin introduced a 4:6 (inhaling for the count of four, exhaling for the count of six) yogic three-part breath (dirga pranayama) in the first session to provide her with a felt sense of how she actually did have more control than she believed—that she could actually induce a sense of comfort. "Her reaction was 'Wow!'" said Lubetkin. Suzanne was relaxed enough to begin the work of therapy during the very first session.

According to Lubetkin, Suzanne benefited from breath work in the very first session and was receptive to learning more. As the sessions progressed, it was clear to Lubetkin that Suzanne came into each session very revved up. Her thoughts were racing, her speech was fast moving, and she had trouble making the transition into the therapy session. "I had carefully assessed her, and she was clearly not bipolar. I had also seen how she was able to calm down significantly after some simple breath work." So Deborah introduced the bee breath (brahmari) as a way to help her transition into the session, to decrease the obsessive thought pattern. "She was very receptive to this, actually becoming silent for the first time since we had met. We continue to use the bee breath regularly." After years of vainly attempting to control the world and her own emotions, Suzanne began to feel her emotions instead of simply reacting to them. For the first time, she cried in sessions. "She is always amazed," said Lubetkin, "by the space she has learned to create in both mind and body."

Specialty yoga trainings for mental health and yoga professionals can offer healing practices from the yoga tradition that empower their clients to be an active participant in managing their moods, that strengthen the therapeutic bond, and help their clients focus, relax, and prepare them for successful work in therapy. Such trainings support yoga professionals who are already working in prisons, halfway houses, substance abuse facilities, and mental health clinics. They benefit from learning a basic understanding of the underlying imbalance, from both a Western and yogic perspective. There are a compendium of yoga practices that do not require a yoga mat and can empower students and clients to reestablish a homeostatic balance in all of the koshas. (Again, in yoga, the koshas are sheaths representing the simultaneous aspects of human existence—physical, breath/energy, emotions, beliefs and bliss or a sense of interconnectedness with all beings.)

Yoga teaches us that when there is a constriction in one area of the body-mind, it is simultaneously affecting other aspects of our being. If there is tightness in the chest, for example (anamaya kosha) the breath may be affected (pranamaya kosha) and there may be a corresponding emotion or mood state (manomaya kosha), and perhaps a belief about the self or the world (vijnanamaya kosha). And if, through a pranayama breathing practice or a simple posture held with attention to sensation and breath, a release of that tightness in the chest occurs, then all of the koshas are affected, and there may even be a momentary experience of bliss (ananadamaya kosha). A window may open through the gloom of the present emotion that allows the practitioner to feel that although she has an emotion, she is more than that emotion, and so much more than that self-limiting belief about herself or the world.

Whether an individual carries the label of depression or anxiety (psychology model) or tamasic or rajasic (yoga model), there are yoga strategies that can move us back into balance. With training, both yoga and mental health professionals can offer students a set of practices that meet the current mood, as assessed by the student or client, and empower the practitioner herself to find her way back to a sattvic (balanced) state.

Yoga supports students and clients in knowing who they are beneath the labels and empowers them to take control of their optimum mental health. Psychotherapist Sherry Rubin, LICSW, who is also a yoga teacher and a LifeForce Yoga Practitioner, reports that her client, who returned to therapy after a couple of years absence, said, "When I came before, you helped me understand and get where I wanted to go. Now you show me yoga practices I use to help myself understand and get where I want to go."

Questions for the Reader

This is a three-day practice that allows you to clear your inner space of whatever is limiting your clear seeing.

Day One: After a practice of gentle movement (asana), breath (pranayama) with attention to all that is arising—sensation, thoughts, feelings—take a moment to write this question at the top of a blank page:

> What am I doing when I am the happiest?

Close your eyes and imagine yourself as a small child, perhaps seven or eight. As though looking at a picture in a photo album, see yourself doing something you loved, something that fully absorbed your body, mind, and spirit.

Now turn the pages of your photo album until you find a picture of yourself at seventeen or eighteen. What were you doing at seventeen or eighteen that fully absorbed your body, mind, and spirit? See yourself doing that now.

Continue turning the pages of your photo album through each decade in your life, stopping at pictures of yourself doing something that brought you great joy.

Finally, stop at a picture of yourself in the recent past. See yourself doing something you love, something that absorbs you completely.

Now take ten minutes to write about the images that came to you in this visualization. What are you doing when you are the happiest?

Day Two: After a practice of gentle movement (asana), breath (pranayama) with attention to all that is arising—sensation, thoughts, feelings—take a moment to write this question at the top of a blank page:

> What are my true gifts?

Close your eyes and imagine yourself as a small child, perhaps seven or eight. As though looking at a picture in a photo album, see yourself doing something that made someone you cared about feel good about herself or himself and that also made you feel good about yourself.

As on Day One, go through your photo album, stopping at a picture of yourself in each decade where you are doing something that not only serves yourself but also serves another.

Finally, stop at a picture of yourself in the recent past. See yourself doing well at something that you appreciate. Perhaps there is another being in the picture appreciating you too.

Now take ten minutes to write about the images that came to you in this visualization. What are your true gifts?

Day Three: After a practice of gentle movement (asana), breath (pranayama) with attention to all that is arising—sensation, thoughts, feelings—take a moment to write this question at the top of a blank page:

> How does what I am doing when I am the happiest align with my true gifts?

Think about where the images from each of these exercises merge. See those pictures throughout your life.

Now take ten minutes to write about the images that arise. How do my true gifts inform what I am doing when I'm the happiest? Let this question inform your dharma. Write about how your life choices are aligning with your joy and your gifts and how they are not. Explore in your writing how you might fully merge the paths of happiness in your life with the path of your highest abilities, your truest gifts.

Blessings on fulfilling your dharma.

References

Brown, R., Gerbarg, P., & Muskin, P. (2009). *How to use herbs, nutrients, and yoga in mental health care.* New York: W.W. Norton & Co.

Cope, S. (2000). *Yoga and the quest for true self.* New York: Bantam.

Emerson, D., & Hopper, E. (2011). *Overcoming trauma through yoga: Reclaiming your body.* Bekeley, CA: North Atlantic Books.

Emmons, H., & Kranz, R. (2006). *The chemistry of joy: A three-step program for overcoming depression through Western science and Eastern wisdom.* New York: Fireside.

Forbes, B. (2011). *Yoga for emotional balance: Simple practices to help relieve anxiety and depression.* Boston, MA: Shambhala Publications, Inc.

Gerbarg, L. G., Wallace, G., & Brown, R. P. (2011). Mass disasters and mind-body solutions: Evidence and field insights. *International Journal of Yoga Therapy*, 21, 97–107.

Gordon, J. S. (2008). *Unstuck: Your guide to the seven-stage journey out of depression.* New York: Penguin Press.

Lake, J. (2009). *Integrative mental health care: A therapist's handbook* (Norton Professional Books). New York: W.W. Norton, Inc.

Liebier, N., & Moss, S. (2009). *Healing depression the mind-body way: Creating happiness with meditation, yoga, and Ayurveda.* Hoboken, NJ: John Wiley & Sons, Inc.

Miller, R. (2011). Personal correspondence with author.

Telles, S., Nagarathna, R., Nagendra, H. R., & Desiraju, T. (1993). Physiological changes in sports teachers following 3 months of training in yoga. *Indian Journal Medicine Science*, 47, 235–238.

Van der Kolk, B. (2007). Personal correspondence with the author at Kripalu Center, 2007.

Weil, A. (2011). *Spontaneous happiness.* New York: Little Brown and Co.

Weintraub, A. (2004). *Yoga and depression.* New York: Broadway Books.

Weintraub, A. (2012). *Yoga skills for therapists.* New York: W.W. Norton & Co.

14 Yoga for Anger Management

Sheri Kreher

Perhaps all the dragons of our lives are princesses
who are only wanting to see us once beautiful and brave.
Perhaps every terrible thing is in its deepest being
something helpless that wants help from us.

Rainer Maria Rilke

Figure 14.1

The Misunderstood Emotion

Anger is a misunderstood emotion. We feel instinctively, or may know from personal experience, that anger can be dangerous. We fear anger in others, and ourselves and given the apparent increase in random violence in our society, who can blame us? However, that fear can impair our ability to respond effectively to one of our most important survival tools.

Like anger itself, people with anger management problems are also misunderstood. To be clear, there is no justification for aggressive, intimidating, or violent behavior. At the same time, people with problematic anger suffer a great deal, and their need for healing is crucial to the wellbeing of our families, communities, and society as a whole.

In my experience facilitating anger management therapy groups, I find that most clients have been victimized, bullied, rejected, or abused throughout their life. Some have endured chronic pain or illness, betrayal, grief, poverty, domestic violence, prejudice, or social injustice. I usually find the root cause of their anger understandable. However, their escalating and often misdirected efforts to be heard, to assert power, or to pre-empt rejection creates unintended chaos. Often these actions lead them to lose employment, housing, relationships, custody of their children, or even their personal freedom if incarcerated. Worse yet, they may bear the guilt of harming another. Alternatively, some people suppress their anger, becoming extremely depressed and self-loathing. They hide from anger's warnings and remain stuck in passive, indirect, or victimized patterns. Aside from those with severe personality disorders (which is beyond the scope of this chapter), most of the people in my anger management groups feel powerless, lonely, and ashamed.

> I'm a bad person, that's just a fact. Why else would I act like this?
> I know I should control myself, but sometimes I don't want to!
> I'm always judging people; I'm looking for an excuse to go off on someone!

Teaching individuals to be skillful with their anger is life changing. When people can learn to listen and stay present to the "alert system" of anger, then they can make empowered choices, and take effective action (or non-action). Most importantly, beyond any skill is compassion. Having the courage to know and love the terrible, helpless dragon within shifts the core struggle, so that one no longer needs to fight or flee from others or oneself. This is the yogic core of mediating anger.

In this chapter I will explore how the teachings and practices of yoga facilitate empowered thinking, skillful action, self-compassion, and the sense of inter-connection needed to manage angry feelings in a healthy way. This chapter will use the "eight limbs" of yoga outlined in Patanjali's Yoga Sutra as practical guideposts, and draw broader purpose from The Bhagavad Gita and Narada Bhakti Sutra (Devi, 2007; Easwaran, 2007; Shearer, 1982).

The Anatomy of Anger

> Within this fathomlong body is found all the teachings,
> is found suffering, the cause of suffering, and the end of suffering.
>
> Buddha

Anger is a physical event, an uncomfortable alarm system designed for rapid response. When the sabre tooth tiger threatened our caveman ancestor, he needed the boost of adrenaline to survive, commonly known as the "fight or flight" mechanism. Understanding this stress response is helpful to understanding how yoga is an effective intervention. In addition, providing psycho-education about the anatomy of anger to clients is extremely validating; it helps affirm intense emotions and universalizes experience. Instead of feeling like *a bad person*, one can realize that he/she is simply an organism fighting (albeit misguidedly) for survival.

Today, there are no sabre tooth tigers chasing us, but our primal limbic system cannot differentiate between mortal danger and perceived threats—such as a close call on the highway or a passing stranger on a dark sidewalk. The threat may occur only in our mind, like a worry or insecurity, and may not even be happening in the present moment; the stress response can trigger even when reminded of past events such as in Post-Traumatic Stress Disorder.

Interestingly, social or emotional threats, like an insult or emotional letdown, draw on the same biological networks (Eisenberger & Liebermann, 2004). This explains why people become inflamed by a negative look (or social slight).

Regardless of how a threat trigger starts, the amygdala activates the Sympathetic Nervous System (SNS) and the endocrine system. An ensuing surge of stress hormones, such as epinephrine (adrenaline) and cortisol, increases the heart rate, results in vasoconstriction, and shunts blood to large muscle groups. The "stressed out" individual now experiences increased heart rate and respiration, agitation, muscle tension, and perspiration (Hanson & Mendius, 2009).

While some systems are "revved up," other non-essential functions shut down, such as digestion and libido. The prefrontal cortex function also decreases, leading to impulsivity, racing thoughts, negative perceptions, and poor recall of events while under stress (Uyterhoeven, 2006). People with rage episodes often report that they "black out" or can't remember events clearly; I've commonly heard clients say, "I don't know what happened, but, the next thing I knew, I was in the back of a police car."

Though the stress response was meant for emergency use only, we are increasingly living in a state of SNS arousal. Our modern sabre tooth tigers are busy schedules, media overload, financial stress, long commutes, relationship discord, health problems, violence, and social injustice to name a few. Chronic stress and anger have been linked to 1) increased risk of heart disease, stroke, diabetes, insomnia, depression 2) decreased immune system, gastro-intestinal functioning, sex drive, mood, and 3) correlated with cardiovascular disease (Licinio, Gold, & Wong, 1995; Wenner, 2008).

Fortunately, our body has the key to end this suffering through the Parasympathetic Nervous System (PNS). The PNS helps the body to maintain homeostasis; it promotes rest and regeneration (Uyterhoven, 2006). In this state, all body systems are functioning normally, including the cardio-vascular system, digestive system, and immune system. This state is characterized by a calm, positive mood state, and sense of safety and peace. For thousands of years, yogic practices have been used to achieve this equilibrium. Today, more and more scientific evidence supports the effectiveness of yoga to tame rampant stress hormones and create the relaxation response in our bodies (Cobb, 2008; Granath, Ingvarsson, von Thiele, & Lundberg, 2006; Hanson & Mendius, 2009; Lee, 2005; Simpkins & Simpkins 2011). Through yoga, we can access our body's wisdom to end its own painful patterns.

Mental Suffering

> How can the mind, which is so restless, attain lasting peace? Krishna, the mind is restless, turbulent, powerful, violent; trying to control it is like trying to tame the wind.
>
> *Bhagavad Gita* 6.33–34

Before action, there is thought. The body only reacts when the mind perceives a threat, and as we know, the mind is not always a reliable source. Anger often arises from our own mental chatter; assumptions, unrealistic expectations, old wounds, false impressions, generalizations, automatic thoughts. Yogic literature and its grandchild Buddhism have addressed mental suffering, for thousands of years. Many of the practices are ancient predecessors for modern cognitive-behavioral, psychodynamic, and dialectical behavioral therapies; teaching us how to think clearly, act intentionally, release old wounds, and live mindfully.

The cognitive behavioral perspective attributes anger to misinterpretation of events, negative self-talk, lack of problem solving skills, and failure to consider consequences. Cognitive behavioral therapy (CBT) focuses on methods of self-control, thought restructuring, psycho-education, relaxation, and self-monitoring of arousal. Research indicates that CBT successfully decrease levels of aggression (Pica, Engel, & Welches, 2003).

The psychodynamic perspective frames anger as a defense mechanism against underlying feelings of shame, fear, inferiority, perceived abandonment, hurt, envy, depression, guilt, and self-loathing (Shelder, 2012). Dialectical behavioral therapy frames anger as emotional reactivity, and uses mindfulness and acceptance to teach distress tolerance, emotional regulation, and interpersonal effectiveness skills (Linehan, 1993).

Yogic practices, echoed in all of these therapies, transform our mental agitation (vritti), emotional wounds (samskaras), and false identifications (gunas) through practical, healthy behaviors and the belief in our inherent goodness to end mental suffering, and bring acceptance and calm.

About Yoga

> [Yoga] is the true union of our will with the will of God.
>
> B. K. S. Iyengar

What is yoga? That depends on whom you ask. Most Westerners associate yoga with a series of body postures, a healthful exercise. The Sanskrit word "yoga" is often translated as "union," or "to yoke oneself to God" (Iyengar, 1966). It is understandable why some may feel a wide gulf between understanding yoga-as-exercise and yoga as a spiritual path. This can be explained by the fact that there are so many forms and practices in the vast yogic literature. In *The Bhagavad Gita,* for example, the possible forms of practice include *Karma-Yoga* , the path of action, *Jnana Yoga*, the path of knowledge, *Bhakti-Yoga*, the path of devotion and *Dhyana Yoga*, the path of silent meditation (Bryant, 2009). In the

Gita, Sri Krishna encourages us to find the path that we are most capable of performing, and doing it to the best of our ability.

Yogic philosophy and practices have been evolving since at least 3000 BCE, which also accounts for its rich complexity and diversity. In simplistic terms, two main goals of yoga are to know oneself (Dharma) and to know God (Cit, a Sanskrit word for Truth). From this understanding, the seeker aspires to his/her highest potential and to align in Truth; this process is known as yoga.

Patanjali's Yoga Sutra outlines practical steps towards this optimal alignment. The text is a discourse of the "eight limbs" of yogic practice: the yamas (ethical restraints), niyamas (ethical observances, virtues), asanas (body postures), pranayama (conscious breathing), pratyahara (withdrawal of senses), dharana (concentration), dhyana (meditative contemplation), and samadhi (spiritual oneness). The Yoga Sutra is useful in many contexts, including therapy in secular settings because of its instructional quality. It should be noted that Patanjali, of the classical school of yoga, subscribed to a dualism between spirit (purusha) and the material world (prakrti) including one's body, mind, and emotions. Ironically, this sets up a conflict for ongoing suffering, emphasizing subjugation of human nature. Other schools of yoga, including Tantric philosophy, embrace a holistic understanding of purusha and prakriti as a compassionate path for all seekers.

What the ancient yogis understood is that the practices of yoga have the power to still the mind, to ease internal suffering, and to calm our nervous system. Science is catching up, validating the power of meditation, breathing techniques, postural alignment, and even the positive effects of contemplating yogic principles.

Setting Personal Intention

> For those who lack resolution,
> the decisions of life are many-branched and endless.
>
> *Bhagavad Gita* 2.41

Most of the people in my anger management programs have been mandated to attend; they typically present with crossed arms, slumped postures, and angry expressions. When asked why they have come, they report external reasons: "My probation officer made me come." "My wife moved out until I can control my anger." "I'll lose my job." "Child Protective Services won't let me see have my kids until I complete this class."

It is essential for individuals to "buy in" to a desire for change (Miller & Rollnick, 1991) so I always start group with setting personal intentions. After their initial response, I have people close their eyes, take a few breaths, and I ask them again, "Why did you choose to come? What's happening inside of you that brought you here today?" In those moments, they are having their first experience with yoga; aligning with their Dharma, with their purpose. Why am I here? What do I want for myself? The softening is apparent in people's second answers, "I'm tired of always feeling so angry." "I just want to enjoy my family." "I need to keep my job, I can't take another failure." "I swore I would never treat my kids the way I was treated. I want better for them."

Their pain is so apparent. They are suffering and feel hopeless about their ability to change. Connecting with their personal resolve keeps them coming back, and will support them in the difficult change process ahead.

Pratyahara—Withdrawing the Senses

> Encouraging the senses to draw inward is pratyahara.
> Glimpsing the inner light, the senses contentedly dwell within.
>
> Devi, 2007; *Yoga Sutra* 2.54–55

The foundational skill for anger management therapy is awareness. It is crucial for a person to be able to self-monitor, to notice when he/she is stressed out or escalating in anger before "blowing." However, most people are unskilled at this self-awareness:

> I don't know what happened. I was fine one minute and exploding the next.
> I go from zero to ten with no warning!

Chances are there is plenty of warning; listening may be the issue here. Pratyahara is the yogic practice of withdrawing the sense from the outside world and directing attention inwards. I ask this of my anger management clients with full appreciation that I am asking them to enter a terrifying war zone inside. It takes courage to stop and notice how you are doing and it takes utter faith to journey with those starting on this path. It's important to alert people that the process of pratyahara will not be comfortable at first; it's not uncommon for people to become more uncomfortable or angry as they begin this practice. It's important to teach this skill in small doses, along with other relaxation skills of pranayama and asana.

There are endless ways to practice pratyahara, but it is essential to provide guidance for the beginner or those experiencing intense emotions. "Centering" is a very accessible pratyahara meditation developed by Michael Lee's Phoenix Rising Yoga Therapy (1997). In this exercise, the facilitator guides the receiver(s) to notice breath, body sensations, thoughts, and feelings. Centering teaches angry clients how to safely unwrap the question, "How am I doing right now?"

To begin pratyahara, I ask people to either close their eyes or gaze softly at the floor. This can be challenging for many people with anger problems who are hypervigilant due to trauma or trust issues. Therefore, it is important to explain the why this inward attention is important and I role model a relaxed, soft gaze at the floor.

"Notice your breath." Breath awareness is often a revelation for many people. Because most of my clients are breath awareness beginners, I usually provide detailed instruction, directing them to notice the various qualities of breath: depth, pace, movement, etc.

"Notice your physical body." Many of the people I work with have some of the most severe reasons to disconnect from their body: everything from chronic pain, disability, traumatic memories, and intense somatic symptoms related to their mental illness (e.g., anxiety, panic, and agitation). As I invite people to notice their body, I make sure to include both negative and positive possibilities. "Notice tension, notice any parts that feel relaxed. Notice agitation, notice calm. Notice pain or illness, notice parts that feel healthy and well."

"Notice your thoughts." Many people with anger problems suffer with racing, intrusive, anxious, negative ruminations and self-destructive thought patterns and they believe they are "stuck" like that. "Just noticing" thoughts introduces the concept of witness consciousness; that you can have thoughts without being your thoughts. This is a very powerful understanding.

"Notice your feelings." Asking a client to actually feel their feelings can seem counterintuitive and frightening to them. They want to stop feeling depression, anxiety, panic, and anger. Again, using a steady voice, I invite them to a place of acceptance for their experience of emotions. I encourage them to notice their feelings without making any judgments about them. "Practice the skill of noticing your emotions without needing to fix or change them." Here, they learn that emotions do not require action.

"With all that you've noticed, give yourself a number between 1 and 10, one is absolutely calm, ten is totally out of control." Instructing clients how to use a simple self-rating scale gives them a tool to measure and talk about how they are doing moment to moment. Following pratyahara, members are invited to "check in" with the group, which provides valuable witnessing, validation, and compassion.

> I thought I was a 2, but, now I notice I'm really upset about what my partner said last night. I'm really angry about it, I feel like I'm actually a 7, which explains why I yelled at my kids this morning.
>
> I'm so used to being mad and in pain all the time, that I just walk around in a bad mood cause my life sucks. But, when I did the check in, I realized that my back isn't really hurting today. And, it's sunny out. I had a nice talk with someone in the lobby. I'm actually in a better mood than I thought.
>
> I kept thinking and thinking about that fight and I couldn't stop thinking about it. I'm so angry that I can't even feel my body. But, at least I know I have a body that I can't feel.

Individuals in my anger management groups report that "The Pause Button" is the single most important skill they develop during the course of treatment. Teaching an individual to stop-and-notice helps them to feel in control of themselves, rather than a reactive victim of circumstance. Sometimes, pratyahara alone is enough to radically change problematic behavioral patterns.

Pranayama—Breath Control

> As the movement patterns of each breath – inhalation, exhalation, lull – are observed as to duration, number, and area of focus,
> breath becomes spacious and subtle . . .
> And the mind is now fit for concentration.
>
> Hartranft, *Yoga Sutra* 2.50, 51

Yogis have long recognized that attention to breath stills the mind. Now, science explains that slow, rhythmic breathing stimulates the vagus nerve, and activates relaxation response (Uyterhoeven, 2006). By intentionally creating slow, deep, steady breathing, we are signaling the autonomic nervous system that "everything is okay."

Teaching clients first to notice their breath and then control it is an essential tool to anger and stress management. There are virtually no barriers to practicing pranayama; the breath is with us wherever we go, it's free, and there are few physical or intellectual limitations.

The numerous pranayama practices can be quite technical, and are beyond the scope of this chapter. With beginning students, simple is better. Here are four pranayamas that I use most often for anger management.

Falling Out Breath

This is a beloved Phoenix Rising Yoga Therapy breath that is just as it sounds (Lee, 1997; 2005). Take a deep breath in, and let it fall out of your mouth with a big "haaah" sound. The "haaah" is important as it encourages an open throat and soft jaw; both areas that tend to constrict when angry or tense. It's the most "portable" pranayama; simple and easy to use at any given moment. The effect of simply giving a moment of awareness, as well as an extra dose of oxygen, can immediately de-escalate emotions.

Heavy Bucket Swings

One complaint many people have is when they are angry and agitated, the last thing they can do is "sit down and do a stupid breathing exercise!" I couldn't agree more. It's important to have a breathing skill in the toolbox that helps ride the wave of adrenaline.

Heavy Bucket Swings is another Phoenix Rising Yoga Therapy invention perfectly suited for someone in the heat of anger. From a standing position, reach forward and pick up two imaginary buckets, one in each hand. Inhale deeply, lift the buckets high above your head, hold momentarily, then swing your arms down and behind you, bending your knees and exhaling with a loud "haaah" sound. Repeat by standing, inhaling your arms up overhead again. Hold. Exhale with a loud "haaah" while swinging your arms back and down. Repeat as many times necessary to "ride out" the intensity. As you are moving, you may even imagine what is IN your heavy buckets and if, at some point, you'd like to put them down. When you are ready, simply end and exhale, letting go of the buckets and fold forward with your arms dangling loosely (Lee, 2006).

Sama-vritti

This classic pranayama means "equal movement" (Iyengar, 1966). In this practice, one simply brings attention to the breath, attempting to make the inhale and exhale equal. For example, "breathe in for three counts, breathe out for three counts." If desired, a pause or "hold" of equal length can be inserted between the inhale and exhale. This simple technique is easy to remember, can be performed subtly in any circumstance, and brings steadiness to the mind and breath. Consequently, this may successfully distract from angry thoughts, if caught early enough. It is also ideal for regular stress management practice.

Full Yogic Breathing

This practice is best performed in a reclined position, and is suitable as a prophylactic stress management technique, or as a way to regain equilibrium following a rage. Lie supine on the floor or bed with a cushion or folded blankets supporting the torso, arms open out to each side. This position facilitates opening and airflow through the belly, chest, and throat. Be sure to be comfortable and warm: an additional head prop, eye pillow, or blanket may be desired. Close your eyes, breathe fully, and deeply. No specific breath instruction is needed, though sama-vritti may also be employed. Relax and allow the fullness of breath for an extended period, 10–15 minutes.

When I teach simple breathing exercises to people with anger management problems, they are usually skeptical at first. Therefore, it is important to practice them in session, rather than simply prescribe it as homework. They notice the results immediately:

> Wow, I never pay attention to my breathing. I can't believe how much better I feel.
>
> I didn't realize how tense my neck and throat are.
>
> Making that "hah" sound actually loosens me up, I feel less tense everywhere.
>
> I feel like I just tricked myself into feeling calm!

It's important to remind people that if they notice any discomfort at all during pranayama, to return to their normal breathing until they feel ready to continue. It is important for pranayama to be easeful, otherwise, the stress response will inadvertently become triggered and all gains will be lost.

Asana—Postural Techniques

> The postures of meditation should embody steadiness and ease.
> This occurs as all effort relaxes and coalescence arises, revealing that the body and the infinite universe are indivisible.
>
> Hartranft, *Yoga Sutra* 2.46–47

Traditionally, "asana" refers to a "seat" or cushion, and this sutra refers to a posture that supports prolonged meditation. Hatha Yoga positions as we know them today were not developed until hundreds of years after Patanjali's *Yoga Sutra* (Hartranft, 2003). While it is beyond the scope of this chapter to teach specific postures, I will suggest some classes of poses that can be useful in managing anger. Seeking a qualified Hatha Yoga teacher is highly recommended for beginners who want to practice asana.

Working with the physical body is extremely useful with anger, a way to match the intensity and safely ride its wave. Four classes of poses can be useful for anger management, either as a person is noticing escalation, or as part of a stress management regime.

Standing Poses

These poses require a degree of physical strength and mental focus. Postures such as warrior, extended side angle, triangle, and chair pose (*utkatasana*) can help exert extra energy, direct concentration and create a sense of empowerment and control.

Forward Folds

Postures that fold the front side of the body are extremely soothing, as they activate the parasympathetic nervous system. Poses like standing forward bend, seated forward bend, and child's pose. They create a sense of inward focus and safety. They can easily be combined with pranayama to increase their relaxation effect.

Inversions

An inversion is any posture where the heart is higher than the head. Shoulder stand is the inversion most commonly recommended for anger management. However, this posture should not be attempted by beginners without a teacher. If shoulder stand is not accessible, bridge pose or a modified shoulder stand using props can accomplish similar benefits.

Restorative Yoga

Restorative yoga is a fully developed style of yoga focused on relaxation, and is an essential practice for stress and anger management (Lasater, 1995).

Restorative poses are characterized by supported postures and extended periods of stillness. Finding a restorative yoga teacher, book, or DVD is highly recommended for anyone seeking ongoing stress or anger management techniques.

Yamas and Niyamas: Ethical Abstentions and Observances of Yoga

> The five external disciplines are not harming, truthfulness, not stealing, celibacy and not being acquisitive.
> The five internal disciplines are bodily purification, contentment, intense discipline, self-study and dedication to the ideal of yoga.
>
> *Yoga Sutra* 2.30 and 32

The *Yoga Sutra* outlines ten ethical teachings, known as the yamas and niyamas. The practices support cognitive-behavioral interventions, framed as healthful and sensible behaviors. These ethical guideposts make natural themes for group discussion and individual contemplation. Here is a brief overview of these principles and how they can benefit anger management:

Ahimsa: nonviolence or non-harming. This yama asks us to avoid harming others, and ourselves, including physical, psychological, emotional, or spiritual harm. By implication, it also expects that we are gentle and compassionate. A commitment to ahimsa is an important starting point for those with anger management problems.

Satya: to abstain from falsehood. This means to be truthful in thought, word and deed, to think, speak and act authentically. It's necessary for those with anger management issues to be honest about how their behaviors have impacted themselves and others. Striving for satya can also inspire people to align with their true Dharma, rather than acting out the old, angry roles that no longer "fit."

Asteya: non-stealing. Asteya refers not only to stealing property but also to coveting what is not ours. This may include resentment over another person's success, relationship, or some quality they have. Asteya is also about releasing jealousy and appreciating what you have.

Bramacharya: control or restraint, and was traditionally linked to celibacy. Bramacharya is useful in anger management as this yama calls for moderation in all aspects of life, including emotional reactivity.

Aparigraha: to avoid greed and cultivate non-attachment. Anger is often rooted in false expectations or attachment to specific outcomes. Helping people to assess the validity of their expectations and attachments often helps avoid unnecessary suffering.

Saucha, the first niyama, is purity. Saucha impacts many levels of existence, from cleanliness of body, purity of thoughts and order with one's home and possessions. Saucha asks us to maintain a healthy lifestyle, including regular sleep, nourishing food, exercise, and other forms of body purification. For those with anger and stress management problems, the practicality of saucha cannot be underestimated. Many people I work with have insomnia, poor diets, and get little or no exercise, which only increases their irritability, stress, and emotional dysregulation. Learning the importance of saucha, and how it impacts stress and anger, helps people feel empowered to take specific action step towards their overall wellbeing.

Santosha: contentment. People with anger and stress management problems often have habitually negative thought patterns. Teaching people to focus on what is good, beautiful, delicious, and serene changes the focus in a crucial way. It also challenges the false notion that happiness needs to be over-the-top-ecstatic. Contentment happens in simple, quiet moments that we might otherwise overlook.

Tapas: austerity and fiery devotion. Anger is a form of tapas. Individuals often need help finding a constructive direction for that energy. Tapas can be channeled towards a commitment to therapy, poured into their practices, or mobilized towards a social cause that may speak to the root of their personal pain, for example, directing tapas towards the end of bullying, domestic violence or childhood sexual abuse.

Pratyahara: self-study. Anger management clients have already engaged in a form of pratyahara through self-reflection and therapy. It's validating for them to find that they are also engaged in an ancient spiritual practice, and to know that throughout the ages, people have endeavored towards self-improvement.

Ishvara pranidhana: dedicating oneself to a higher power. When you ask, most people identify some force outside of themselves as a higher power. Helping people to identify and connect with that "something greater" helps to contextualize their struggles, and gives meaning to their efforts. People with anger problems often feel alone, and forsaken. Reminding them of their Spirit is a crucial point of hope and healing.

Dharana and Dhyana—Concentration and Meditation

> Closing their eyes, steadying their breathing, and focusing their attention on the center of spiritual consciousness, the wise master their senses, mind, and intellect through meditation. Self-realization is their only goal. Freed from selfish desire, fear and anger, they live in freedom always.
>
> *The Bhagavad Gita* 5.27–29

The advanced practices of dharana and dhyana meditation help to deepen an individual practice. Dharana is "single-pointed concentration" on a focal point. Common focal points are pranayama, asana, a mantra, a candle, flower, a meaningful image or icon, or a positive intention. Dhyana is a meditation of "free play" contemplation with the hope of arriving at samadhi, absorption in spiritual oneness.

Research is mounting on the positive effects of meditation practice. Scientists are finding that regular meditation can actually change the structure of the brain, and form new neuro-pathways, making positive thoughts and behaviors more habitual the longer they are practiced (Cobb, 2008; Uyterhoeven, 2006).

Samadhi: Spiritual Oneness

> When individual consciousness unites with the Divine Consciousness,
> the illusion of separateness dissolves; this is Samadhi.
>
> Devi, 2007; *Yoga Sutra* 3.3

No one has ever come to my anger management group asking for "spiritual oneness." However, people with problematic anger are sorely disenfranchised; they feel judged, rejected, and alone. Not only do they feel shunned from others, but also they experience an inner abandonment. They live with deep shame about their reactive behaviors or thoughts; they've given up on themselves.

> I've pushed everyone away with my anger. I'm totally alone now.
>
> My wife won't let me see the kids until I get help, but, I don't even deserve my family.
>
> I hate myself for being this way. I'm a monster!

Once a person has given up on him or herself, he/she tends to give up on others too. Yet social instinct drives many towards the strange companionship of reciprocal hurt. Feeling stuck in an "angry role" may be the only way he or she knows how to relate.

> The only time anyone listens to me is when I'm screaming like a lunatic.
>
> At least she looked at me when I punched the wall out. That got her attention.
>
> I don't care if I'm mean. At least people will know how I feel.

The "illusion of separateness" must be addressed for any change to be possible. No amount of therapy or yogic practices can help if a person's "heart" is in despair. People need to feel that they are inherently good and worthy of belonging. They need permission to forgive themselves and encouragement to outgrow their angry patterns. Angry people long to be loved.

Yoga teaches that we are, and always have been, united in Divine Love. The rich yogic teachings on universal love, as in the *Narada Bhakti Sutra*, support the kind of compassion needed for inner and outer healing:

> To turn toward Love – to return to Love – is to open our hearts to its presence within us and within others, and then to live our lives in steadier alignment with it. The turn toward Love thus implies a movement of sorts, a transformation of our existence. (Mahony, 2010)

This kind of Bhakti Yoga must be offered and felt, rather than taught and learned. A genuine facilitator may never name it "Love," but embody humanistic qualities such as congruence, humility, unconditional positive regard, openness, acceptance, hope, humor and encouragement (Rogers, 1961). Group members are encouraged to offer each other witnessing, validation, acceptance, honesty, and compassion. This may truly be their first experience of community, of connection, of Love.

A group member once said, "I've been in a lot of anger management groups, but, it never worked for me before. There's something different about this class." That "something" is the felt sense of being cared for. Bhakti opens the door to much-needed self-acceptance and the possibility of softening to the world. With courage, individuals can love the helpless dragon within and take their rightful place in the fabric of humanity.

Questions for the Reader

1. Take a few moments to practice pratyahara; tune in to your own breath, body, thoughts, and feelings. What do you become aware of that you didn't notice before you hit the "pause button"?
2. How do you feel about yourself when you lose your temper? What judgments do you have about others with angry behaviors?
3. How can yoga help you to be more compassionate to yourself and others? How can your yoga practice help you be more effective with your emotional needs?

References

Bryant, E. (2009). *The Yoga Sutras of Patanjali, a new edition, translation, and commentary*. New York: North Point Press.

Cobb, E. (2008). *The forgotten body: A way of knowing and understanding self.* Hartwick: Satya House.

Devi, N. J. (2007). *The secret power of yoga: A woman's guide to the heart and spirit of the Yoga Sutras.* New York: Three Rivers Press.

Easwaran, E. (2007). *The Bhagavad Gita.* Introduced and translated by Eknath Easwaran. Tomalas: Nilgiri Press.

Eisenberger, N.I., & M.D. Lieberman. (2004). Why rejection hurts: A common neural alarm system for physical and social pain. *Trends in Cognitive Science*, 8, 294–300.

Granath, J., Ingvarsson, S., von Thiele, U., & Lundberg, U. (2006). Stress management: A randomized study of cognitive behavioural therapy and yoga. *Cognitive Behaviour Therapy*, 35(1), 3–10.

Hanson, R., & Mendius, R. (2009). *Buddha's brain, the practical neuroscience of happiness, love & wisdom.* Oakland: New Harbinger Publications, Inc.

Hartranft, C. (2003). *The Yoga-Sutra of Patanjali: A new translation with commentary*. Boston: Shambhala Classics.

Iyengar, B. K. S. (1966). *Light on yoga*. New York: Schocken Books.

Lasater, J. H. (1995). *Relax and renew: Restful yoga for stressful times*. Berkeley: Rodmell Press.

Lee, M. (1997). *Phoenix Rising Yoga Therapy: A bridge from body to soul*. Deerfield Beach: Health Communications, Inc.

Lee, M. (2005). *Turn stress to bliss: The proven 8-week program for health, relaxation and stress relief*. Gloucester: Fair Winds.

Levin, S. (1989). *A gradual awakening*. New York: Anchor Books.

Licinio, J., Gold, P. W., & Wong, M. L. (1995). A molecular mechanism for stress-induced alterations in susceptibility to disease. *Lancet*, 346, 104–106.

Linehan, M. M. (1993). *Skills training manual for treatment of borderline personality disorder*. New York: Guilford Press.

Mahony, W. (2010). *Exquisite love: Heart-centered reflections on the Narada Bhakti Sutra*. The Woodlands, TX: Anusara Press.

Miller, W., & Rollnick, S. (1991). *Motivational interviewing: Preparing people to change addictive behavior*. New York: Guilford Press.

Pica, M., Engel, S., & Welches, P. (2003). An experiential approach to the inpatient anger management group. *International Journal of Group Psychotherapy*, 53(2), 177–200.

Rogers, C. (1961). *On becoming a person: A therapist view of psychotherapy*. New York: Houghton Mifflin Company.

Shearer, A. (1982). *The Yoga Sutras of Patanjali, translated and introduced by Alistair Shearer*. New York: Bell Tower.

Shelder, J. (2012). The efficacy of psychodynamic psychotherapy. *American Psychologist*, 65(2), 98–109.

Simpkins, A. M., & Simpkins, C. A. (2011). *Meditation and yoga in psychotherapy: Techniques for clinical practice*. Hobokin: John Wiley & Sons, Inc.

Uyterhoeven, S. (2006). Yoga and the autonomic nervous system: Re-educating the mind. *Yoga Therapy in Practice*, August, 23–25.

Wenner, M. (2008). The dangers of stress; getting stressed isn't just a state of mind. It can also harm the body. August 15. *Scientific American*, 24. Retrieved January 20, 2013, from www.scientificamerican.com/article.cfm?id=stress-dangers.

15 Music of Yoga/Yoga of Music

François Raoult

Music is therapy. Music moves people.
It connects people in ways that no other medium can.
It pulls heartstrings. It acts as medicine.

Mackelmore

Figure 15.1

Prelude

When we separate music from life we get art.

John Cage

Is music therapy to music what yoga therapy is to yoga? Perhaps. But in this case, all music is therapeutic. In fact everything is potential therapy—a moment, an event, a meeting— if there is consciousness. And "everything is music," as the mystic poet Rumi wrote. Yoga is music and music is yoga in so many ways: the practice of an art, the deepening of perception, the emotional layers unfolding. The blueprint of a yoga practice or a yoga class, from a student or teacher point of view, is like a raga, (e.g., a melodic mode used in Indian classical music). First there is the *alap*, a gradual opening (warm-up, or to understand more fully, a creating of space previews) then a rhythmical aspect (*tala*) and a climax—even a trance—before a resolution toward silence (back to the drone, all sounds merging into one, all asanas merging back in savasana, deep relaxation). Sure, we can apply specific practices to specific needs but the music itself is a specialization. What is therapeutic is to reconnect with the original nature of *Sound*, of which what we call music is a *small part*. We are made of sound, vibration, frequencies, so it is deep ecology to recognize ourselves in a sonic vibratory universe. Music is omnipresent in society, that is one thing that has not changed since time immemorial, from the early shamanic chant of South Africa to The Beatles, symphonic concert halls, church music, military bands, and airport background muzak. Both music and yoga help us reconnect with the pleasure of being alive and avoid anhedonia. It is all about peace of mind and clear perception. This is why breath practice, pranayama, is a form of deep listening. Actually, the sound of the breath itself may be the original mantra.

We know that stress creates all kind of pathologies and disturbances in the form of somatization. These pathologies are a direct consequence of stress overdose on the sympathetic nervous system. It is possible (but more difficult and we cannot always guarantee) that the relaxation response, meditation, deep listening, restorative yoga, meditation on music, or silence could reverse them. It requires consciousness, clarity of mind, and consistent practice to succeed, and all these require discipline and a positive attitude. The vicious circle is that stress can cloud the mind and make it difficult to access that state of being. Therefore, we have teachings (traditional and innovative), guides and practice suggestions, hoping these will heal the wounds and build mental and physical health.

> All that is visible, clings to the invisible, the audible to the inaudible, the tangible to the intangible: Perhaps the thinkable to the unthinkable.
>
> Novalis

Nada Yoga

On one of my first journeys to India and Nepal, I visited an old antique shop in Bhagdaon in the Katmandu valley and searched for a singing bowl. I didn't know much about resonance or overtones, but the object itself fascinated me, made of shiny golden metals. So I brought one back to France and it took the dust for years. I could have served peanuts in it, or appetizers. Then I started to study Tibetan music and began to investigate harmonic chanting. I also listened to bells of all kinds and searched for overtones in contemporary music from Bartok (Mikrokosmos) and Stockhausen (Stimmung) to free jazz like Sun Ra. I would not call it easy listening. All sounds are in one sound. This is why Indian musicians tune their instrument from the drone of the radiating, shiny harmonics of the tanpura, (a long-necked, instrument originating from Central Asia (Mesopotamia and Persia/Iran).

Then the bowl started to have a life on its own. I heard how the sounds travel through space in multiple layers. I touched it, rubbed it with various clappers and sticks to get the best resonance. In savasana, deep relaxation, I was beginning to have deeper experiences of the prana, the flow of energy moving, what we call in yoga the vayus, the winds of the breath. And I began to explore the space I was projected into after the resonance of the bowl vanished into silence. It felt like being suspended in time or in bahia kumbakha, the silent state following the exhalation, which Patanjali, the great Indian philosopher, refers to in the Yoga Sutras chapter 1, 34.

Mystical texts from a traditional Indian point of view say silence is essential; all sounds come from silence and they return to silence. Anahatanada (unmanifested sound) is associated with Brahma, universal soul. Ahatanada (manifested sound)—which could be speech, any kind of music made with instruments, or singing—has a tangible existence with which we can play. And the overtones would be a bridge between the not manifested and manifested. It is possible to hear them but most people don't. Watching the film Genghis Blues, a documentary about a blues singer traveling to Mongolia for a throat-singing contest, would be a good introduction. I have the pleasure to recognize overtones/harmonics in every sound, soundscape, or when any groups of yoga students chant the mantra OM. Overtones are a bridge between the not manifested and manifested world, but most people don't know what to listen for. By analogy, look at wine or olive oil tasting; overtones would be the subtle qualities behind the gross level first impression. It is truly esoteric.

In ancient texts related to yoga of sound (Nada Yoga), it is suggested to practice listening to inner sounds and to meditate on sound or music between midnight and 2 in the morning. A little while ago I had a dream in which I was swimming in an ocean with giant waves and big rocks, and gradually swam to the shore, seeing teepees and fires in the distance. A shamanic dream, perhaps. It woke me up and here I was at 2 in the morning, writing about sound, the sound of silence, not the beautiful song by Simon and Garfunkel, but the presence of silence, the vibration of the universe.

Nada Yoga, or any yoga, gives you the opportunity to dive into sound, as you can dive into the essence of matter. These journeys are reflected in the great paintings of Max Ernst, Jackson Pollock, and in great compositions of all times. If you were playing a piece called *Soundscape of the World* or composing it, it would be the same. You would just have to meditate and listen; the music would unfold itself as it goes, as a giant complex global multilayered symphony, moment to moment.

In fact, as Alain Daniélou (1991) writes in *The Myths and Gods of India*, a classic work on Hindu polytheism, "Ancient grammarians and theoreticians of the Sanskrit language considered the separation of spoken language, gestural language and music as a late phenomenon and never completely realized." Nada Yoga listens to life as music and music as a reflection of life. Everything is music, from the audible to the inaudible.

Let's look at how yoga and music interpenetrate each other. There is yoga of music and sacred sound. It is a Path in India. Classical musicians are considered yogis; in fact, they usually look down at Hatha Yoga as a gross form of practice. There is also a music of yoga, with its complex and beautiful harmonies, resonances of the body as an instrument playing asana and pranayama, heartbeat, breath cycles, pranic flow, vibration of life, rhythms, and all music related at a primal level. But is there also music for yoga, like there is music for airports, music for aerobics, music for dance (Cervine, 2013)? Is it an obstacle to concentration or an opportunity to go deeper within? Let's see (hear) if we can widen our field of possibilities and rehabilitate Western classical music as well as ethnic music of other cultures. In this way, perhaps we can avoid becoming ethnocentric all over again and over-focusing on Western Kirtan songs when there is so much else to explore. Sound is sound; it is non-denominational in its essential nature!

What I teach often in meditation while sitting at the beginning of a session or lying down at the end of class is to listen deeply to whatever there is to be listened to. This could be internal sound, whatever is in the room (light frequencies, the heater, or the cracking of the wood, etc.), the sounds of other people, the sounds of the city, the sounds of nature, near and far, subtle and not so subtle, a global listening, the live soundtrack of life's movie. Just receive and absorb, making the whole body a microphone. This is a powerful experience. I've done it in all kinds of different places, way lost in the jungle, in the middle of the city, in the crowd, by myself. With no pre-existing labeling agenda, listen with the innocence and wonder of a child seeing the ocean for the first time. As you read these words, take a moment to just listen to everything around you and within you, just the sound vibrations, as if you didn't know what they were, no words, no labels, no categories, just sound for the sake of it, as if it was the first time you ever heard them.

I have for decades investigated so-called meditation music, sacred music of all periods and cultures: "prehistoric" music, free jazz, acoustic and electro-acoustic, "world" music, new and old age music, classical Indian, contemporary, Gregorian chant, and, best for me, "unclassifiable." In every category I have found a soundscape that is able to create a yogic state of mind, maybe even a glimpse of samadhi.

Practice Guidelines. A Musical Map: Posture for Music Meditation

Your posture has to be comfortable and suitable for long timing, from ten to forty-five minutes. Make sure you're warm enough. Cover yourself with blankets if needed.

Sitting meditation poses: Ensure the knees are lower than the hip joints and the natural spinal curves are respected. So, sukhasana, siddhasana, virasana, ardha padmasana, padmasana, sitting on a chair all are suitable. If the posture is held effortlessly, the posture will hold you.

Supine positions: All variations of lying down poses suitable for savasana, with the chest and head supported, or calf muscles on the chair, are suitable for music meditation, even supta baddha konasana with a bolster.

Inverted poses like sarvangasana, supported halasana, and sirsasana are suitable, if they are functional and effortless. As a musicology and yoga student, I used to listen to Mahler and Bruckner symphonies in head balance and shoulder stand (a multi-tasking, pitta-induced idea). In those days, we had to turn the LP every twenty-five minutes or so; it was a perfect inversion and Nada Yoga practice combined!

Music Meditation Practice

> If you give it good concentration, good energy,
> good heart and good performance the song will play you.
>
> Levon Helm

Listen with eyes closed. If lying down, cover them with an eyebag or some cloth. Eyes, being the windows of the brain, have to be completely soft, receptive, introverted, relaxed, as must all sensory organs, including the skin, so that the whole body can become a giant listening ear. Volume should be at moderate but intense enough so frequencies can reach your fluid body. If you find one piece you like in particular, listen to it on loop. If you have a computer, click on controls, then on repeat, and on one! Quite a mystical agenda! Enjoy the ride, let yourself go. In an article on savasana by B. K. S. Iyengar in an ancient *Yoga Journal* magazine, he ended with: "You have to lose yourself to find yourself." A challenge, sure, but one with a payoff!

Listen first to slow movements, adagios and/or music that have loops/ repetitive music, because it will be closer to your biologic rhythms; the heart-beat, the breath, walking, and will create a sense of timelessness. In traditional therapies, music is a way to reach a trancelike state towards liberation. And the concept of time in those traditional cultures is more like a snake biting its tail or an endless screw; a divided line with a beginning and an end. Any music that waves, cycles, loops, or breathes within the breath will be more likely to induce a state of trance or absorption. Any drone-based, and therefore modal-like, music will also play better through you, just as life is also repetitive but never the same from moment to moment. If the drone can be seen as the ground, the ocean, the river, the melody would be the flight of the musician. If the music has substance, it will create a pranic awakening. If the music (a song, or anything from Ave Maria to OM) touches and moves you, then the upper chakras will be highlighted. This is especially true of the fontanel or a bit above it. You may feel a kind of buzzing, something like pins and needles in the fascia and skin; this means the sounds have resonated deep into your whole being. Whether it's a slow piece or a fast piece, no matter what you do with your breath, you are going to feel like it is somewhat in sync with the musical sentences, the flow of the music. This works particularly well with Mozart; if you practice deep, slow yogic breathing, you are always in sync with the melodic or harmonic wave patterns. You are part of the same play. Some small bits of melodies may just make you cry and your whole being may be swept by deep waves of music.

Music Selection: Contemporary, Repetitive, Minimalist

> Already very early I thought of a microphone
> as a musical instrument, like a bow
> or like a percussion instrument, whatever you use.
>
> Karlheinz Stockhausen

Contemporary

We cannot avoid Philip Glass, like it or not, because he practices meditation and his music is very open-ended, with a concept of time not unlike ritual Tibetan music. Even though he has been prolific, it's not always interesting. There are two CDs I recommend by Glass. One is *Glassworks,* featuring a piece called *Facades.* Then there is the music he wrote for the silent movie *Koyaanisqatsi,* based on a Hopi revelation text. This work includes a deep voice (bass) organized around a chaconne structure, a type of musical composition used for variations on a short, repeated bass-line. The piece is powerful, abyssal and works well with savasana. As far as Steve Reich, who is part of the same group of so-called minimalist composers, I recommend *Music for Mallet Instruments,* which is very hypnotic. I also recommend *A Rainbow in Curved Air* by Terry Riley; it's nice for an early-morning rise, if you can transcend the outdated synthesizers. And there is the mythical string trio from the composer La Monte Young.

Ethnic/folk

> Once we are inside a tune, we can do anything with it.
>
> Keith Jarrett

I am a big fan of Armenian music. There's an instrument called the duduk, an ancestor of the oboe, a double reed, and it's heartbreaking. The main duduk player is Jivan Gasparyan. The CD I enjoy the most is *I Will Not Be Sad in this World.* Some of his students, like Levon Minassian, are also mind-blowing and can take you into deep otherworldly space.

Try early polyphonies and water drumming of the Aka and Baka Pygmies; South African tribal music from the Xhosa women; Amazonian Indian, etc. It's a rich field of exploration resonating in the collective unconscious layers.

Classical Western Music

> The music is not in the notes, but in the silence between.
>
> Wolfgang Amadeus Mozart

In the classical department, there are several concerti that work well, though of course I refer to the slow movements. Listen to Baroque composers such as

Marcello, Albinoni, Locatelli, and Vivaldi. You will find gems. Making a big jump in time, Ravel's *Piano Concerto in G* is a beautiful, extremely meditative piece.

Back to Mozart. His music can be a little bit too nice and peppy sometimes, so you have to search for pieces more on the spiritual, introverted side of the spectrum. His compositions for glass harmonica are ethereal, rich in overtones, and quite wonderful. They are played on wet glasses that are turning, creating a singing bowl kind of sound. On the concerti side, best are the Piano Concerto No. 23 (Keith Jarrett recorded it and did a wonderful improvisation in the final cadenza) and, of course, his pieces for the clarinet, flute, and harp, etc. Check out the Adagio from Mozart's Symphony No. 40, the Adagio from the Gran Partita (conducted by Pierre Boulez), and the dark Masonic music he wrote for his friend's funeral. Mitsuko Uchida has recorded all the Mozart sonatas. As a yogini, she masters the art of silence and has laser-beam precision, reminding me of my teacher B. K. S. Iyengar, who likewise possesses sharpness, precision, and so much spirit and presence.

Then you have Arvo Pärt, a Christian mystic. His music sounds like it is from the Middle Ages or Early Renaissance, but with a twist and some surprises. Actually, it was composed in the last twenty years. He retains the purity of the Cistercian Abbeys. I particularly enjoy *Alina –Spiegel im Spiegel* and *Lamentate.*

Classical Indian

> The interpretation of the raga is let the sound die when sculpting it until it dies. And it is believed, continues to sculpt the silence. Then the music becomes visible around the musician.
>
> Rene Daumal

On the Indian side of the spectrum, classical Indian music is, by its essence, meditative. It is a form of yoga, actually; the ragas are very long, several hours, though they cut them down usually when exported to the West to an hour or less. This takes place because Westerners, in general, have the Sesame Street attention span of little kids compared to the Indians! Pandit Jasraj, the best known classical singer in India, has recorded almost everything from ragas to bhajans to the Upanishad verses. These recordings will keep you content for several years.

I was blessed to hear Pandit Jasraj twice in concert. Once was in Pune, when B. K. S. Iyengar suggested we go on Sunday morning and Jasraj sang for five hours non-stop. Trance, deep emotion, meditation. A few years later I heard him sing in Rishikesh, where we were having a Pranayama intensive on the banks of the Ganges. He sang for us and our guru in the evening, ragas under the tent, reminiscent of our nomadic roots and literally common ground as Proto Indo-Europeans. The presence of the Ganges nearby and the transcendent voice of the singer after a day of intense Pranayama are still interwoven in my mind decades later.

Search for ragas for the surbahar (a bass sitar), the santur (ancestor of the cymbalum), the flute, the shennai, all great Indian instruments. I have a soft spot for the jalatarangam, an instrument resembling the glass harmonica, which uses small bowls filled with water played with little sticks.

Raga-like meditative improvisations on lute in Iran, Iraq, and North Africa create deep soundscapes and bring us close to the birth of music. There's a group called Ghazal, more on the Iranian side of the spectrum, which recorded Lost Songs of the Silk Road. These are extremely shamanic in feeling, very suitable for restorative practice and Nada Yoga.

Postlude

> Oh wisest ones!
> This body's a splendid tambura.
>
> Kabir

Great music, as is sound, vibrates through all cells, generates an emotional response. It can make you cry. I've had experiences like this in many sacred places, like the Temple of the Sea in Mahabalipuram or in small chapels like the one at the top of the Pic Saint Loup in the south of France. At moments like these you just cry out of nowhere, because it's so beautiful and you know it is tapping into a very deep, primal, preverbal, pre-religious, prehistoric layer of yourself. It's a cry of joy or ecstasy, generated by the overtones of your own voice, the quality of the silence, the sacred music and pipe organ of the cathedral, the accordion of the drunk beggar in the subway, the song of a little boy in the Rajastani desert singing the song of all gypsies. It's powerful because something is reaching deep into the nervous system and into the heart center, *anahata* again. Unstruck.

So finally here is a top 40-like list that I have selected from thousands of possibilities over the years. It could have been much longer and the choices are of course subjective. You may want to create your own version someday according to your sensitivity, with serendipity leading the way.

Having a list does not mean that I do not listen to other sources like Joan Baez, Neil Young, French singer-songwriters, The Beatles, or reggae. Good music is something that moves you and you are moved by. In every category of music there is a wide range of material: gems, good finds, less exciting pieces, and things not worth listening to. The following pieces would not do well in a nightclub, unless the definition of a nightclub is a yoga center in the dark with candles! Enjoy the ride!

More Practices for Sound Meditation and Ideas for the Reader

1. Chant Om with a drone (sruti box) or any other drone (block keys octave and fifth) on a basic synthesizer. Find a pitch matching with the drone, low pitch, middle range, and head voice. Play with the all the vowels of the OM.
2. Om alone! Chant long OMs by yourself as an emitter receptor.
3. Om vinyasa. Stay on each vowel, "A o oo m" and between "o" and "m" invite other vowels like "e" and "i" in your mind. The convergence will make overtones appear.
4. Bhramari pranayama, humming breath. Change volume of mouth cavity as you hum; it will sound like a mouth harp with harmonics.
5. Om from bhramari. Humming on exhalation, then open lips a little for a soft "o" then back to humming. So, the mantra is "MOM"!
6. Listen to all sound, global listening, far and close, inner and outer, the ongoing composition of the soundtrack of life! Listen to it as music written on purpose to be listened to by you with full attention, even though it has no purpose. That will bring into play various filters, sensory organ limitations, education, vrttis of all kinds, projections and judgments.
7. Reverse experience. Listen to what we call music as Sound, as if it was random or just sound happening in nature with no specific intention. Listen to the vibration of the sound mass, almost as if you were deaf—skin, bones, organs resonating.
8. Listen to Antonio Vivaldi's "Spring" concerto from *Four Seasons*, four versions. Listen to the version recomposed by modern composer Max Richter, then to interpretations by Nikolaus Harnoncourt, Yehudi Menuhin (a former famous student of Sri B. K. S. Iyengar!), and John Halloway, in that order if possible. The pulse, the tuning, and the interpretation, the aesthetics of each are different. Same piece, four commentaries. Which one has the most precision, the most authenticity, the most presence? Which one is the closest to the Source? Which one moves you the most? Imagine if the Largo by Vivaldi was a Patanjali sutra or a sacred text.
9. Finally John Cage's *4'33"*. Buying this piece MP3 version online is a strange experience, as buying 4'33" of silence in 3 silent parts means you are purchasing nothingness! Something always happens when you listen to a certain amount of purposeful silence. Then everything else comes into the picture. Acute mindful focus. Global listening. Realizing Silence is not the absence of Sound!

Suggested Playlist

Baird Hersey: *The Eternal Embrace*; *Awakening the Cobra*
Krisna Das and Baird Hersey: *Gathering the Light*
Steve Reich: Music *for 18 Musicians; Music for Mallet Instruments; Proverb*
Philip Glass and Ravi Shankar: *Passages*
Andrea Bauer: *Cello Songs for Silence*
Dagar Brothers and Gundecha Brothers: Various alaps of ragas
Vivaldi: *Four Seasons*, by Halloway, Harnoncourt, Richter and Menuhin
Ancient Treasures: *The Best of Singing Bowls Healing Sounds*
Karma Moffett: *Golden Bowls of Compassion*
Sacred Treasures II: Gregorio Allegri, *Miserere*
Pandit Jasraj: Everything!
Vellard and Chaudhuri: *Two Worlds of Modal Music*
Accentus Choir: Barber's *Adagio* Transcription
Philip Glass: *Glassworks; Koyaanisqatsi*
Jivan Gasparyan: *I Will Not Be Sad in this World*
Arvo Pärt: *Lamentate; Alina; Spiegel im spiegel*
Paul Horn: *Inside the Taj Mahal, Vol. 2*
Ghazal: *Lost Songs of the Silk Road*
Joseph Haydn: *The Seven Last Words*
Sheila Chandra. *ABoneCroneDrone*
Pauline Oliveros: *Deep Listening*
Pergolesi: *Stabat Mater*
Keith Jarrett: *The Koln Concert, Part 1*
Terry Riley: *A Rainbow in Curved Air*
Jordi Savall: *Ostinato*
Levon Minassian: *Songs Form a World Apart*
Marcello, Albinoni, Locatelli and Vivaldi: most adagios
Mozart: *Fantasia in C Minor*, (Mitsuko Uchida); *Adagio for Glass Harmonica; Gran Partita* (Boulez conducting); *Piano Concerto 23*
Jan Garbarek: *Officium*
Ravel: *Concerto in G* (Alicia de Larrocha)
Guillaume de Machaut: *La Messe de Nostre Dame*; Motets
Pérotin: *Alleluia nativitas.*
Johann Sebastian Bach: *Passacaglia in C Minor* for organ
Central Asia and Siberia: Epics and Overtone Singing

Recommended Movies

Genghis Blues
Touching the Sound
Latcho Drom

References

Cervine, D. (2013). *How therapists dance: Poems and essays.* Austin, TX: Plain View Press
Daniélou, A. (1991). *The myths and gods of India.* Rochester, VT: Inner Traditions Bear & Company.

16 My Other Yoga

A Patient's Journey through Healing On and Off the Mat

Frances Sommer Anderson and
"Laura" (Pseudonym)

In Memory of Mary Sinclair
(Thank you, Mary, for putting your hand on the brow of my soul and caring so much about whether the bud would flower.)

Figure 16.1

Introduction and Explanation

Several months after this chapter was completed, Mary was diagnosed with cancer and passed away shortly thereafter. We had just returned from a Patricia Walden yoga retreat. I will always feel blessed that we shared those last happy and precious days together. While Mary had read an earlier draft of this article and likely had her own views about my healing process, I regret that she did not live to see it published. With gratitude to Dr. Anderson for helping me through this most painful period.

I am profoundly grateful to all of my yoga teachers, but especially to Mary Sinclair, my first and primary teacher, and to Patricia Walden, Boston-based senior Iyengar teacher with whom I try to study as often as possible, and of course to Dr. Anderson. Although I have tried to use my own words to describe my yoga experiences, my teachers, who have studied in India with B.K.S. Iyengar, have in large part influenced my descriptions. Mr. Iyengar's teachings and writings have helped shape the modern vocabulary of yoga, particularly yoga taught according to the Iyengar method. Although I have never studied with Mr. Iyengar, I wish to acknowledge his influence on my yoga practice (and in my life) through my teachers. Phrases and descriptions directly attributable to him without quotation are unintentional.

Laura's Story[1]

It seems not so very long ago that yoga was one of the last places I could see myself. Actually, the same was true for therapy. Sometimes I look back in wonder, is this really the same person I was?

I came to yoga indirectly, through therapy, or rather therapy opened me to the possibility of yoga. I started therapy reluctantly. There was a secret part of me that probably knew I needed it, but a stronger more dominant side could not acknowledge I might need help. Fortunately for me, my inner pain began manifesting itself, insistently and increasingly over time, as physical pain. Thus began my journey, first to Dr. John Sarno and from there to Dr. Fran Anderson, my therapist now for over seven years.[2]

I am not quite sure where or when exactly the idea of learning yoga began to take shape. I had heard about yoga but was not really sure what exactly it was. In my mind, it was just some kind of exercise that involved stretching, a New Age bendy, twisty kind of thing. Definitely not something I was thinking about adding to my exercise routine.

Early in our work together, Dr. Anderson tried to introduce me (gently, it seems in retrospect) to some basic yogic concepts such as breathing exercises and simple restorative positions, but it didn't really take, at least not at first. In fact, several months later I vaguely recalled that Dr. Anderson had suggested I try to do something at least twice a day, but I could not for the life of me recall what it was. When I asked about it, she just smiled and reminded me it was breathing exercises. Not the most auspicious start, to say the least.

So (admittedly, with some skepticism), I began slowly to incorporate breath work into my day, pausing for five minutes mid-morning and again mid-afternoon to focus just on my breath: slow, even inhalations through the nose, followed by slow, even exhalations, listening to the quiet sound of my breath, cool on the interior surface of the nostril on the way in, and warm on the way out, feeling first my body and then my mind begin to let go and relax. Initially, it was difficult not to let my thoughts wander, but gradually through practice, I could stay with the soft sound of the breath for longer periods. It also began to take less and less time to start feeling the sense of relaxation sweep through my body. Over time, I found that the effect would carry over throughout the rest of the day. I would feel refreshed and less stressed and was able to return to my work with increased focus. I think it also carried over into my work with Dr. Anderson, helping me to feel more relaxed and to open up in ways that before had seemed unimaginable. Dr. Anderson would also incorporate some breath work at the end of a particularly difficult session so I could return to work in a less agitated state.

Beyond this humble, almost overlooked beginning, Dr. Anderson never suggested or encouraged me to begin yoga, but somewhere about nine months into our sessions I had the idea that maybe I might want to try it. Perhaps it was the breath work I had integrated into my daily schedule that encouraged me to seek out more of what seemed to be helping or maybe it was the yoga magazines in the waiting room I would flip through before my sessions (or did I somehow want to please her?). However, not only was the idea of going to a yoga class a little too intimidating at the time, but I was still dealing with a variety of painful, emotionally-triggered physical conditions. Private lessons seemed like the right way to get started—better first to work alone with a yoga teacher until I was comfortable enough to try a yoga class.

I was blessed to have been introduced to Mary Sinclair, a truly gifted and compassionate teacher, and began working with her privately on a weekly basis. I remember feeling self-conscious and awkward, especially since the first thing she asked me to do was walk around the studio so she could observe my posture and gait. This was not quite what I expected, and I remember thinking to myself, "just stay open to it, just stay open." Fortunately, we soon moved on to some basic poses. Mary would first demonstrate what the pose should look like, then adjust the position of my foot or hip, gently reminding me to breathe or to unfurrow my brow. She also encouraged me to breathe through the nose, deeply from the abdomen (instead of shallowly from the chest) and to chant *om* while feeling its deep vibrational quality as the sound moved through my body. We spent over two hours that first day working quietly together, and while most of the other details of that first lesson are a little blurred now, what I remember most was that when we were finished I was tired but blissfully calm and relaxed. I did not know at the time that this was the beginning of something that was going to change my life.

Dr. Anderson began referring to my work on the yoga mat as my "other yoga." Although she said it jokingly, it was beautifully illuminating. In so many ways the work I was doing with her was so very much like the work I was doing on the mat with my yoga teacher, although I am sure I did not fully appreciate this insight at first. I often think back to something Patricia Walden, said at a retreat I attended about four years ago. Patricia is a phenomenal and inspiring teacher, compassionate and with a sly sense of humor, and her classes are always a masterful blending of yoga poses, breath work, and sutra philosophy study. That evening she was talking about how yoga can be helpful for depression, but then went on to say, "sometimes yoga is not enough." It had been difficult for me to admit to myself, let alone to Dr. Anderson, that I was suffering from depression, but hearing a teacher I admired and respected speak openly about seeking professional help affected me profoundly. I remember thinking, "and sometimes, therapy is not enough." By these simple words, Patricia had somehow helped me close a circle. I will always be deeply grateful to her for the inspiration of that evening's yogic connection.[3]

In the beginning, however, it was not clear to me what therapy was doing for me, nor was it clear what yoga would do for me. But I was suffering from a lot of physical pain and had come to realize through Dr. Sarno that much, if not all of it, was emotionally triggered. This was a radical way of thinking for me, so radical that I knew I needed to stay open to new experiences and give everything time. I started working with Dr. Anderson to find help healing the body through the mind, and, although I did not realize it at the time, the yoga would help me heal the mind through the body. Yoga has over the years helped shape the way I have come to regard my work with Dr. Anderson. In many ways my "other yoga" has helped me progress with my therapy, and at times, the work I have done with Dr. Anderson has helped me through the emotional challenges of my yoga practice on the mat.

When I first started yoga, I had so many painful physical conditions (lower back pain, tight hamstrings, stiff knees—these are only the ones I remember now, the list seemed endless then) that most of the poses seemed hard. Mary worked carefully with me, slowly releasing, bit-by-bit, the painfully knotted parts of my body. The sessions quickly became the highlight of my otherwise stressful workweek. No matter how challenging the practice I would always leave her studio feeling calm and happy. Soon I began to think of Mary as my healer, and what started out as "just a few private lessons" to help me transition to a group class has continued to this day, and Mary has become a special and beloved friend.

My yoga practice evolved tentatively; I added some yoga classes, first at Mary's studio, and eventually trying classes with other teachers. Eventually, with Mary's encouragement, I tried some weekend workshops and, after several years, weeklong retreats. I also gradually developed my own home practice, at first just 10–15 minutes here and there to work on a challenging pose and then daily, trying to squeeze in as much time before work as my schedule might permit. In addition, I started spending a few minutes before bed doing one or two calming poses or some breath work, which helped with the sleeping difficulties I was experiencing. The more consistently I practiced, the better I felt, and I began to notice that the sense of calm and wellbeing would carry over from the mat and stay with me throughout much of the day. I think that in my new, calmer state I was also able to make more progress in my sessions with Dr. Anderson.

After a couple of years, I added a yoga class directly after my weekly sessions with Dr. Anderson. Although she would always leave time at the end to transition, sometimes after a particularly difficult session had stirred up a lot of strong emotions, it would be hard to let everything settle back down. But once in yoga class, I could turn my focus to the alignment of my body and the flow of my breath, and gradually let go of the difficult topics we had discussed. I think that this sequencing of therapy followed by the calming effects of yoga gave me the confidence to explore difficult issues more deeply with Dr. Anderson because I knew I would have a way to return to a more calm state afterwards.

In the beginning, however, everything about yoga just seemed so hard. I could not remember the Sanskrit names of the poses or how to do them, my legs would tremble and I would break out in a sweat. Even basic poses that looked really easy were not, like *viparita karani* ("legs-up-the-wall" pose), a passive position with the back on the floor, the buttocks supported on a bolster, and the legs flush up against the wall. I could not stay even in this pose for more than a few seconds without experiencing pain in my lower back and legs.

Although I now enjoy this restorative pose, I remember thinking, even after a year of practice, how can everyone stay in this position for so long and look so peaceful?

Mary's teaching was thoughtful, skillful, and creative. She would not just teach me how to do the pose, she would link the various poses so I could understand how they were related; for example, how the muscle action that was relatively easy to find in one pose was like what I needed to find in another pose. Over time, my practice developed a more inward focus. I was able to find a stillness of mind within the stillness of body, working with less physical intensity directed towards "doing" a pose and instead, allowing myself to experience "being" in the pose. I was no longer practicing yoga exclusively from the outside in, I was also finding the pose by working from the inside out and experiencing the more meditative qualities of the pose. I also gradually began to devote more of my attention to *pranayama* (yogic breathing exercises) and meditation, but my yoga practice had itself become a kind of meditation.

Mary would make generous use of various yoga props (blocks, belts, blankets, chairs) to help my body find more ease in the pose. If I could not bend over with straight legs and touch the floor, she would use blocks to bring the floor closer to my hands. If I could not sit comfortably on the floor, she would add more and more blankets until I could. Sometimes it seemed like there were more props than pose and that I was barely doing anything. At first I was not entirely convinced that I liked the props, which felt a bit like cheating to me. I wanted to be able to do the pose by myself, to be strong enough or flexible enough to do it without help. As I practiced more, with Mary's gentle guidance and careful instruction I began to understand better the use of props. Props not only could make a pose more accessible, but with the support of a strategically placed prop I could find a muscle I needed for the correct alignment in a pose and bring intelligence to the physical body. Some props were used temporarily until muscles were lengthened or space created, others were used from time to time as teaching aids to improve a pose. But some poses, such as *sarvangasana* ("shoulderstand") always required props, in this case blankets to support the curvature of the neck and avoid injury. In retrospect, my experience with yoga props was much like my therapy experience. Deep down, I knew I needed help, but it was difficult to seek support and acknowledge how much I needed it. Most important, I came to accept that Dr. Anderson's help could also be long-term, like one of those props that always improves the pose.

One of the most concrete examples of how yoga has affected my life off the mat came after I had been practicing yoga regularly for about a year. As a lawyer, I often have to deal with demanding clients and difficult opposing counsel. On this occasion, I had a challenging negotiation with a belligerent opposing counsel who was particularly hostile and obnoxious and who punctuated his weak arguments with gratuitous, demeaning, and snide remarks. His comments were inappropriate by any objective standard. I remember distinctly a moment when I found myself calmly acknowledging that he was a jerk and not reacting at all, verbally or emotionally, to his rantings. The angrier he became, the more calm I felt. I experienced a sense of detachment from the interchange as if I were observing it from a distance. What made this experience even more memorable was that I had a similar experience a week or two later with a different opposing counsel and was joined on both calls by different junior lawyers. After the calls, both of the junior lawyers said "I don't know how you stayed so calm, I was so angry for you!" Hearing these reactions, I realized that my pre-yoga self would have been angry too. Seeing their anger helped me realize how experiences like these would make me wound-up, agitated, and tense. I would respond in an outwardly calm manner, but this pent-up anger would leave me feeling exhausted and drained. So much wasted energy!

This experience helped me see, in a way I had not been able to articulate to myself before, that the calm and non-attachment I was able to find in my yoga practice could be transferred to my life off the mat. This was a profound and transformative experience for me, brightly illuminating the importance of my yoga practice in all aspects of my life. It also helped me see in a very physical way the themes I was working on with Dr. Anderson, and yoga (my "other yoga" on the mat) became a useful metaphor for our work off the mat, a point of reference I could turn to when I was struggling with some issue we were working through. I could tell myself, "This work we are doing here in therapy, this work off the mat, is so very much like the work on the mat. So have patience with it, have patience with yourself, just like on the mat. It takes time and practice, but the change will come, even if progress is not always in a straight line." At times I am frustrated that it is so difficult to apply the lessons learned on the mat to life off the mat, to effect emotional change in the same way that I have been able to effect change on the mat. But like my yoga practice, there has been change, and it has come with time and patience. As B. K. S. Iyengar once said, "enlightenment comes through change, which comes only with constant practice."

I have come to think of my yoga practice as a way of putting all the brain chatter on pause, a mini-vacation for the mind. Once, for example, I was working in the office over the weekend with the hope of rewarding myself with an evening yoga class after I finished. As the day wore on, I found myself becoming increasingly agitated because the work was taking much longer than I expected and it looked like I might not be able to go. Although ordinarily I would have continued working until I was finished, I ultimately decided I should go to the class. This was definitely a good decision, because I returned to the office feeling so refreshed that I was able to finish quickly. In retrospect, the choice probably should have been obvious, but at the time it was not, despite Dr. Anderson's efforts. Of course, any kind of pause during intense work can be helpful. But it was more than just a break that made the difference. This particular experience was so memorable because I was able to return to my work with incredible clarity and focus. The yoga practice, with its shift in breathing patterns and focus on the body, helped clear my mind. The effects of the practice also carried over to later that night when, after completing the work, I was able to shut down the mental activity and fall asleep quickly (which in the past would not have been possible).

Often my yoga practice illuminates some of the issues I have been working on with Dr. Anderson, providing a useful and physical point of reference to apply to my daily emotional life. For example, many yoga poses involve physical balance, such as balancing on one leg in *vrksasana* ("tree pose"). For a long time, a weakness in my right leg has made balancing poses on that side particularly challenging. As a beginning student, I worked hard on these poses, bracing myself to prevent toppling over. Over time, I came to appreciate that the balancing was not just physical, not just an effort to firm up wobbly parts, but also a mental balancing. I realized that it is hard to achieve physical balance if the mind is churning through yesterday's upsets or ticking through tomorrow's to-do list. I also learned that in focusing on the breath and letting go of everything, including the effort to stay in the pose, a sense of quiet and calm would emerge, even though my right leg might waver in its balance. As my practice evolved, I also realized that it was more important not to be disturbed by the trembling than to eliminate every quiver, and that it is not possible to eliminate all of them, even on my stronger left leg. I also came to accept that some days the balance comes more easily, and some days it does not come at all.

These are lessons that apply to life as well. One of the key issues I have been working through with Dr. Anderson involves trying to find emotional balance, learning to tolerate inevitable emotional ups and downs, and working to observe them with a more detached mind. Most important, I try to remember that little emotional wobbles do not necessarily mean a free fall into a prolonged depressed state. I have found over time, both on and off the mat, that it is easier to maintain my equilibrium. I have also learned that I can calmly return to a pose after being off balance, just as I can more quickly return to a more balanced emotional state after a period of unhappiness. In *Yoga Sutra* I.13, Patanjali describes yoga as "the steadfast effort to still the fluctuations of the mind" (Iyengar, 2002). I cannot think of a better way to also describe the work I have been doing with Dr. Anderson.

I also have come to realize that often the difficulties I am experiencing on the mat reflect the issues I am working on off the mat. In the beginning, for example, I wanted to be able to *do* the pose, working hard at it and pushing myself to get there, getting frustrated when I could not accomplish what I thought I should be able to do. So very much like how in my life and work I have pushed myself harder and harder (and sometimes too hard) to achieve a goal. In my professional life, much of my success came from working harder and longer than everyone else; it was only natural that I would apply that same work ethic to my yoga practice. However, while discipline and will power are important components of a yoga practice, it is also important not to push to the point of injury and to practice with the intention to bring the body and mind to a quiet state. The poses all require a certain amount of hard work in the beginning: understanding how to position the body, finding the correct alignment, activating the right muscles, remembering to keep the breath soft and even. There is so much to do, so much to think about. But as the body gradually becomes more familiar with a pose, it is possible to do it with less effort and less thinking and to bring quietness to the mind, and ultimately (according to Patanjali) to achieve the pose with "effortless effort." "Perfection in an *asana* is achieved when the effort to perform it becomes effortless and the infinite being within is reached" (*Yoga Sutra* II.47; Iyengar, 2002). This has now become my work, to "do less" (as my teachers often remind me), and through doing less, eventually, to find more effortlessness in my practice.

When I first started working with Mary, even though she was incredibly wise and experienced, I would often think that I could do more than she thought I could or should do. She would always patiently explain why I was not yet ready for the next step or simply demonstrate why my approach was not correct. Gradually I began to trust that she was right, even though I really wanted to do more. For example, there is a seated pose in yoga called *paschimottanasana* ("seated forward bend") where the legs are stretched out straight in front, the feet are held by the hands and the trunk rests on the thighs, the head on the shins. I immediately liked this pose because I knew this was one I could do! I could touch my head to my knees! Mary would then show me how my pose came from the flexibility in my lower back and how my upper back was a big round lump. She would acknowledge that it might feel satisfying to reach my head down to my knees, but it was not correct. She asked me to pull back from the final pose, to focus on keeping my back straight, even though it meant not reaching my head to my knees. I remember feeling unhappy to be doing less than I wanted to do, especially when I was in a class and could see that others were doing more. However, I followed her advice, reminding myself that her guidance and teaching had been so helpful in all other respects. I was able to recognize that it was really my ego that wanted me to bring my head to my knees, even if it was incorrect. Mary was right. It did not really matter if I "completed" the pose, I could still benefit from it as long as I was doing it correctly. I practiced this way for almost two years, focusing on lengthening my back and keeping it straight and not reaching my head lower, until over time I found that I was able to lower first my abdomen, then my ribs to my thighs, and ultimately my forehead to my shins. By doing less, I was gradually able to do more—a valuable lesson in patience (and how the ego can lead to injury) to which I often return for inspiration, not only in my yoga practice, but in yoga as metaphor for my daily life off the mat, including in my work with Dr. Anderson.

If I am honest with myself, I know I have not always welcomed Dr. Anderson's advice, even if deep in my heart I knew she was right, and I have not always wanted to give our work the patience and time it has required. And so through our difficult periods I have tried to look at our relationship through the lens of my yoga practice to remind myself that her advice is sound and that change takes time (and that it is my ego that is resisting). And like my yoga practice, it is a journey, a work in progress. I have come to think of her as my healer too, the healer of the mind and through the mind the body. Just as in my "other yoga" Mary has been my healer of the body and through the body the mind. And where does the one yoga begin, and the other end? I am not sure anymore that it matters.

Commentary by Frances Sommer Anderson, PhD, SEP[4]

Ellen Horovitz invited me to contribute to this volume in the context of having read my chapter, in my edited book, *Bodies in Treatment: The Unspoken Dimension.* In the throes of trying to complete that chapter when Laura and I began psychotherapy, I was struggling with how much to disclose about my 30 years of experiencing adjunctive bodywork modalities while a patient in mainstream psychoanalysis.

In *Bodies in Treatment,* I described my yoga teacher's calm and centered attunement as a consummate "holding space," literal and figurative, within which I learned to identify, tolerate, and regulate emotional experiences that sometimes seemed both inaccessible and overwhelming. I illustrated how physical holding in yoga and in other "hands-on" bodywork, over the course of 30 years, had enabled me to discover, at a visceral level, residues of pre-, peri- and post-natal trauma. Since early childhood, I had heard my mother's narrative about her ordeal of 48 hours in delivering me into this world. In my personal psychoanalysis, I had discussed these experiences and knew, theoretically, how significant they were. Accessing them experientially in the "talking" framework of psychoanalysis had proven impossible.

When *Bodies in Treatment* was published, Laura read my chapter. It was clear to her that I had benefitted greatly from adjunctive bodywork outside the psychoanalytic treatment frame. My disclosure has had both facilitating and inhibiting reverberations in the years of our work together. It is difficult to know all the ways in which it may have influenced her pursuit of yoga and her healing process. In her narrative above, for example, she wonders if she began yoga in part to please me.

As I pondered the focus of this book, I thought of Laura's discovery and use of yoga during her treatment with me. I have found that first-person accounts of treatments of all kinds are invaluable to practitioners and to people who are considering experiencing these treatments. After careful reflection about the impact of inviting her to co-author this chapter, I brought it up for discussion. In time, Laura decided to try to write about her experience. She has beautifully articulated the mutually enhancing combination of the talking framework and the freedom and challenges of being on-the-mat. I consider her to be the senior author, as her account of her healing process is the primary contribution in this chapter. As the chapter evolved, it seemed natural that my role would be to comment on her incisive reflections. As commentator, I will offer observations focused on treating people in pain, showing how Laura's experiences can be useful to psychotherapists and body-focused practitioners.

Laura arrived at my office physically limited by musculoskeletal pain: In her words, "lower back pain, tight hamstrings, stiff knees." At times her pain was almost intolerable and, on at least a couple of occasions, she required medical intervention in the form of lidocaine injections. Being constrained in moving was equally intolerable. "Holding" her in this state of mindbody anguish was the immediate challenge, one that therapists of mind and body always encounter when their patient is in pain.

How do we "hold" adults who are in pain? How do we help them tolerate their reactions to the musculoskeletal pain? Research in the field of pain science documents that the more negative our reaction to unpleasant sensations, the more intensely we experience these sensations, *i.e.*, the perceived intensity of the pain increases. Accordingly, it is incumbent upon the healthcare practitioner to begin by helping the person in pain "dampen" or "modulate" their reactions to painful sensations. Images of parental figures holding and soothing children who are in pain come to mind readily. In the talking therapy relationship, we "hold" our patients with words that are empathically attuned to their mindbody state, while being mindful of the prosodic features of our speech. Bringing our patients' awareness to their breath, we can teach simple breathing practices that decrease sympathetic nervous system hyperarousal, thereby decreasing hypervigilant monitoring of pain sensations. We can encourage the development of soothing imagery in all sensory modalities. In hands-on bodywork, the therapist can literally hold the person in pain, using touch to modulate distress. In *Bodies in Treatment*, I describe how useful I found this kind of physical contact during my personal healing from headaches.

Pain that interferes with movement, that constrain our activities of daily living, and that makes us reliant on others for assistance can trigger extreme fear in the most physically fit, highly functioning adult. I remark on this in my chapter in *Relational Perspectives on the Body* on treating musculoskeletal pain in the psychoanalytic framework. When we are compromised in these ways, our earliest childhood experiences of needing help can be vividly evoked. Knowledge about our patient's developmental history in this area becomes important in order to fine-tune our treatment interventions.

The person's capacity to acknowledge the need for help and to be able to accept help has to be considered as treatment begins. Laura evocatively describes her early ambivalence about therapy: "a stronger, more dominant side could not acknowledge I might need help." Referring to her attitude toward using "props" in yoga, Laura illustrates this dilemma: "I wanted to be able to do the pose by myself, to be strong enough or flexible enough to do it without help." She depicts the process of learning that props can improve the pose, and that, similarly, therapy can improve her life off the mat. "Deep down, I knew I needed help, but it was difficult to seek support and acknowledge how much I needed it."

Laura extends the discussion of help when she takes up the topic of learning to be patient: "in my life and work I have pushed myself harder and harder (and sometimes too hard) to achieve a goal. In my professional life, much of my success came from working harder and longer than everyone else." Her determination is similar to many people I have treated with stress-related musculoskeletal pain, working collaboratively with physiatrist John E. Sarno, MD. Relentless internal pressure to accomplish at the highest level as quickly as possible creates an extremely stressed mindbody system. We have found that these kinds of self-induced pressures, combined with tendencies toward perfectionism, can create the conditions in which musculoskeletal pain can develop and become chronic.

As I read Laura's drafts of her journey, her discussion of the importance of "doing" and learning to "do less" stood out as a prominent theme in our work. I have encountered this theme often, since 1979, in my treatment of other people like Laura who was referred with stress-related musculoskeletal pain diagnosed by Dr. Sarno. In writing about another patient referred by Dr. Sarno in *Relational Perspectives on the Body*, I reported that "Ellen" had described herself as a "human doing, not a human being." She was referring to a period in her life just before she developed severe, disabling musculoskeletal back pain. Her pain was even more incapacitating and long lasting than Laura's pain.

Many of my patients have had to learn to "do less," in Laura's words. She describes how she discovered the importance of this new attitude in her yoga practice, how to "have more effortlessness in the pose." With her first teacher, Mary, Laura would "often think that [she] could do more than [Mary] thought [she] could or should do." She goes on to say: "By doing less, I was gradually able to do more—a valuable lesson in patience (and how the ego can lead to injury) to which I often return for inspiration."

Another salient conclusion to be noted by talking and body therapists/teachers is Laura's discussion of how using her body in yoga helped her "to feel more relaxed and to open up in ways that before had seemed unimaginable." She is referring to opening both in the *asanas* and in the treatment relationship with me: "I think that in my new, calmer state I was also able to make more progress in my sessions with Dr. Anderson." "I think that [the] sequencing of therapy followed by the calming effects of yoga gave me the confidence to explore difficult issues more deeply with Dr. Anderson because I knew I would have a way to return to a more calm state afterwards." "I was able to find a stillness of mind within the stillness of body, working with less physical intensity directed towards 'doing' a pose and instead, allowing myself to experience 'being' in the pose."

Laura further discusses the concept of balance in yoga and in psychotherapy, a topical subject in the field of contemporary psychoanalysis and the neurobiology of attachment and trauma. Later in our work together, I introduced Laura to the work of Peter Levine (2010) and his thesis that recovery from overwhelming experiences requires the individual to learn how to regulate sympathetic arousal in response to inevitable "ups and downs." She was able to use the fundamentals of Somatic Experiencing® creatively, including incorporating it into her yoga practice. In her narrative above, she describes "trying to find emotional balance," how to return to a balanced state from surges of positive and negative feeling states, and finding it "easier to maintain equilibrium." As she states: "I can calmly return to a pose after being off balance, just as I can more quickly return to a more balanced emotional state after a period of unhappiness." As Laura notes, the yogic quality of our work together off the mat is beautifully stated in the *Yoga Sutras* as a "steadfast effort to still the fluctuations of the mind."

It is my hope that this collaboration with Laura about her healing process on and off the mat will be enlightening to psychotherapists, body-focused therapists, yoga teachers and students, people in pain, and those who love them and try to help them heal. In sharing this journey with Laura, I have learned a great deal about myself and about helping people in pain. As Laura indicates about her own journey, it is a work in process and progress has not always been in a straight line. To paraphrase one of my inspiring teachers, may we all be "blessed with curiosity" when we encounter pain.

Questions for the Reader

This chapter describes the evolution of Laura's yoga practice in the context of how it enhanced her psychotherapy treatment. Although yoga has now become more popular, not every patient will be receptive to beginning a yoga practice. As Laura notes, the gentle introduction to yogic breathing almost didn't take; and after the chapter was written, she acknowledged that at the time, she found Dr. Anderson's encouragement to try "child's pose" and "corpse pose" a little weird and off-putting.

As a psychotherapist:

1. How might you best identify a patient who could benefit from and be receptive to "simple" breathing practice?
2. Under what circumstances would you suggest that a patient explore a yoga practice?
3. This chapter describes a yoga practice in the Iyengar tradition that has both a physical component and an inward focus, are both necessary?
4. How would you decide which kind of yoga practice to recommend?

As a yoga teacher:

1. How would you discern that a student feels embarrassed or reluctant to take support? Laura mentions that at first she did not like the use of yoga props, she wanted to be able to do the pose without help. In the Iyengar method, props are discouraged for beginners, but in Laura's case she had so many physical limitations that her teacher felt she needed the props for support.

2. Do you believe that there can be a connection between the work of talking therapy and the work on the mat?
3. If yes, how would you help the student make those connections?
4. If your student is not in psychotherapy and you feel that it would be beneficial, how would you communicate with your student about your recommendation?

Editor's Notes

1. This chapter was written by "Laura" (a pseudonym) and is followed by a commentary written by her therapist, Dr. Frances Sommer Anderson. Laura is a partner at a prominent New York law firm and for obvious reasons wishes to remain anonymous. She is in her mid-50s, is married and has an adult daughter. Laura practices Iyengar Yoga, which is characterized by an emphasis on correct alignment of the body (and through the body, the mind), use of props such as blocks, blankets, chairs, and belts, and sequencing of poses to create a cumulative effect. Iyengar Yoga is also characterized by poses that are held for long periods of time to permit the pose to penetrate more deeply. With an experienced teacher, it can also be used therapeutically for certain medical conditions.
2. John E. Sarno, MD is best known for his books that explain how most back pain and certain other musculoskeletal and medical conditions are related to emotional stress, e.g., *The Mindbody Prescription* (1991). Laura was initially a patient of Dr. Sarno, who referred her to Dr. Anderson.
3. Patricia Walden is one of the most senior-qualified teachers in the Iyengar Yoga method and only one of two Americans to hold a senior advanced Iyengar teaching certificate. She has trained with B.K.S. Iyengar since 1976 and is internationally renowned for her teacher training, workshops and retreats. Along with her teaching, Patricia Walden is also known for yoga videos, including *Yoga for Beginners* (2002), and writings, e.g., *The Women's Book of Yoga and Health* (Walden & Sparrowe, 2002).
4. Dr. Anderson is a psychoanalyst, licensed psychologist and Somatic Experiencing Practitioner (SEP) with expertise in treating people with medical conditions, physical disability and trauma. She has specialized in treating back pain and other stress-related physical symptoms, using an approach that integrates contemporary psychoanalytic theory, research in the neuroscience of emotional and cognitive processing, and the neurobiology of attachment, trauma and pain. She incorporates techniques from mindfulness meditation and body-based talking therapies for treatment of trauma. She co-edited *Relational Perspectives on the Body* with Lewis Aron (1998) and edited *Bodies in Treatment: The Unspoken Dimension* (2007). She is a co-author of *Pathways to Pain Relief* with Eric Sherman (2013). Dr. Anderson has written about her own experiences with yoga in her chapter in *Bodies in Treatment* "At a loss for words and feelings: A psychoanalyst reflects on experiencing bodywork," and has taught yoga teachers and other body-focused practitioners about the relationship between pain and trauma. Her favorite pose is *savasana* ("corpse pose"), a restorative position with the entire back-body resting on the floor; it requires total relaxation of the mind and body, making it one of the most challenging *asanas*.

References

Anderson, F.S. (ed.) (2007). *Bodies in treatment: The unspoken dimension* (Relational Perspectives Book Series). New York, NY: Routledge Press.

Anderson, F. S., & Sherman, E. (2013). *Pathways to pain relief.* Amazon: CreateSpace Independent Publishing Platform.

Aron, L., & Anderson, F. S. (eds.) (1998). *Relational perspectives on the body* (Relational Perspectives Book Series). New York, NY: Routledge.

Iyengar, B. K. S. (trans.) (2002). *Light on the yoga sutras of Pantanjali.* SanFrancisoc, CA: Harper Collins.

Levine, P. (2010). *In an unspoken voice: How the body releases trauma and restores goodness.* Berkely, CA: North Atlantic Books.

Sarno, J. (1991). *The mindbody prescription: Healing the body, healing the pain.* New York, NY: HachetteBook Group.

Walden, P. (2002). *Yoga for beginners.* Louisville, CO: GAIAM.

Walden, P., & Sparrowe, L. (2002). *The Woman's book of yoga and health.* Boston, MA: Shambhala Publications, Inc.

Appendix A
Yoga Health History Form

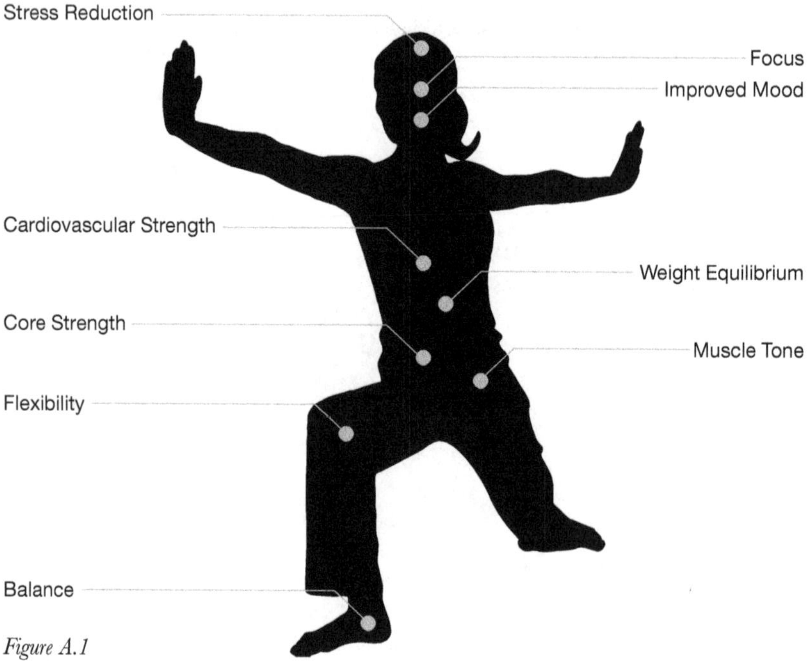

Figure A.1

2014, Dr. Ellen G. Horovitz

Your answers on this form will help your yoga practitioner to better understand your medical concerns and conditions before starting Yoga. This form is to ascertain any medical information that might be pertinent to your treatment and will be placed into your file. If you are uncomfortable with any question, you need not answer it. If you cannot recall specific details, please provide your best guess. Thank you!

Name ____

Address ____

____

Age ________ DOB __________

Email ______________________ Phone ____________________

How would you rate your general health?
❑ Excellent ❑ Good ❑ Fair ❑ Poor

Main Reason for Today's participation in Yoga ______________________

Have you ever practiced Yoga and if so, for how long? __________________

Have you ever practiced meditation and if so, how long? _______________

Other Concerns ____

Review of Symptoms: Please circle all that apply:

<u>Constitutional</u>
Recent fevers/sweats
Unexplained weight loss
Unexplained fatigue
Weakness

<u>Eyes</u>
Change in vision

<u>Ears/Nose/Throat/Mouth</u>
Difficulty hearing
Ringing in ears
Hay fever/allergies
Congestion
Difficulty swallowing

<u>Cardiovascular</u>
Chest pains/discomfort
Palpitations
Short of breath

<u>Breast</u>
Breast lump
Nipple discharge

<u>Respiratory</u>
Cough/ wheeze
Coughing up blood

Gastrointestinal
Heartburn/reflux
Blood in bowel movement
Nausea/vomiting
Diarrhea
Pain in abdomen

Genitourinary
Painful/bloody urination
Leaking urine
Nighttime urination
Discharge: penis/vagina
Vaginal bleeding
Concern w/ sexual functions
Musculoskeletal
Muscle/joint pain Recent back pain

Skin
New mole or mole change
Rash

Neurological
Headaches
Memory loss
Fainting

Psychiatric
Anxiety/stress
Sleep problem

Blood/Lymphatic
Unexplained lumps
Easy bruising or bleeding

Endo
Cold/heat intolerance
Increased thirst/appetite

In the past month, have you had little interest or pleasure in doing things, or felt down, depressed or hopeless? ❑ Yes ❑ No ❑ Sometimes

MEDICATIONS: Prescription and non-prescription medicines, vitamins, home remedies, herbal supplements, birth control pills, Ayurvedic prescriptions, etc.

Medication Dose (e.g. mg/pill) How many times per day?

____

____

____

Allergies or reactions to medications ______________________

PERSONAL MEDICAL HISTORY:
Heart Disease
Specify type__________
Asthma/Lung Disease
High Blood Pressure
Diabetes
Other
(specify)________
High Cholesterol
Thyroid Problems
Kidney Disease
Cancer (specify)
____

SURGICAL HISTORY: Please list all prior operations (with dates):
____
____
____
____

FAMILY HISTORY: Please indicate the current status of your immediate family members: please indicate family members (parent, sibling, grandparent, aunt or uncle with any of the following conditions:

Alcoholism ________________________________
Cancer, Specify type ________________________
Heart Disease ______________________________
Depression/Suicide __________________________
Genetic Disorders ___________________________
Diabetes __________________________________
High Cholesterol ____________________________
High Blood Pressure _________________________
Stroke ____________________________________
Bleeding or Clot Disorder _____________________
Asthma ___________________________________
Other Concerns _____________________________

SOCIAL HISTORY
Tobacco Use:
❑ Cigarettes ❑ Never Quit Date ________________
❑ Current Smoker packs/day _____ # of years______
❑ Other Tobacco ❑ Pipe ❑ Cigar ❑ Snuff ❑ Chew
Are you interested in quitting? ❑ Yes ❑ No

ALCOHOL USE:
Do you drink alcohol? ❑ No ❑ Yes
drink per week ____________________
Is your alcohol use a concern for you or others?
❑ No ❑ Yes

DRUG USE:
Do you use any recreational drugs?
❑ No ❑ Yes
Have you ever used needles to inject drugs?
❑ No ❑ Yes

SEXUAL ACITIVITY:
Sexually active ❑ No ❑ Yes ❑ Not currently
Current Sex partner is/are ❑ Male ❑ Female
Birth Control method _____ ❑ None needed
Have you ever had any sexually transmitted diseases (STDs)?❑ No ❑ Yes

OTHER CONCERNS:
Caffeine Intake ❑ None ❑ Coffee, Tea, Soda ____ Cups/day
Weight: Are you satisfied with your weight? ❑ No ❑ Yes
Diet: How do you rate your diet? ❑ Excellent ❑ Good ❑ Fair ❑ Poor
Do you eat or drink four servings of dairy or soy supplements or take calcium supplements?❑ No ❑ Yes

SOCIOECONOMICS HISTORY:
Exercise: Do you exercise daily? ❑ No ❑ Yes
What kind of exercise? _______________________
How long (minutes)? _________
How often? ________________
If you do not exercise, why? ____________________
Safety:
If you bike, do you use a helmet? ❑ No ❑ Yes
Do you use seatbelts consistently? ❑ No ❑ Yes
Is violence at home a concern for you? ❑ No ❑ Yes
Have you ever been abused? ❑ No ❑ Yes
Do you have a gun in your home? ❑ No ❑ Yes
Have you completed a living will or durable power of attorney for health care?
❑ No ❑ Yes

Occupation ___________________________
Employer___________________________
Years of highest degree__________
Marital Status: Single Partner/Married Divorced/Widowed
Other ________________________________

Spouse /Partner's Name_______________
Number of Children__________________
Who lives at home with you? ____

WOMEN'S HEALTH HISTORY:
# of pregnancies __________________
deliveries ______________________
abortions _______________________
miscarriages _____________________
Age at start of periods ______________
Age at end of periods ______________
Any additional comments:
____
____

I am aware that the instructor of Iyengar Yoga is here to serve me by sharing knowledge of yoga and health. I understand that the practice of yoga involves physical movement and exercise which may from time to time be strenuous, and that such practice carries some risk of injury. I also understand that I must judge my own capabilities with respect to practicing yoga with any instructor. By my participating in classes, I agree to take full responsibility for not exceeding my limits in the practice of yoga and for any injury I may incur in the practice of yoga. I acknowledge that it is my responsibility to inform Dr. Horovitz immediately if an injury occurs during class. I understand that, from time to time during classes with the instructor, she may physically adjust students' form when making a yoga posture. If I do not want such physical adjustments, I will so inform the instructor. I also acknowledge that if I do not wish to receive physical adjustments, it is my responsibility to inform the instructor when an adjustment has gone as far as I desire at that time. I hereby waive and release any claim that I might have at any time for injury of any sort against Dr. Horovitz.

I have carefully read, fully understand, and agree to all the above.

______________________________ ____________________
Signature Date

2014, Dr. Ellen G. Horovitz

Appendix B

Release For Information Form

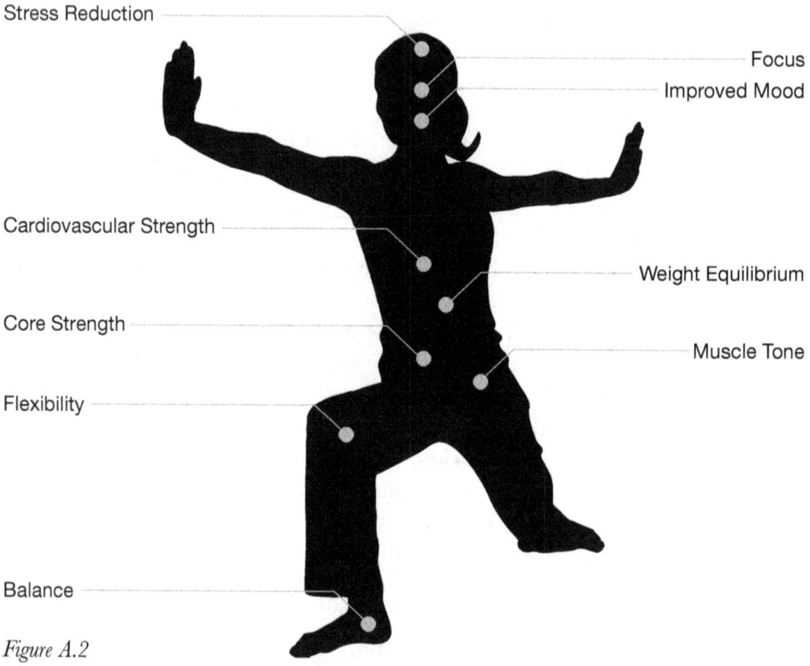

Figure A.2

2014, Dr. Ellen G. Horovitz

I hereby give Dr. Ellen G. Horovitz, PhD, ATR-BC, LCAT, E-RYT, LFYP permission to communicate with: ______________________________
regarding medical information and / or clinical information of:
____ (client)
The purpose behind gathering this information is to create a clear and comprehensive treatment plan for the aforementioned client.

____________________________ ____________________

Patient or Parental Guardian Date

Dr. Ellen G. Horovitz, PhD, ATR-BC, LCAT, E-RYT, LFYP

Appendix C

Art Therapy/Yoga Therapy Research Release/Confidentiality Agreement

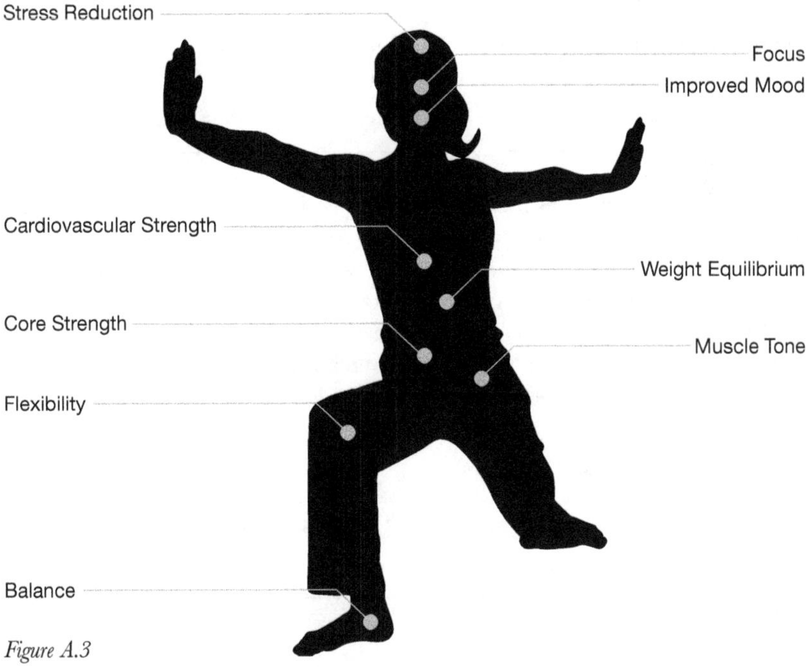

Figure A.3

2014, Dr. Ellen G. Horovitz

Name ____

Date ________________

I understand that by signing this document, I, ________________________ (client's name), give my permission to give the practitioner ______________ and Dr. Ellen G. Horovitz, PhD, ATR-BC, LCAT, E-RYT, LFYP to do the following with my artwork:

(*Please check all that apply*)

❑ Photograph the artwork

❑ Photograph the client

- ❑ Duplicate
- ❑ Display
- ❑ Video tape the sessions
- ❑ Audio tape the sessions
- ❑ Use the artwork in teaching, publication and educational presentation
- ❑ Use the session dialogue in teaching, publication and educational presentation
- ❑ Use the artwork in research
- ❑ Use the session dialogue in research
- ❑ Use videotape in teaching, publication and educational presentation
- ❑ Use artwork in World Wide Web publications (internet)
- ❑ Use videotaped/ filmed sessions in World Wide Web publications (Internet)

I understand that this agreement is valid for the following time period, if defined by examinee:

Dates ____

I understand that that all measures will be made to ensure that my identity will be protected and that any confidential material will remain confidential. I understand that if at any time I choose to withdraw my permission that I can do so by contacting Dr. Ellen G. Horovitz, PhD, ATR-BC, LCAT, E-RYT, LFYP and that my request will be taken care of immediately. I understand that if this work has been already shared for research, teaching, publication, and educational presentations that my withdrawal of permission cannot be retroactive.

Client's signature____
Client's Parental Guardian's signature (if under legal age)

____
Author's signature

Index

Page numbers in *italics* refer to figures.

CPSIA information can be obtained
at www.ICGtesting.com
Printed in the USA
LVHW021722140620
658048LV00018B/2368

9 781138 816169